CONVICTED AT BIRTH

CONVICTED AT BIRTH

Stories from the World's Largest Penal Colony

Jennifer Wynn

LITTLE, BROWN AND COMPANY

A *Little, Brown* Book

First published in the United States in 2001 by
St Martin's Press, New York
under the title *Inside Rikers*
First published in Great Britain by
Little, Brown 2002

A CIP catalogue record for this book
is available from the British Library.

ISBN 0 316 85567 7

Typeset in Plantin by M Rules
Printed and bound in Great Britain by
Clays Ltd, St Ives plc

Little, Brown
An imprint of
Time Warner Books UK
Brettenham House
Lancaster Place
London WC2E 7EN

www.TimeWarnerBooks.co.uk

For my parents, who never doubted what I did;
for Raymond Acevedo, who inspired me to do it;
and for Barbara Margolis, who made it possible.

Many men on their release carry their prison about with them into the air, hide it as a secret disgrace in their hearts, and at length, like poor poisoned things, creep into some hole and die. It is wretched that they should have to do so. . . . Society takes upon itself the right to inflict appalling punishment on the individual, but it also has the supreme vice of shallowness, and fails to realize what it has done. When a man's punishment is over, it leaves him to himself; that is to say, it abandons him at the very moment when its highest duty toward him begins. It is really ashamed of its own actions, and shuns those whom it has punished as people shun a creditor whose debt they cannot pay, or one on whom they have inflicted an irreparable, an irredeemable wrong.

Karl Menninger, *The Crime of Punishment*

CONTENTS

CONTENTS

INTRODUCTION

I came to work with prisoners unintentionally. My background is in journalism, and it was as a reporter that I first entered Rikers Island in 1991. I was writing a crime story for the *New York Post*, and the man I needed to interview was incarcerated out on the dreaded island. Although Rikers lies just six miles from midtown Manhattan, it took me one subway ride, two buses, clearance through numerous metal detectors, and two pat frisks before I arrived in the visiting room of the world's largest penal colony – nearly two hours later. When a correction officer asked me to pull my bra away from my body to see that I wasn't concealing drugs, I closed my eyes and swore I would never return.

But return I did, hundreds of times over the following years, to teach a writing class to adult male inmates in a unique rehabilitation program known as Fresh Start. Run by the Osborne Association, Fresh Start begins on Rikers and continues after the offenders are released. I became editor of the *Rikers Review*, a jailhouse magazine produced by Fresh Start inmates, and for two years I served as the program director.

I returned because the men I met behind bars defied my stereotypes of criminals. 'They don't all have horns and tails,' Fresh Start's founder, Barbara Margolis, told me before I started teaching. Aside from a few exceptions, most of my inmate-students seemed eager to learn and to better themselves. They were far more sharp, expressive, and polite than I'd imagined. Not once in six years of teaching have I left the classroom without the prisoners thanking me for coming. Inmates appreciate us 'civilians' who brighten their drab world, almost as if they can breathe the fresh air of freedom right from our clothes. They are grateful to people who treat them as regular men, the kind of men they aspire to be and whom some of them become.

There were many times in my first years of teaching that I struggled to reconcile the 'good' men I knew in jail with the destructive things *some* of them did – and I stress the word 'some' – before or after their incarceration. My predictions about their either staying off drugs or away from criminal activity were often wrong. The class stars, the ones I thought would make it, often didn't. The ones I thought would never succeed somehow did.

To gain a theoretical understanding of my students' motivations, I enrolled in a graduate program at John Jay College of Criminal Justice. Many classes, books, and a master's degree later, I came to see that there are a host of factors underlying criminal behavior: Social, psychological, and even biological factors have all been correlated with crime and deviance. Today, having worked closely with hundreds of inmates on Rikers, men ranging in age from sixteen to sixty, I can see that my students share several characteristics: Nearly all of them come from one of the city's 'dead zones' (a police term used to denote areas with extremely high rates of homicide): Central Brooklyn, Southeast Queens, Spanish Harlem, the Lower East Side, the South Bronx. Most of the older men (over thirty) are drug addicts; the younger men (in their teens and early twenties) are drug dealers. The majority have lost a family member or close friend to murder, street violence, or drugs. Many have a father, brother, or uncle in prison upstate. Few have studied past the tenth or eleventh grade. Nearly all have been to Rikers or state prison before.

Like everyone, my students have good traits and bad. Unlike most people, however, they are convicted criminals, and because of this, they will usually be known by their single worst deed. This is a sentence worth rereading. Think about all the decent things you've done over your life and then imagine that you committed a crime and got caught. For the most part, you would be known first by your single worst deed, not by the sum of all your good deeds minus a few bad ones. 'The ex-con label never leaves you,' Angel Rivera, the first Rikers inmate I met, tells me to this day.

Because these convicts let me into their lives and tell me their stories, because they call me when they relapse and ask for help when they're ready, Rikers, for me, became a transforming experience. It transformed me from a dispassionate journalist into a teacher, social worker, and advocate for criminal-justice reform. It added purpose to my life, and it made me compassionate.

Despite the difficulties of penetrating the vast penal colony, I return because working behind bars offers a glimpse into a hidden world, a world of contradictions and extremes, a world where little is sacred and anything can happen. I return because my students teach me things I could never learn about in books. These men in 'greens,' as jail uniforms are called, tell me how it feels to bump into a son in line in the cavernous mess hall; about the despair that sets in when you're looking for a job as an ex-con and your only credential is a certificate from prison attesting to your ability to buff floors; about the choices you make when you're holding the bullet-ridden body of your best friend in your arms, knowing that if you don't drop him and run you'll be facing twenty-five years to life – as the accused murderer. I return because my students show me that untapped talent languishes behind bars and that good programs save money and lives.

There's a story the older inmates like to tell about a plane crash in the 1950s, off of La Guardia International Airport, which lies less than a hundred yards from Rikers Island. When the plane skidded off the runway and plummeted into the East River, inmates were called to the rescue scene. For their service of saving lives, some were granted freedom.

When the inmates tell me the story, their faces light up and their eyes widen. They shake their heads and talk about how things were different then, before prisons became bloated, when wardens had souls, when a job paid a livable wage. Today, they tell me, freedom doesn't offer much, and that's why nearly 75 percent of Rikers inmates return. It doesn't take many visits to 'the Rock,' as the inmates call it, to see that Rikers Island is the dirty secret of the richest city on earth, a caged city floating in the East River that most New Yorkers couldn't find on a map.

NOTE TO THE READER

Some of the men portrayed in this book are far from sympathetic. More than a few have committed violent crimes: assault, arson, armed robbery, even murder. Many have been locked up before and some are back in jail or prison today. But one day they will all be released, to live among us or near us, to return to criminal behavior or not.

WELCOME TO THE ROCK

The vilest deeds like poison weeds,
Bloom well in prison air;
It is only what is good in Man
That wastes and withers there. . . .
  – Oscar Wilde,
  The Ballad of Reading Gaol

When I first met Angel Rivera in March of 1991, he was handcuffed to a chair at NYPD's Central Booking. I couldn't believe my luck: The elusive con artist whose scams I'd been writing about had finally been caught. The lieutenant from Special Frauds called and said I could interview him. I left my office and headed for One Police Plaza.

As the cab sailed down the FDR, I tried to conjure up an image of Rivera. Although his female victims described his appearance as ordinary, I figured he must have some kind of charisma given the effect he'd had on them and the money he'd conned from them. Special Frauds described him as a 'predator,' a highly skilled con artist who posed as a casting director and promised his victims he'd make them stars.

'He'd approach attractive females in the street,' the lieutenant said, 'wanna-be actress types – they're a dime a dozen in Manhattan – and tell 'em everything they wanted to hear.'

Baiting his 'mark' with a stream of compliments and a phony business card, Rivera would say she had 'just the look' he needed for an upcoming movie. He'd buy his victim a cup of coffee and display a portfolio of the actresses he'd made famous, luring her into his web with promises of one-hundred-dollar-an-hour all-day shoots. When he knew he had her, he'd let the ax fall.

'You have a SAG card, right?' he'd ask. To work on a movie, actors must belong to the Screen Actors Guild and have a union card to prove it. Rivera hoped his victim didn't have a SAG card, and most times he was right.

Feigning disappointment, he'd wrinkle his brow, take a sip of coffee. 'Damn shame,' he'd say. 'As I said, you're perfect for the part. You got just the look we need.'

Then he'd fake the flash of an idea. 'Wait a minute – I think I know someone at SAG. . . . Lemme see what I can do.'

Now he was doing her a favor, implying that she was worth a risk. He'd excuse himself, head to the nearest pay phone, and return with a smile. 'Done deal,' he'd gloat. 'Today's your lucky day. He'll give it to you for a steal. Five hundred bucks and you're in.'

In most cases, if he'd gotten this far the woman would go to a cash machine and withdraw the money. Rivera would tell her to meet him later in the evening and the card would be ready. When she arrived, he'd be nowhere in sight.

And now here he was, sitting in front of me, handcuffed to a metal chair, head bowed as if he were sleeping. In one of the strangest arrests Special Frauds ever made, Rivera had been caught by an off-duty cop. Attesting to the sheer volume of women he'd scammed, Rivera actually approached a woman he'd conned before. He'd forgotten her, but she hadn't forgotten him. He'd been thirty seconds into his rap when she started screaming: 'Scam artist! Scam artist! This man's a thief!'

A cop happened to be walking by, straight into the scene of the crime. He took off after Rivera and nabbed him as he ducked into an idling cab.

'Mr. Rivera?' I asked.

He raised his head: large, bloodshot eyes; strong features; an oval-shaped face. He was a light-skinned black, of average build, and looked to be in his early forties. He wore a Yankees cap, khaki pants, and a dirty denim jacket. He looked exhausted.

'How can I help you?' His voice was softer and more conciliatory than I'd imagined. In fact, his appearance was anticlimactic. Rivera was the first 'real criminal' I'd met and he looked more like a high school janitor than a swashbuckling con artist.

'I'd like to ask you a few questions,' I said. 'I've been writing about your scams in the paper. . . .'

'I know. I've seen the stories. I figured I was gonna get caught one of these days.' He shrugged and shifted in his chair.

'About the women you conned . . .' I started. 'The women you promised to make stars . . . do you feel any remorse for taking their money?'

'Listen, those women *gave* me their money,' he said wearily. 'I didn't force them to do anything. I didn't hurt anybody.'

A cop came over and told us to wrap it up. He was anxious to finish his shift and take Rivera to the holding cells beneath the courthouse where detainees await arraignment.

'If you wanna know more,' Rivera said, 'you'll have to come interview me on Rikers. That's where I'll be for a while.'

I slipped him my card and said I'd see him there.

For a month I tried to arrange the interview, but my calls to the Department of Correction's Public Information Office went unreturned. I was about to give up when I received a letter from Rivera. Somehow knowing my predicament, he explained it was far easier to get security clearance as 'a friend' of an inmate rather than as a journalist. To help me out, he said, he put my name on his list of approved visitors. He enclosed the following week's schedule and circled the days I could visit.

Immediately I thought he was setting me up. Like most crime-spooked Americans, I figured that he was a criminal and couldn't be trusted. Then again, I thought, what could he really do to me? He was in jail, on his way to prison upstate, and he wouldn't be out for a while. So I followed his advice, pretended I was his 'friend,' and set out for the dreaded Rikers Island.

New York's 'carceral archipelago,' to borrow from French philosopher Michel Foucault, squats in the East River about 100 yards from La Guardia International Airport. It was once a green and leafy oasis, eighty-seven acres of farmland owned by a Dutch family by the name of Rychen. Since the first jail opened in 1935, the island has been expanded by landfill to encompass 415 acres and hold ten separate jails, capable of housing over 16,000 inmates. There is a jail for women, which contains a nursery, and a jail for boys sixteen to eighteen years old. Two Staten Island ferries, converted into floating detention centers, are docked off the northern tip of the island and together hold over 300 prisoners. A modern 800-bed barge, known by inmates as the 'slave ship,' is moored off the South Bronx just opposite Rikers Island. With a huge power plant, three high schools, a firehouse, a hospital, a courthouse, a tailor shop, and a bakery, Rikers Island could be its own town. Its budget costs taxpayers $860 million a year, yet most New Yorkers have no idea where it is.

Like most prisons and jails in America, Rikers Island performs an expert magic trick: It makes people vanish. It not only hides prisoners from public view, but in a double sleight of hand it keeps *in* those who want to get out and keeps *out* those who want to get in. As any visitor can attest, penetrating Rikers Island is a punishing experience.

The journey begins on Queens Plaza South, a trash-strewn strip lined with fast-food joints, pawnshops, and after-hours clubs, a place where the pay phones are either out of order or so grimy you don't want to touch them. During the weekends, every twenty minutes or so, a small crowd gathers to await the Q101, the city bus to the Rock. The regulars, mostly mothers (or grandmothers) with toddlers, collect their inmate care packages, flick their cigarettes, and board the bus to Rikers.

Half an hour later, you're traveling over the Francis R. Buono Memorial Bridge, a two-lane ribbon of highway separating the land of the free from the land of the jailed. The inmates say it's 'the longest bridge in the world,' taking 'just minutes to cross over, but eternity to cross back.' At the entrance to the bridge looms an intimidating billboard: CITY OF NEW YORK – CORRECTION DEPARTMENT, RIKERS ISLAND – THE BOLDEST CORRECTION OFFICERS IN THE WORLD.

At the high point of the bridge, the view is surreal. From behind, the dazzling Manhattan skyline beckons like the Land of Oz. Whitecaps ripple the expanse of water below. Ahead sprawls a massive, low-lying detention complex ringed by coils of razor wire and a lethal electric fence.

Visitors file into the Control Building, where they must produce valid photo ID before they proceed deeper into the bowels of the jails. If they cannot, it's back on the bus. Signs prohibiting cameras, tape recorders, cell phones, beepers, and weapons plaster the walls. An odd and enduring relic, the Rikers Island 'amnesty box,' sits off to the side. At first glance it looks like a mailbox. It is not. The amnesty box is where visitors can deposit contraband (drugs or weapons) without fear of arrest or reprisal. If they are caught smuggling contraband, however, they are arrested. In 1999, nearly 350 visitors were arrested on Rikers. Imagine that – being arrested in jail.

As if on the set of a science-fiction movie, you then enter a bright red cylindrical booth. A bulletproof door seals shut behind you while an X-ray machine scans you head to toe for metal. If no metal is found, the door slides open and you're released to begin part two of the journey: boarding a small 'route bus' that takes you to your designated jail.

However, if metal is detected on (or in) your person, an Orwellian voice from inside the chamber bellows: 'We beg you to come back and deposit metal objects in the chest on the doorway.' I marvel at the choice of words – they *beg* me to come back? They are *begging* me to come to Rikers? What happened to 'please'?

Correction officials say that the futuristic scanners, which cost $50,000 apiece and were installed in June 2000, have been pulling in four times the usual amount of contraband. Among the most recent collection of castaways were knives, razors, scissors, dental picks, Walkmans concealing drugs, balloons stuffed with crack and marijuana, a knife that was hidden in a pen, and – get this – a stun gun.

Even when the sun shines on Rikers, little cheer penetrates the dreary penal colony. Huge jets from La Guardia rip through the sky with a deafening roar; alarms and sirens sound off with regularity. Cars, commercial trucks, and blue and orange Correction Department buses crammed with inmates chug along the roadways. Black and Hispanic prisoners till the vegetable gardens surrounded by razor wire, bringing to mind images of slavery. On an average day, Correction Department buses log more than 3,500 miles transporting shackled inmates to courthouses in the city, or to reception centers on their way 'up north' – to one of New York's seventy state prisons.

From their tiny jailhouse windows, some Rikers prisoners are treated to a spectacular view: the orange rays of a Manhattan sunset reflecting off the city's gleaming skyscrapers. Freeworlders on the Rock describe the view as breathtaking; the inmates say it's heartbreaking. 'So close and yet so far,' they lament. I often think they have no idea just how far away the city is.

Literally and figuratively, the mile-long bridge to Rikers Island is a dividing line between the Big Apple's haves and have-nots. About two-thirds of Rikers inmates are pretrial detainees who have been charged with, but not convicted of, a crime. They are detained because they cannot afford bail. Illustrating their poverty, one-quarter of Rikers inmates face bails of $500 or less. 'Unlike white, employed, middle-class persons, who are perceived as being reputable and thus are generally released on their own recognizance or are able to make bail,' writes criminologist Albert Roberts, these 'disreputable persons are detained.'

When Ronald Lauder (son of Estée Lauder, founder of the cosmetic company) was campaigning for mayor in the 1980s, he took a trip to Rikers and was outraged to see that inmates were permitted to watch TV and spend an hour in the recreation yard. 'If it were up to me, I would have them breaking stones to pebbles,' he said, failing to realize that 65 percent of Rikers inmates are pretrial detainees, 'innocent until proven guilty.'

Lauder's confusion about the basic difference between jails and prisons is common. Many people are not aware, for example, that whereas prisons house convicted felons (with sentences of one year or more), jails hold mostly pretrial detainees. In addition, jails house people convicted of misdemeanors (serving sentences of less than one year) as well as convicted felons awaiting transfer to state prison.

Not surprisingly, criminologists have described jails as the 'strange social hybrids' of the correctional landscape, as 'detention centers for suspects.' They have been called the 'poorhouses of the twentieth century,' the 'ultimate ghettos,' the 'social garbage cans' used to discard 'society's rabble.'

Indeed, Rikers Island is primarily a melting pot of recidivist inmates: drug users, dealers, and disorganized street people. Less than a quarter have been charged with violent crimes; the majority were arrested for possession or sale of drugs. Other demographics speak volumes about this exiled population:

- 92 percent are black or Hispanic, though blacks and Hispanics represent 49 percent of the city's population;
- 90 percent lack a high school diploma or GED;
- 30 percent are homeless;
- approximately 20 percent of female and 10 percent of male inmates are HIV-positive;
- 25 percent have been treated for mental illness;
- 80 percent have a history of substance abuse;
- about 75 percent return to Rikers within a year.

Back in 1991, I wasn't aware of these statistics as I sat in the visiting room waiting for my 'friend' to arrive. More obvious was that I was the only white person among a sea of black and brown faces. I felt like a lightbulb. This is liberal, integrated New York City, I thought, home of a hundred different cultures and ethnicities, certainly not the homogenous Midwest, the Deep South, or even South Africa, for that matter. Today I have grown used to the sight of so many black and Hispanic men behind bars, but my first glimpse of Rikers prisoners astounded me. Did blacks and Hispanics really commit all of the crime in this city, I wondered, or were they just the ones who got caught?

ANGEL: PART I

After spending a couple of hours with Angel Rivera, another contradiction emerged: Far from the picture of a 'conniving predator' NYPD's Special Frauds Squad had painted, Rivera was a rather likable fellow. Surely he was a hustler, and his scams had left a trail of disappointments and lighter wallets in his wake. But he was also witty and warm and seemed surprisingly honest when I asked him about his crimes.

Before meeting Angel, I had interviewed two of his victims. One was a petite blond waitress who had recently moved to New York to become an actress. The other was a striking black woman in her late twenties with a master's degree in philosophy. Listening to their stories, I sympathized with the humiliation they experienced and the money they lost. But after coming to know Angel and his sisters, I felt worse for him.

Angel Rivera was born and raised in one of New York's poorest neighborhoods, El Barrio, also known as Spanish Harlem. Here, he and his three sisters slept two to a bed in a three-room tenement on 100th Street and First Avenue. His mother died from a 'home' abortion when he was five. His father was a drunk whose idea of punishment was making his children kneel on grains of rice until their knees bled, or beating them with wire hangers.

Throughout high school, Angel shined shoes on the streets of Harlem and later found work as an elevator operator. But he was bright and ambitious and had higher aspirations.

'I hated that no matter how hard I worked I was still poor,' he said. 'I'd come home after twelve hours on the job and see things on TV I wanted for myself. I felt I deserved them as much as anyone else.'

It was out of frustration to obtain 'the good things in life,' he told me, that he turned to conning women. For the first time in his life he felt powerful.

Over the following years I spent many hours speaking with Angel and his sisters in a tiny, padlocked apartment in Washington Heights. They invited me to their cookouts and birthday parties and treated me like one of the family. I visited Angel when he was sent to prison upstate and when he thought about suicide at Christmastime. I assigned him the job of undercover prison reporter and penology tutor so that I could learn about prison from a prisoner and crime from a criminal. I helped him find a job when he was released, and today I consider him a friend.

Like most things 'New York,' Rikers Island represents an extreme: an extraordinarily expensive, vast, and complicated penal colony. It houses more inmates than the entire prison systems of thirty-five other states and has been described in the literature as 'a more dangerous institution to manage than even maximum-security state penitentiaries.'

Not only is Rikers one of the most complex jailing systems in the United States, it is also one of the most expensive. While the average annual cost to house a person in state prison is approximately $25,000, New York City spends approximately $68,000 annually (about $175 daily) for every prisoner confined on the Rock. That's more than eight times what it spends to educate a child in public school, or as much as a college education. As the Reverend Jesse Jackson likes to say, 'It costs more to go to jail than to Yale.'

Rikers stands out in another way as well: in the tremendous growth of its inmate population. Between 1980 and 1990, the number of inmates on Rikers *tripled* from 7,000 to 21,000, while the U.S. prison population at large 'only' doubled from 500,000 to 1 million people.

Between 1990 and 2000, the U.S. prison population doubled again. In fact, the United States, 'the land of the free,' rang in the year 2000 as the world's number-one jailer, with 2 million of its citizens behind bars. Another way to look at it is this: 'In the early 1970s, there were about 200,000 people locked up in the United States,' says Robert Gangi, executive director of the Correctional Association of New York. 'Today, there are 2 million people behind bars – a growth of over 1,000 percent.'

'The situation we're in now is completely unprecedented,' says Marc Mauer, author of *Race to Incarcerate*. 'The number of people going through the system dwarfs that in any other period in U.S. history and virtually in any other country as well.' Indeed, the United States has 'overtaken Russia for the honor of having the world's highest incarceration rate,' writes Anthony Lewis in *The New York Times*. Although America comprises fewer than 5 percent of the world's population, it holds a quarter of the world's prisoners. 'I've been studying criminal justice trends for twenty-five years,' says Todd Clear, one of the country's leading authorities on corrections. 'And each year I think this can't continue. We can't keep doubling our prison population every decade. But we do. It's astounding.'

To comprehend the size of the American prison landscape, picture the entire populations of Atlanta, St. Louis, Pittsburgh, Des

Moines, and Miami behind bars. Then calculate your chances of becoming part of this landscape: For an American born in 1999, the chance of living some part of life in a correction facility is one in twenty; for black Americans, it is one in four.

Undeniably, the country's unbridled prison expansion has hit people of color the hardest. Today, one out of every three young African-American men is in prison, on probation, or on parole. In big cities, the number is one out of every two. The conservative economist Milton Freidman reports that the rate of incarceration of African-American men in the United States is four times greater than the rate of incarceration of black men in pre-Mandela, apartheid South Africa. And Hispanics now comprise the fastest-growing group of prisoners.

'All this has a profound social cost,' writes the *Times*. 'Since 1995 the states have spent more on prison than on university construction.' Operating prisons in the year 2000 cost about $40 billion, up from just under $13 billion in 1985. These figures are so extraordinary that even some experts known for taking a hard line on crime think it's time to re-evaluate our criminal-justice policies.

One of the sanest ways to end our incarceration binge was suggested by an unlikely source: conservative criminologist John DiIulio. In 1999 DiIulio made an impassioned plea in *The Wall Street Journal* for 'zero prison growth,' stating that 'two million prisoners are enough.' He observed that 'the value of imprisonment is a portrait in the law of rapidly diminishing returns.' He singled out New York for its bulging inmate population and harsh drug laws that are responsible for 'landing legions of nonviolent drug offenders in the state's prisons for mandatory terms ranging from 15 years to life.'

I imagine *The Wall Street Journal* ran DiIulio's editorial because businessmen more than anyone can appreciate the bad returns and bloated budgets of prisons. New York is home to the some of the best business schools and sharpest business minds in the country. How is it that with all this bottom-line acumen a New York City agency can spend $860 million a year on inmates, of whom 75 percent return?

The lawyers, criminologists, and CEOs at the Milton S. Eisenhower Foundation posed another good question. In a 1999 report they asked whether the rosy picture of declining crime rates is altogether accurate. 'What we call the "crime rate" measures the activity of those criminals who are still on the street,' they write. 'But as a measure of the deeper problem of criminality – as an indicator of the tendency of our society to *produce* criminals – it is obviously defective.'

The problem, they say, is that our crime rate ignores the fact that we've simply shifted some of the total pool of criminals in our society from one location to another. We haven't stopped *producing* lawbreakers; we have just *moved* them.

'Measuring crime this way is like measuring the extent of some physical illness in our society while systematically excluding from the count all those people who are so sick we've had to put them in the hospital,' they write. 'In a reasonable culture we would not say we had won the war against disease just because we had moved a lot of sick people from their homes to hospital wards. And in a reasonable culture we would not say we have won the war against crime just because we have moved a lot of criminals from the community into prison cells.'

In many ways, Rikers Island is like the big white elephant sitting smack in the center of New York City that no one sees. Its invisibility symbolizes the kind of dense national fog that enshrouds the country's thinking when it comes to people who break the law. Our current strategy of 'make them pay and keep them far away' simply incapacitates lawbreakers temporarily and at a ridiculously high price. It ensures that the 130,000 people who pass through Rikers Island every year, many of them prison alumni, will continue pursuing the two things they know best: doing crime and doing time.

One of my inmate-students wrote an incisive article for the *Rikers Review*, aptly titled 'A Fool's Resume.' Lending human voice to the findings of countless studies, it shows that prison does little to deter criminal behavior and much to perpetuate it:

> My name is John B. I am 37 years old and if memory serves me well my first time being locked up on Rikers was in 1977. That's almost 20 years ago. I have been a regular guest ever since.
>
> I did, however, take a long vacation from 1979 through 1982. During that time, I visited Attica, Auburn and Elmira

state prisons. Inside those great walls of education, I earned my GED, as well as a bachelor's degree in the art of stealing and a master's in lying to myself. These diplomas have prepared me well for spending an average of four months a year on Rikers playing spades, scrabble and watching TV. I have also, during my stays on the Rock, acquired several job skills.

Let's see, I now know how to mop floors. I can also take food orders. Working in the jail commissary taught me how to follow instructions. 'How many boxes of cookies shall I put in your basket? How many bags of coffee did you say?'

I can paint, too! In 1985 I painted the stairwells and lower hallways of the jail. I also know the how-to's of working in the kitchen. My job was to put six sugars on each tray. I guess you could say I'm somewhat of a chef.

I worked in the storehouse as well. I can lift heavy boxes and stack them one on top of the other. I learned how to spot a crate of Frosted Flakes a mile away. Not to mention my ability to hide those frosted corn flakes from the guards to assure that my fellow workers and I ate a hearty breakfast for the next week. I can even get past the guards in the mess hall on chicken day to eat twice. Now to do that you have to be super slick, so I suppose you can say I'm skilled at covert operations as well.

After 20 years of incarceration I can honestly say: 'I am true to this, not new to this.'

John finished his article with the following words: 'After pausing to read what I have written, I am saddened and disgusted. I am afraid that my past may very well become my future.'

Unfortunately, it did. Shortly after he was released from Rikers at four in the morning, John walked into a hotel in Manhattan, picked the lock on a guest-room door, and swiped the first item he saw on the dresser. On his way out, he asked the concierge for a pen.

I know this because John told it to me himself. True to his word, he came to our office his first day out to attend a Jails Anonymous meeting, a support group for Fresh Start graduates. When I saw the fancy watch on his wrist and the hotel pen in his hand, I asked him where he'd stolen them from, and he casually filled in the blanks. He talked about how it made him feel 'powerful' and 'smart' to 'get one over on the system,' about the rush he felt as he sailed out of the hotel, no alarms or racing footsteps behind him, knowing that he was scot-free.

'Didn't you care about the man whose watch you stole?' I asked.

'Come on.' He rolled his eyes. 'Why would I care about him? I didn't even know him.'

He had a point, I thought. To John, the man in the hotel room was as rich and faceless as a corporation. He was a 'have' and John was a 'have-not.' And living, as he did, on the margins of society, John wasn't likely to know many haves.

'You know,' he added, 'I could've taken his wallet or the plane ticket that was sitting on the dresser. But I thought, Why be greedy? The watch is enough.'

For a moment I marveled at his thinking; the distinctions in his conscience showed, at least, that he had one. I quickly snapped out of it.

'Enough for what? To get high? Did you steal the watch to sell it for heroin?'

'No. I'm trying to go straight. That's why I came to your office. Can you help me get a job?'

I used to be amazed when my students would tell me about their crimes so openly, as if somehow I would find humor, cleverness, or a Robin Hood–like heroism in their heists. Only a sociopath, I thought, could speak about sticking people up or 'boosting' (shoplifting) with such bravado or, more commonly, with complete nonchalance. Certainly for some, getting away with a crime meant they had succeeded at something, and the pride in their voice was unmistakable. For most of my students, however, certain crimes just aren't a big deal. Their backgrounds, associations, and return trips to Rikers not only impart but reinforce criminality. As criminologist Ronald Akers observes, crime and deviance result when people 'differentially associate' with individuals who expose them to crime, and when deviant behavior is 'differentially reinforced over conforming behavior.'

The social controls that deter most people from stealing – shame from peers and family members, being fired by an employer, the fear of incarceration – don't exist for state-raised convicts who have a low investment in conventional society. Breaking the law and going to jail become what sociologists describe as 'normalized' experiences. Criminal behavior loses its stigma; sanctions lose their sting.

'The more often the sanction of imprisonment is employed, the less it deters,' writes Todd Clear in a groundbreaking article on how incarceration actually increases crime. For people like John, prison is no deterrence. How could it be? It's a familiar environment where he knows how to function, how to 'get his props,' as the inmates say. In a jail full of losers, John was a star. In society he was nothing.

KENNY

Despite their sporadic and inadequate schooling, my students are far from ignorant. I remember a homework assignment I gave to my first class: Write an essay on one of three questions: *How do you feel about the baseball strike – do you side with the players or the owners?* (The Major League players' strike made headlines in the spring of 1994); *Discuss the pros and cons of President Clinton's 1994 Crime Bill*; or *If all of your insecurities disappeared, how would your life look a year from today?*

I assumed most of them would write about the baseball strike. Instead, I received seven informed articles on the crime bill, six essays about life without insecurity, and two pieces about the baseball strike.

Twenty-year-old Kenny wrote the following essay about the crime bill. He was raised in Harlem by a single mother and sentenced to a year on Rikers for selling drugs. His father is serving a life sentence in Attica prison for a murder he committed in his teens. 'He's never comin' out,' Kenny said when I asked him if he'd see him anytime soon. 'He'll die in there.' Of President Clinton's crime bill, Kenny wrote:

Simply stated, the recently passed crime bill is a joke. The crime bill costs taxpayers $30 billion but you can be sure it'll hurt blacks and Latinos. See, when you're young and black, you're guilty first. The rule for cops when it comes to people like me is shoot first and ask questions later – when the paramedics come.

The 100,000 new police officers on the streets will be trying hard to make arrests to keep their jobs. Given the recent police scandals we've seen, it's probably safe to say that at least 10% of them will be corrupt. Poor urban areas are unknown jungles for them, and they draw their weapons too quickly.

Unfortunately, the bill did not include enough money for community centers, homeless shelters and jobs. Seems like a lot of money passes by but never stops in our neighborhoods.

And then came the anger.

This crime bill is a piece of shit and a waste of taxpayers' money. Instead of educating people in low-income communities, politicians just want to lock motherfuckers up for the rest of their lives. Society should remember that most prisoners get out one day. Who do they want on their streets? Animals or educated, reformed ex-cons?

Several years later, I was on my way to class and bumped into Kenny on the campus of John Jay College. I wondered what he was doing there, at a criminal justice college attended mostly by law-enforcement professionals. He'd shaved his head, and the earring was gone. Standing six-three with a Tommy Hilfiger jacket draped over his broad shoulders, he turned more heads than mine. 'I told you I wasn't goin' back to jail,' he said. 'A few more semesters and I'll have my degree.'

I remembered a Saturday morning in June two years before, when Kenny came to my apartment with a box of doughnuts and a worn SAT book under his arm. He had been out of jail for almost a year and was working part time in our office. He was determined to get into college, and I offered to help him study vocabulary words on the weekend.

I remember the look on my boyfriend's face when he answered the door. Like Kenny, Keith was tall and muscular, but I saw a flash of apprehension as his eyes took in Kenny, how he fumbled through his best version of a 'boy-from-the-'hood' handshake. Our Rottweiler, Jake, wouldn't back off. Too many alpha males in one room, I thought, and suggested that Kenny and I go to the roof to do our work.

On a stack of index cards Kenny had written definitions, synonyms, and antonyms. 'Here,' he said, handing me the cards. 'Quiz me.'

'Okay . . . pecuniary . . .'

Kenny closed his eyes. 'Money? Something to do with money?'

'Right, good job.' We went on like this for a couple of hours.

Today Kenny is putting himself through college. He attends classes four nights a week and works as a counselor at a detention facility for juvenile offenders. 'I tell them I've been in their shoes,' he says, 'and if they don't wake up soon, they'll be headed for state prison just like I was.'

CHARLIE

The last day of class is always bittersweet: I know I won't see some of my students again but I'm proud that they made it through the rigorous program. In the last hour, I ask each man to go to the front of the room and describe to his peers the kind of life he visualizes for himself upon release. I sit in the back and take notes as they speak. The notes go in their files, which we show them when they're out as reminders of their goals.

At first, some of the men shake their heads or pretend they don't understand the question. Then one man, usually riding more on bravado than bravery, swaggers to the front of the room and begins.

The most memorable experience was with my first class. Charlie, a peaceful heroin addict and one of the best students in the program, waited until everyone had gone before he slouched to the front of the room. I thought he was feeling self-conscious; the dentures he received from the jail dentist didn't fit right and chattered in his mouth when he spoke. But the students respected Charlie because of his writing skills. He had written some of the best articles in the *Rikers Review* and had a gentleness of spirit that made him instantly likable.

Charlie walked slowly to the front of the room. At age forty-five he had the appearance of an old man. (Doctors say inmates have the 'medical age' of people ten years their senior because of 'at-risk behaviors,' inadequate preventive care, and years of neglect.) When Charlie turned and faced his classmates, whose expectations of him were high, he opened his mouth, mumbled something, and then buried his face in his hands. When he lifted his head his face was wet with tears. I knew something terrible had happened; behind bars, crying is the ultimate sign of weakness, a shameful act that breeds contempt and ostracism.

All eyes were on Charlie, but he had no dreams to present. That morning he had learned that he was HIV-positive. He told the group he didn't know how he would find a foothold in society once he was released.

'I am an outcast four times over,' he said. 'Ex-con, ex-junkie, black, and HIV-positive. I'd be lyin' if I told you I had any dreams.'

Silence. Open mouths. Staring at the floor. I prayed someone would reach out to him. And then someone did: the class tough guy, the stubborn, fiercely independent inmate and occasional bully, Milton, pushed his chair aside and approached Charlie. He hesitated, thrust out his chest, and then wrapped his arms around him. 'Hey – you my man. You gonna make it,' Milton told him. 'I believe in you, man.' The ice was broken.

One by one, each of Charlie's classmates, the men society knows only as coldhearted thugs, rose from their chairs and walked to the front of the room. They shook Charlie's hand, slapped him on the back, and hugged him.

'You're my hero,' one of them said. 'You ain't gonna die. You gonna make it. We're here for you, man.'

Two days after Charlie left Rikers, he started shooting heroin again. But this time he did something different: He called his counselor at Fresh Start and agreed to enter a six-month drug-treatment program.

I didn't hear from Charlie for a while. Three years later, I bumped into him in a dark holding cell under the Supreme Court building in Manhattan. The agency I had moved to, the Correctional Association of New York, monitors conditions in the city's court pens, mini-jails in the bowels of the courthouses where detainees are held before arraignment. As we toured the cell blocks and spoke with the inmates, one of them called out my name.

Charlie rose from a bench in the back of the cell and squinted as he approached the bars. He was bone thin and stooped. I stuck my arm through the bars to shake his hand. A correction officer told me to step back.

'Charlie? Is that you? What are you doing here? I'm so glad to see you!' I instantly regretted my poor choice of words. Of course he couldn't tell me why he was there with twenty men pushing up on him and a guard within earshot. And telling someone you're glad to see him in jail just doesn't work.

'It's a long story,' he said. 'I'll write you a letter.'

I slipped him my card, doubting he would.

A week later I received his letter. I noticed that the return address was the Anna M. Kross Center on Rikers Island, the jail where inmates facing hard time in state prison are held. Charlie wrote that after he completed the drug program, he finally started getting his life together. 'I wanted to take some courses, creative writing among them,' he said, but was back in jail before he had a chance. 'In my situation, having the Monster [AIDS] as they call it here, I have to rely on public assistance to get on my feet,' he explained. 'The places the city houses me in are always in the middle of the war zone. Just when I had almost pulled myself up by my bootstraps, I was stopped by the police, arrested and charged with drug sale.'

He swore he was innocent; the cops got the wrong guy, he said. 'All I had on me was $13. No drugs, no money that was marked, nothing. It took me eleven months to get to trial and be acquitted.' Because he was innocent – or some might say foolish – Charlie refused to 'cop a plea,' meaning he declined the plea bargain the prosecutor offered: a reduction to a misdemeanor charge and a couple of months on Rikers. But proving his innocence and the cops' mistake cost him about a year of his already shortened life.

According to Michael Jacobson, delayed justice in the Big Apple is all too familiar. Michael Jacobson is a professor at John Jay College who has studied court-case processing; he is the former commissioner of the New York City Department of Correction and the former commissioner of the Department of Probation. 'New York City has one of the most pathologically delayed court systems in the country,' he tells me. 'Inmates who can't make bail are held on Rikers Island and can be taken back and forth to court fifteen times before their case is resolved.' New Yorkers charged with felonies spend an average of 140 days on Rikers before they are convicted and sentenced or, as in Charlie's case, acquitted and released.

'I was released into the streets with nothing,' Charlie continued. The material loss was bad, he said, but what 'hurt the most' was the personal loss. Before he got locked up, Charlie had met a woman who was also in recovery and also HIV-positive. They had fallen in love and planned to marry. 'She waited for me while I was detained, not knowing if I would be out in twelve months or twelve years,' he wrote. 'But eventually she gave up on me and moved back to Florida with her mother.'

The episode 'took the heart out' of him, he said. 'I went to war in my own little way. I just said "fuck society" and ended up doing everything I had been accused of. I sold drugs, I started using again. I didn't care. I started packin' (carrying a gun) 'cause I swore I wasn't going back. In short, I went buck wild.' The day I saw him in the holding cell in the Manhattan supreme court building, he was awaiting sentencing for gun possession and drug sale.

'I figure I can't just lie down and die,' he wrote. 'I got to rise. I want to go higher next time. One day I hope to make you proud to say you know me.'

Chances are strong I will not see Charlie again. As a second felony offender, he will serve, at a minimum, ten years in state prison. By then, the Monster will have killed him.

When stories like Charlie's make me feel like giving up, I remember the advice of my former supervisor at Fresh Start, Alice Layton. She told me that if we save one man in thirty, we've beaten the odds. 'We need to be the safe people our students can count on for second, third, and fourth chances. Our mission can't be affected by individual successes or failures.'

Beginning in the 1980s, the Department of Correction contained the swelling inmate population by building more jails, grafting prefab units onto the old-style penitentiaries, and launching several jail barges. The city purchased two 350-bed ships, former POW ships from the Falkland Islands war, to the tune of about $50 million. When the jail population dipped slightly in the mid-1990s, the city closed the old POW ships. Since tens of millions had been spent on them, Commissioner Michael Jacobson toyed with the idea of a floating hotel, a novel idea that landed his picture on the front page of the *New York Post*. 'We even had a name for it,' he joked. 'The Holiday Inn-mate.' The ships ended up sold as scrap metal.

Taxpayers bore a steep price for the flurry of jail construction: a more than 600 percent increase in the Department's operations budget between 1980 and 1990. Despite the spending on correction, both the jails and the city were a mess when I started teaching on Rikers in 1994. Revelers rang in the New Year as two cops fell to sniper fire. Over 2,000 New Yorkers had been murdered the year before. Crack was on the downswing but heroin use was up. Newly elected Mayor Giuliani declared war on 'a city out of control.' He ushered in zero tolerance and quality-of-life policing, which landed scores of low-level offenders and drug addicts in jail. With intensified law enforcement, arrest rates soared and Rikers brimmed with prisoners.

Compounding the problem was the stock market crash of 1987, which left in its wake a budget crunch that lasted through the mid-1990s. Throughout the city, social services were cut; in the jails, they were decimated. Scores of Rikers counselors and teachers were fired; entire programs were closed down, leaving the inmates idle and more frustrated than usual. In 1994 alone, the jails racked up over 1,000 inmate stabbings and slashings. An October 1994 cover of *New York* magazine featured the headline *IS RIKERS ABOUT TO EXPLODE?*

In one of the most alarming breaches of security in the history of Rikers Island, an inmate on Rikers was shot. (Not even officers are allowed to have guns inside the jails.) 'I'll never forget that phone call,' former commissioner Jacobson tells me. 'It was four in the morning and the chief of security is on the line telling me an inmate's been shot. I'm thinking, *Shot?* Shot with what? A slingshot?' Jacobson later learned that a visitor had smuggled in the gun, a tiny derringer pistol, with which four inmates had planned to

WELCOME TO THE ROCK

shoot each other. The deal was that one inmate would shoot the other three, then himself, and they'd all sue the city for damages. 'It was so unbelievably stupid,' Jacobson says. 'The gunman almost died when he shot himself.'

When I entered my classroom that spring, tension on the Rock was palpable. A CO warned me that a riot was likely. The jails were averaging more than 100 violent incidents a month. I took solace in the fact that Fresh Start was located in CIFM, known as the calmest jail on the island. CIFM houses only sentenced inmates who, because they want to go home on their scheduled release date, are more invested in following the rules.

Still, the jail was far from orderly. Gangs ran the dorms, and 'red alerts' signifying an inmate disturbance, which could mean any-thing from a simple stabbing to a full-scale riot, were frequent occurrences. During red alerts all jail movement ceases. The doors slam shut to 'freeworlders' (civilian staff and correction officers alike); no one is allowed to enter or leave the facility; traffic on the bridge comes to a stop.

In my classroom in the basement of the jail, I'd be shut in with fif-teen male inmates sporting doo-rags and gang colors (both of which have since been banned) while edgy correction officers roamed the halls. 'Don't worry,' my students would say. 'You're safe in here with us.'

For the most part I felt that I was, because one thing I knew about convicts was that they have a soft place in their hearts for mothers and teachers, particularly female teachers. It also helped that I was a contributing editor at *Prison Life*, a glossy magazine for America's captive readers known as the 'voice of the convict.' Because of that, my students saw me as an ally. If a riot broke out when I wasn't there, they said, they'd be good reporters and get me the scoop from the inside.

Fortunately, a riot never did occur, and over the ensuing years violence on the Rock declined precipitously. Since 1995, inmate stabbings and slashings have dropped 90 percent. Stories of what some believe is a Rikers Island renaissance have been featured in *The New York Times,* the *New York Post,* the *Daily News,* and even a prestigious criminology journal.

ALFONSO

One of my students, Alfonso, interviewed some old-timers on Rikers for an article he was writing about brutality in the jails before the current reforms. I told him we would never be able to publish his story in the *Rikers Review* – the Department prohibits any mention of gangs, weapons, or violence – but Alfonso wrote it anyway. 'Maybe I'll get it published on the outside,' he said, and asked me to hold onto it for him.

According to his sources and the ten years he spent on and off Rikers Island, 'the Rock was a violent and crazy place' until the late 1990s. 'Most of the fights were along racial lines. Blacks and Hispanics fought constantly. Gangs ran the dorms and controlled the phones.' Of the two phones in each dorm, one belonged to the Bloods, a black gang, and the other to the Latin Kings, a Hispanic gang. 'If you weren't part of a gang, you had to split a motherfucker's face open to get on the phone,' he wrote. 'Extortion, stealing, rape . . . I'd need an encyclopedia to complete the list.' Jailhouse thugs 'would extort punks for their commissary' [goods purchased from the jail store] 'or try to make you their wife.' Predatory inmates known as 'booty bandits' forced weaker inmates into becoming their personal sex slaves and sometimes traded their sexual services for cigarettes and food from other prisoners.

'Inmates organized into gangs for security,' he wrote. 'Even today, anyone who goes to a CO (correction officer) for help is a "rat" and the consequences are severe. Back then, death was not out of the question.

'All the officers would do for you after the inmates done fucked you up was move you to another dorm. And when the inmates in that dorm found out you snitched, you were dead meat.'

Alfonso called me a week after he was released. He'd managed to make it home safely from Rikers without getting high or into trouble. He'd kept his appointment with the college counselor who visited the program on Rikers and planned to begin classes in the fall. He even got his old carpenter's job back. His only problem, he said, was loneliness.

'Everyone I know is in the mix. I don't know what to do with myself when I'm not working.'

He lived with his sister and her husband in the projects and didn't feel safe leaving the apartment. 'I don't wanna get caught up in a drug sweep,' he said, 'or be tempted to buy drugs myself.' He asked if I'd like to do something with him that weekend so I invited him to church, hoping that the Unitarian sermon wouldn't offend his Catholic sensibilities.

When I arrived, he was standing outside and greeted me warmly. Within seconds, my heart sank – I could tell he'd gone back to heroin.

'You can always tell by the complexion,' a former heroin addict and Fresh Start counselor told me. 'It's darker and yellowish.'

I could also tell by the difference in Alfonso's appearance. In jail, he looked almost elegant: tall, well built, jet-black hair, smooth olive skin. He was quiet and dignified; his many years of 'hard time' in state prison had earned him respect from his peers. One look from Alfonso would silence a disruptive student. To them he was a convict, not an inmate. To his teacher, he was a gentleman.

Most times he'd arrive early to class. He'd straighten the rows of desks and erase the blackboard so I wouldn't get chalk on my clothes. He'd hustle the inmates out of the halls and raise his hand before speaking. But on that cloudy Sunday morning on the Upper East Side, the dark circles under his eyes, his 'yellowish' complexion, and the tremble in his hands as he bent to light a cigarette told me he'd gone back to heroin.

After the service, I took him to lunch. I asked him how he was doing; he said he was fine.

'It's still weird being out,' he said, pushing aside a half-eaten hamburger. 'I know I'm supposed to be happy but it's hard. I've been in prison so much I feel like an outlaw even when I'm free.'

He saw the sadness in my face and it made him uncomfortable.

'Don't worry about me,' he said. 'I'll get over it.'

I tried to approach the subject of relapse but ended up on a soapbox. 'Alfonso, I know it's difficult right now, but it'll get better. I promise. You'll be in school in just a couple of months and you'll make friends there. You'll meet people who aren't in the drug game.

But please, you can't keep getting high. You'll lose everything if you do. You're too good for drugs.' I sounded like a commercial.

'I'm not getting high,' he said. 'I mean, not really. I picked up once but I stopped the next day. I went to an NA meeting right afterward. I'll be fine. Let's change the subject, okay?'

I knew to shut up. Alfonso was proud and he would do it on his own – or not. I also knew that when an addict says he 'only picked up once but will be fine,' he's headed for a return trip to Rikers. I could see how lonely Alfonso was when he asked if he could 'just hang' with me while I did some errands that afternoon.

We stopped in a used bookstore in Greenwich Village and browsed through a table of one-dollar books. I figured he'd buy a thriller, maybe an adventure story, but *The Secret of Male Depression* was the title of the book he bought. A counselor once told me that our clients often use drugs to 'self-medicate' – Prozac for the uninsured.

Outside, a cold rain had begun to fall. He held his book over my head so I wouldn't get wet. I told him to call me or his counselor at Fresh Start if he wanted to talk. He said he would and we hugged good-bye.

As I watched him walk away with his worn book on depression under his arm, I had a sinking feeling I wouldn't see Alfonso again. That time I was right.

Violence on Rikers began to decline when Commissioner Jacobson took over the city jails in 1995. A former city-budget official with a Ph.D. in sociology, he knew not only where to find the funding to make the jails safer, but also how. He expanded education programs, added another month of training for correction officers, and, most significantly, increased the number of drug-treatment slots from 100 to 1,500.

'Michael Jacobson was a truly extraordinary commissioner,' says Anthony Smith, head of the New York City Horticultural Society, which runs a greenhouse program for Rikers prisoners. 'He really cared about inmates not coming back.'

The perfect complement to the humanitarian Jacobson was his tough-minded partner in correction, Bernard Kerik, then a deputy commissioner. Known for his hands-on management style and intolerance for inefficiency, Kerik worked unrelentingly to tame Rikers Island. In an innovative move, Jacobson and Kerik took NYPD's nationally recognized crime-fighting strategies and adapted them to the jails. Known as TEAMS, a sporty acronym for Total Efficiency Accountability Management Systems, the program combines the principles of business management with zero-tolerance policing. It holds both correction staff and inmates accountable for keeping orderly jails. According to Kerik, whom Mayor Giuliani recently appointed Commissioner of the NYPD, the Department now has over 100 performance indicators to assess agency operations. Kerik instituted weekly 7:30 A.M. meetings where wardens are grilled on overtime expenses, inmate violence, and CO sick rates. Many Rikers wardens have been fired or transferred for less-than-pleasing results.

'We gotta name for TEAMS,' says a captain who favors the old-school policy of let-the-wardens-run-their-own-jails. 'Total elimination of all managers systematically. You go to one of those meetings with decades on the job and you come out fuckin' retired.'

For inmates, zero-tolerance means that if an inmate slashes another inmate, he's charged with assault and weapon possession and faces up to seven years in state prison. In the past, assaultive inmates were given sixty to ninety days in 'the Bing,' a disciplinary lockdown unit. In 1999, the Department arrested 1,186 inmates in the jails, a whopping 675 percent increase from 1996. Today, sweeping searches for contraband by helmeted, baton-wielding COs are common occurrences. The Department also introduced electronic stun shields, glowing and crackling with electric currents – 'They scare the inmates more than anything,' a Department official told me – to 'extract' recalcitrant inmates who refuse to leave their cells.

Undoubtedly, the jails are noticeably safer today and my students are calmer, both of which make teaching there easier. It also helped to learn their lingo and know their backgrounds. My first few minutes in the classroom, however, were mortifying. As I stood before my students and began to introduce myself, a few of the men started hissing. 'Whew . . . she's fat,' I heard someone say. My face reddened; my jaw dropped. 'I can't believe you're calling me fat,' I blurted idiotically.

Chuckling and shaking heads. Then one of the inmates went to the blackboard and picked up the chalk. 'P-h-a-t,' he spelled. 'That's ghetto for hot.' I felt both relieved and manipulated.

A half hour later I did it again. I asked the men to introduce themselves to the group, stating their age, where they were from, and why they had joined Fresh Start. When a young Hispanic man began speaking, I noticed a tear-shaped tattoo on his cheekbone, like a teardrop on a clown's face. It made him look less sinister.

'That's an interesting tattoo,' I commented. 'I've never seen one like it. Does it symbolize a state of permanent sadness?'

This time the men didn't chuckle – they howled. The inmate turned and looked me dead in the eye. 'It means I killed someone,' he said. He was a member of the Latin Kings, one of the two Hispanic gangs on the Rock. Tears mean dead bodies, not sadness.

I was also guilty of idealizing my students. They worked so diligently in the program that I couldn't understand how difficult it was for many of them to keep a job on the outside. I learned this lesson the hard way: from one of my favorite students, Benjamin.

BENJAMIN

When I interviewed Benjamin I was surprised when he said he wanted to be in the computer class. Fresh Start offers vocational training in two areas: culinary arts and computers, both major industries in New York City with plenty of job opportunities. The inmates in the computer program also learn word processing so they can type their articles for the *Rikers Review*. But I didn't see how that would be possible for Benjamin. His left hand hung like a rag from his wrist, the result of a gunshot to the back.

'You realize you'll have to learn to type if you're accepted,' I said. 'We don't want to set you up to fail.' I felt bad that I had been abrupt with him. Unlike the other inmates with their convict swagger and 'hood-boy toughness, Benjamin projected vulnerability. He was small – maybe five-five – and spoke in a quiet voice. He had huge, walnut-brown eyes and a smile so warm it could melt the heart of the coldest correction officer.

'I won't fail,' he said. 'I can promise you that. I'm just asking for a chance. I wanna work in an office when I get out. I gotta learn how to use a computer.'

I thought about Fresh Start's mission: rebuilding New York, one life at a time. Benjamin had nearly lost his life. The least we could do was teach him to type.

Like the other inmates sitting in the gym waiting to be interviewed, Benjamin had learned about the program through flyers we posted in the jail dormitories. Unlike some of the other inmates, I noticed, he hadn't ripped the flyer off the wall but wrote down the time and place of the interview. About 250 of the jail's 1,200 inmates sign up for Fresh Start, but because of limited funding we can enroll only twenty-five students in each three-month cycle.

Besides instinct, which comes from knowing the inmate population well, we base our choices on whether the candidate has some work history and doesn't show signs of mental illness. Eye contact, authenticity, and enthusiasm – the qualities that would attract employers on the outside – are the traits we look for in one-on-one interviews.

After fifteen minutes with Benjamin, I told him he'd made it to the next level. 'Consider yourself a semifinalist,' I said. 'The final requirement is to write a one-page essay on life in jail and drop it by the program office by nine o'clock tomorrow morning.'

When he asked if he could write about life after jail, I liked him even more.

To prepare students for jobs on the outside, we simulate a workplace environment. We give them performance evaluations, pay them the highest wage available in the jail (fifteen dollars a week), and dock them a day's pay if they miss a class. In addition to twelve weeks of vocational training, the students attend classes in conflict resolution, relapse prevention, life skills, public speaking, career counseling, and GED prep. Equally as important as cooking or computer skills, these groups address the problems that lead to criminal behavior in the first place.

In the writing class, which I teach, the inmates become reporters and writers for the *Rikers Review*. I use the project of publishing a magazine to build their skills in teamwork, prioritizing workloads, and meeting deadlines. Similar in format, say, to an *Esquire* magazine for convicts, the *Rikers Review* contains feature articles, profiles, true confessions, poetry, short stories, and humor. The men draw illustrations to accompany their articles, or pay other inmates with cigarettes to get the artwork they need. While pieces such as 'Confessions from a Drug Dealer,' 'How to Be a Dad from Behind Bars,' and 'Your Guide to Getting (Legal) Work on the Outside' are common features in the *Rikers Review,* some of the men write rich and gritty short stories in the tradition of prison writers like Chester Himes and Edward Bunker.

In every class, one or two men write with uncommon literary sophistication. Take, for example, the following poem that my student John W. wrote for his girlfriend.

SOMETHING FOR YOUR HEAD

I want to know where you go
When you journey on the wings of your thoughts –
I have watched you take flight
Like a bird in the night.

Do you realize that your imagination
Is the inspiration for life's rhythms
The beat to songs yet sung,
A melody so beautiful it can't be clothed in words?

When you behold your image in life's mirror
Does your spirit dance with the waves
Taking you to places and unexplored spaces
Revealing your face in all of its graces?

Can you believe with conviction
That you alone
Are the source from which all poetry finds its beginning
And its end –

That life is a woman
Like you
Making men, like me
Understand what it means to live.

Some of the men write to release emotions that have been buried under layers and years of mind-numbing drug addiction. Others write for solace, for redemption, or to lash out at the demons that have robbed them of their dreams. A few write to stay sane; others write to pass time, but most come to find that writing is cathartic and publishing builds self-esteem. Seeing their name in print, even in a jailhouse magazine, infuses them with the sweet joy of confidence. Some are so inspired that they continue to write after they're released.

In fact, two of my students have had prominent pieces published in major New York City newspapers alongside their pictures. One of my students completed a novel. Another published a guide to Windows 95 in Spanish. A sixteen-year-old in the one class of adolescents I taught on Rikers went on to become the editor of his college literary journal. More than a few have had letters to the editor published in the *Daily News*. Another graduate performed his poetry at the exclusive National Arts Club off Gramercy Park in Manhattan and now teaches poetry to incarcerated youths. A former drug dealer I never thought I'd see again now designs Web sites for a living, including one for a prominent criminal-defense association. Several times a year he returns to the Rock to lay out the inmate magazine he once wrote for.

All this from society's 'rabble.'

I'll never forget the sight of Benjamin hunched over the computer keyboard, hunting and pecking with one hand. He never complained, and he refused the offers of help from his peers. He learned to type forty words per minute, faster than some men with two working hands. He was the perfect role model, living proof that handicaps needn't kill dreams.

When I asked Benjamin about his life, he said he had two children and that his girlfriend ('my babies' mother') was on public assistance. He had a job at Footlocker paying minimum wage, and started selling drugs after his second child was born. 'I had to make ends meet,' he said. At the time he was twenty years old.

A full-time minimum-wage salary is $16,478. Welfare and food stamps for a family in New York (comprised of one parent, one pre-schooler, and one school-age child) is $10,344. 'Though the federal government says poverty in New York City officially ends at $14,150,' reports *The New York Times*, '. . . meeting bare-bone needs in the city costs two to five times more than the national poverty level for families with children.' A study of basic family expenses in the five boroughs set the 'self-sufficiency wage' for a family living in Queens, for example, at $46,836.

Shortly before Benjamin was released, I told him I had a job waiting for him on the outside. I'd recently become the managing editor at *Prison Life* magazine and we needed help in the office. Our ex-con publisher was happy to give him a chance, and I was thrilled to be able to help him. Benjamin was one of my first students to leave Rikers, and I had the intoxicating feeling, as self-indulgent as it is illusory, that I was saving a life.

On the last day of class Benjamin gave me a poem expressing his gratitude. Using his new skills, he typed it on the computer and framed it with clip art of farm animals. The poem reads, in part: 'Doubt the sun shines in the sky / Doubt the moon illuminates the night / Doubt the truth to be a lie / But never doubt my gratitude for you / No matter what the outcome is / I will always be grateful to you for assisting me in re-establishing my life on the straight path.'

Benjamin's poem was the first of many gifts I have received from inmates over the years, and it hangs in my office today. I say this not to brag, but because I want people to know how generous ex-inmates can be and how much they appreciate the smallest gestures of kindness from freeworlders. My office is filled with hand-painted cards, handkerchief art, origami, a Hallmark plaque about friend-ship, and even several large oil paintings from a prisoner whose work was exhibited at the Whitney Museum of Art in Manhattan. When these ex-cons come to my office, it is not unusual for them to have a box of candy or some flowers under their arm, despite being fresh out of jail and virtually broke. It is also not unusual for them to walk on the outside of the sidewalk, a gentlemanly gesture I rarely see in non-ex-con men under fifty.

Looking back, I can say that Benjamin tried hard and lasted longer than I would have expected today. He started with a bang, arriving early, working through his lunch hour, and even writing a hip-hop column for our magazine using the skills he'd learned in the writing class. One day he went to the doctor for his TB medication (in the early nineties TB had reached epidemic levels on Rikers) and convinced the nurse to write an advice column for the magazine pro bono. We called it 'Ask Da Nurse.' It was the more mundane aspects of office work that baffled him, such as deciphering abbreviations like 'pls' and 're' on memos or understanding the mystery of faxes.

About three months into the job, he left a message saying he wouldn't be in that day. His voice sounded normal on the answering machine. I figured he just wanted a day off and it wasn't a big deal.

'My uncle got shot last night,' he told me the next day when I asked if he was okay. I was beginning to see that his life was more complicated than I'd imagined.

Soon after, Benjamin's absences became more frequent. Sometimes they were related to his TB; other stories were too confusing to make sense of. He's just finding his stride, I'd tell myself. Once he's used to the routine of a regular job he'll straighten out. We'd have a talk and for a few weeks he'd improve, but then it was back to his one day out for every two weeks worked. My boss's patience was wearing thin and I found myself making excuses for him. I knew I'd gone overboard when I heard myself say, 'Just give him one more chance. He's crippled.'

I forget what the inciting incident was, but I remember telling him he was fired. I remember because he started crying, which made me cry too. He apologized over and over, saying he just couldn't 'get it together.' I rode down with him in the elevator and hugged him good-bye on the street.

The next week I was on vacation, and when I returned I couldn't believe what I was hearing: My boss was telling *me* that we should give Benjamin another chance. I think it was a combination of his limp hand, his bright smile, his total lack of ego, and his sweet disposition that made people fall in love with Benjamin. The office was small to begin with, but it was empty without him.

My boss picked up the phone and called him. Benjamin answered and said he'd be there the next morning at nine o'clock sharp. 'He sounded good,' my boss said. 'He must have said "thank you" ten times.'

Benjamin did show up the next day, and continued to show up steadily for the next few weeks. He worked longer and harder than ever. He coordinated a huge mailing I never thought he'd manage with his hand and came in on the weekend to finish it.

The following Monday morning I gave him sixty dollars to pick up office supplies at Staples, a job he'd done regularly and faithfully every week since he'd started.

After an hour or two elapsed, my colleagues would pop into my office. 'Benjamin back yet?' After lunch they knew to stop asking.

It was several months later that I learned the truth about Benjamin. His girlfriend called looking for him, and I told her we hadn't seen him since the day he left with the sixty dollars.

'Sixty dollars? That's nuthin'! That crack head stole my TV.'

Crack head? Our Benjamin was a crack head? He seemed too young and too bright to be a crack head.

I'd like to think that today, hundreds of inmates later, I would have been able to tell – or that Benjamin would have been able to tell me.

2

FROM THE BELLY OF THE BEAST
TO THE NEW YORK STREETS

'Most Rikers inmates are serving a life sentence – one six-month bid at a time.'
> – Former warden James Kane

'I don't have a record – I have an album!'
> – Frankie G., a Rikers inmate who 'grew up on the Rock'

Before the sun rises over the East River each weekday morning, a strange scene unfolds in the heart of downtown Queens. A New York City Department of Correction bus emerges from the darkness and unloads a cheering group of ex-cons in front of Twin Donuts on Queens Plaza. It is here, on this empty strip at four in the morning, that the choices men make will determine whether they – like 75 percent of Rikers inmates – will be re-arrested and returned to jail within a year. For some it's a matter of days.

The 4 A.M. drop-off is one of the strangest (and most shameful) Rikers Island rituals. Years ago, before the surge in population, inmates were dropped off during daylight hours. But as the number of ex-cons descending upon the streets grew with increased admissions, local shopkeepers became nervous. The ex-inmates would scare away customers, they said. They were thieves just waiting to steal. So the Department of Correction agreed to release the inmates at dawn, when no one would be there to see them.

Today, the problem is that all the wrong people are there to greet them – namely drug dealers and prostitutes – and the right people – family members, friends, and social workers – are either too afraid or too tired to journey to Queens Plaza at that hour. My students often talk about the traps awaiting them the moment they step off the bus, and how the decisions they make during those critical first minutes can and often do send them straight back to the Rock.

One student designed a quiz for the *Rikers Review* called 'Rate Your Recidivism Quotient – Will You Come Back to Rikers?' The first question was: 'When you get off the bus on Queens Plaza, which of the following are you most likely to do? (A) Approach the nearest drug dealer B) Call home for a ride C) Grab a 40 [a 40-ounce can of beer made with malt liquor] and drink it with your buddies or D) See if there's some female action in Twin Donuts.'

I was attracted to Fresh Start because it boasted a recidivism rate of about 30 percent, meaning that nearly two-thirds of the program's graduates stay out of jail. Fresh Start succeeds because it continues *after* jail, because the same counselors, instructors, and volunteers who work with the men on the inside help them find jobs, drug treatment, and support on the outside.

'A man who has been in jail once or twice or twenty times is twice as crippled as a man who has lost a leg,' founder Barbara Margolis says. 'It doesn't take a big brain to realize that most people are going to fail.' According to the Vera Institute of Justice, 350 inmates are released into New York City every *day*.

While some of Fresh Start's counselors and volunteers take a more hands-off approach with newly released inmates, Barbara's strategy is simple: 'You smother them,' she says. 'If you surround them and call them and bug them enough, then you have a chance.'

Barbara recalls one of her former students saying that the only reason he stopped getting high and entered a drug-treatment program was to get her 'off his back.' Today, this HIV-positive ex-junkie ex-con works as an outreach counselor for homeless men and has a decade of drug- and jail-free days behind him. Barbara recently told me he'd gotten married. 'I had the thrill of sending a Fresh Start graduate a wedding present,' she said. 'Can you imagine – sending a Fresh Start graduate a wedding gift?'

I don't know many people who would find such joy in sending an ex-con a wedding gift, but Barbara Margolis, like the inmates in the program, defies stereotypes.

'It seems like a situation comedy nobody would believe,' wrote *The New York Times* in a profile of her titled 'Lending a Jeweled Hand to Remorseful Thieves.' She is described, accurately, as 'a rich, sophisticated woman oddly dedicated to helping prisoners. She visits them in her limousine, brings chefs from the fanciest restaurants to teach them the mysteries of soufflés, sends them post-cards from her hideaway in the South of France.' Married to a recently retired CEO of a Fortune 500 company, Barbara served for a decade as the commissioner of protocol under former Mayor Edward Koch. For over thirty years she has volunteered in city jails helping inmates, meanwhile raising four children, building Fresh Start, and serving on the boards of a dozen city agencies and criminal-justice organizations.

One of her early inmate victories was a policy requiring the city to provide toothbrushes for pretrial adolescent detainees, who'd be locked up for months before they saw a judge. The more personal ways she has helped inmates are as innumerable as they are unusual, from arranging for the care of one inmate's dog to collecting bail money from the prostitute-girlfriend of another. The point she emphasized to me when I started was that teaching in jail is the easy part. It's when the inmates are released that their real prison sentence and our work begins.

It didn't take me long to see that she was right. Despite the depressing environment, teaching in jail is a pleasant experience, especially if you're a woman. You have a captive audience that hasn't seen a non-uniformed member of the fairer sex in a long time. Fortunately, my inmate-students usually relate to me more as a maternal figure than a romantic interest, and whether I'm in a relationship or not I always make reference to a boyfriend. The point is, they value contact with any civilian, male or female, who shows them warmth and respect. A compliment can turn them into putty.

Teaching behind bars is seductive because jail is not the real world. It is an illusory place, built on temporary and artificial supports, a place where it is far easier to declare one's dreams than actually pursue them. Helping inmates live out their good intentions in the free world, however, or even to find a foothold, can be a Sisyphean task.

Imagine leaving Rikers Island with only a $4.50 Metro card to your name and the same clothes you were arrested in on your back. If you were arrested in July in a T-shirt and shorts and sentenced to six months in jail, you will be released in January in the same outfit. This is another Rikers oddity. When inmates relinquish their street clothes for jail greens, the Correction Department doesn't bother washing them. They simply stuff them into a bag – vomit, urine, filth, and all – and return them, wrinkled and stinking, to inmates upon release. This and a $4.50 Metro card are the city's parting gift to an inmate.

Imagine re-entering society in such a condition, maybe with a GED or some other certificates from jail. Imagine having the same untreated drug addiction that landed you in the joint in the first place still raging in your system. Imagine you didn't have a home to begin with, or lost the lease on your apartment in the process. These are the challenges facing the men who show up at our office ready to become 'productive members of society.' For the most part, their intentions are good and their staying power is admirable. It's just that the disappointments, for many, become unbearable. Frank is a good example.

FRANK

Frank is a thirty-nine-year-old Hispanic who 'grew up on the Rock.' His father was an alcoholic, a former boxer, and a wife beater who encouraged his son to be the most violent street fighter in the South Bronx.

'He and his friends used to sit outside the storefront and make us kids fight each other,' Frank told me one afternoon on Rikers when I asked him how his conflict-resolution class was going. 'That was how they entertained themselves. If I got my ass kicked on the street, I'd get another beatin' from him when I got home. That man was a tyrant.'

One night, Frank said, his father came home 'all drunk and saw a dead mouse in the trap. I'd left it there 'cause I didn't wanna touch it. I was like eight. I was afraid of it. So he starts slappin' me, callin' me a baby, punching me in the chest. He says, "Here, I'll give you something to cry about," and he picked up the mouse and put it in his mouth.'

When I grimaced, Frank said, 'C'mon, Jennifer. He was just tryin' to make me a man.'

Several years before I met Frank, his mother died. He described her as a fragile and religious woman who lived in fear of her husband and cleaned houses to put food on the table. He loved her more than anyone, he said, but he never got to say good-bye because he was serving a 'three-to-nine' in prison. The shame of losing his mother while he was locked up and the emptiness of his life upon release re-ignited his heroin habit. Soon enough, he was back on the Rock.

On Rikers, Frank was the model inmate. He joined a boot-camp program called High Impact (the country's first inmate boot camp) and responded to the military structure with joy. 'It kept me healthy, mentally and physically. They taught us discipline, things I never learned,' he said. He graduated as the valedictorian.

When he finished High Impact, he joined Fresh Start. In our program, he was exceedingly polite, always responding to the COs and instructors with a sharp 'Yes, ma'am,' or 'No, sir!' He had an avid interest in psychology and could often be seen with a self-help book under his arm. 'You just wait,' he'd tell me. 'It's gonna be different when I get out this time. I've learned from my mistakes, and I'm not coming back. You'll be proud of me; I'll show you. I'm gonna be the greatest accomplishment this program has ever seen.' Frank was always eager to please, and I guess that was what endeared him to me.

On the last day of the program, about three weeks before his release, he gave me a piece of jailhouse art. On a white handkerchief he had drawn a red heart, cracked in two by a lightning bolt, inscribed with a cryptic message he'd written in calligraphy: 'The strong take from the weak . . . the smart take from the strong.'

On Frank's first day of freedom, he stopped by our office. I remember the day well because it was unusually damp and cold. A freezing rain had begun to tap on the window when the receptionist told me Frank had arrived. I went out to greet him and there he was, standing in the same military stance he'd carried off so well in jail. He seemed too stiff, either from habit or the cold, to sit. The combination of his tight purple suit, patent leather shoes, and no overcoat made me want to cry.

Nevertheless, he extended a firm, cold hand and told me he'd told me so. 'Betcha never thought you'd see me again,' he said with a wink.

When he took a seat in my office and a sip from the coffee I handed him, I had the strange feeling of meeting Frank for the first time – a feeling I often experience when I see a man I've known only in jail on the outside, in street clothes, under the glare of office light. On Rikers, in his pressed greens and polished shoes, with his combed hair and shaved face, Frank looked like a model citizen. On the outside, with his garish suit and frozen smile, revealing the teeth of lifelong drug addiction and poverty, he looked insane.

But there he was, sitting across from me, with a grin as wide as a jack-o'-lantern's. He was so happy to be free! He opened his vinyl briefcase nervously – I noticed his hands were shaking – and displayed a dozen certificates from various prison and jail programs he'd completed over the past decade.

Let's see: Frank was certified to buff floors, prep cook, paint walls, and repair computers. 'Were they IBMs or Macs you worked on?' I asked, the gaps in his résumé closing in my mind.

'I don't remember.' He shrugged. 'I did that training five years ago.'

Frank's mission was to get a job – 'ASAP,' he said. Using the goal-setting techniques he'd learned in Fresh Start, he gave himself a deadline of two weeks. 'I got just enough money to last me until then,' he said.

I was able to piece together a résumé for Frank, using the 'functional' versus 'chronological' format, but I knew his employment pickings would be slim and there wasn't a lot I could do to help him. By then another client was waiting, so I gave Frank the classifieds, a phone book, and copies of his résumé and wished him good luck. I told him I felt bad I couldn't do more for him and to come back on a less busy day. 'Don't apologize,' he said. 'You made me a great résumé. I know I can get a job.'

Frank called the next day to say he'd gone on two interviews: one for a messenger's job and another for a sales job that paid commission only. When I asked him how he thought he did on the interviews, I was surprised at his self-awareness. 'I think I scare people,' he said. 'It's obvious I've been locked up.'

After a full week of interviewing, Frank was still without an offer. He came to our Jails Anonymous meeting and spoke of his frustration and how it took every bit of strength he had not to get high. When the counselor recommended a drug-treatment program, Frank refused. He'd been locked up half his life; he didn't want to go from one institution to another without giving freedom the best shot he had. He left the meeting agitated but still determined to get a job.

I didn't hear from Frank for a while, then one day he stopped by the office 'just to say hi.' He hadn't found anything steady but was working off the books doing construction jobs. I noticed a screwdriver protruding from his pack and asked him if it was one of the tools of his trade.

'Well, not exactly,' he said. He explained that he used the screwdriver to break into an abandoned apartment so he could sleep in peace. 'It's better than living in a crack house,' he said. 'And besides, there's a big rat there who keeps me company. I named him Lynwood.' (Lynwood was a Fresh Start counselor and ex-con known for his 'in-your-face' style of lecturing the adult male inmates.)

I asked him if he was using heroin again because I could tell from his complexion that he'd picked up. I also wanted to see if he'd be straight with me, and he was.

'Yeah, occasionally. I'm just dibbin' and dabbin'. I got it under control. Don't worry about me. Everything's great.'

I recommended an outpatient drug-treatment program but he refused. 'I'm a workin' man now. I don't have time to sit around and talk about my problems. I need to make some money so I can get an apartment.'

Several months passed before I heard from Frank again. Then one day he called from a pay phone. The excitement in his voice was palpable. 'I've got something to show you,' he said. 'I know you're busy. I'll only take ten minutes of your time.'

He arrived sweaty and disheveled and took a seat in my office. 'You're never going to believe this,' he said, removing his knapsack. 'Everything's changed. Look at this –'

He pulled a large paper bag from his knapsack and tried to hand it to me, but I rolled my chair away. Instinct told me that whatever was in that bag wasn't good.

'Frank, if there are drugs . . . or a gun . . . in that bag' – I spoke slowly and deliberately to give him a chance to change his mind – 'I really don't want to see it.'

'No, no. It's nothing like that – just open it!' he said, and dropped it into my lap.

I opened the bag. Inside were stacks upon stacks of hundred-dollar bills fastened with rubber bands.

'That's thirty thousand dollars.' He beamed. 'Go ahead – count it.' He thought that was funny and laughed.

I had never even seen, much less held, that much cash. A zillion thoughts raced through my mind: Is this some kind of setup? Why is he showing me this? Is the money marked? Where did he get it?

'Where'd you get this money, Frank?'

'Who cares where it came from? I just wanted to show you. I had to tell somebody, and I wanted to give you some. Here,' he said, reaching into the bag and pulling out a stack of hundreds, 'take what you need. You can't make that much money in this field, and you've always been so nice to me. Please . . .'

His smile now wrapped around his face, and all I could think of was how he should get his teeth fixed with some of the money.

I handed him the bag and tried to think of some therapeutic words, but my mind went blank. My heart was pounding; I went with my gut.

'Frank . . . I don't know what to say . . . so I'll just tell you how I feel, and how I feel is, well, sad.'

I was sad, I said, because whatever drug dealer I figured he stole the money from would probably kill him by day's end. And I was sad he'd taken a shortcut. 'If you ever decide to go straight and get a real job, you won't see this kind of money in a year. Or you'll waste it on drugs and be dead in a month.'

'No I won't,' he protested. 'As soon as my Medicaid kicks in I'm going into a program.'

'Medicaid? You don't need Medicaid, Frank! You could pay for six months at Hazelden with this kind of money.' He didn't get it. He was so used to being taken care of by the state that the thought of paying for drug treatment didn't occur to him.

We sat for a few minutes in silence. I thanked him, in any case, for his offer. 'Would you consider turning it in, maybe giving it back?'

'That's not possible,' he said, and left.

Like many prisons, Rikers Island is home to a colony of stray cats. Occasionally they slip into a jail kitchen, where a cook might toss them a scrap of food. Mostly they roam the island in search of mice; some get run over by correction buses. I was beginning to see a parallel between the cats and my clients. The sack of money Frank brought me was the dead bird a cat leaves at the doorstep of its owner. Like the strays on the Rock, they roam the streets in search of a fix or a hustle. They live scrappy, dangerous lives, then drop by for the occasional bowl of Friskies, or to leave a dead bird.

It was summer before I saw Frank again. Fit and suntanned (or was it the heroin?) in a white Polo shirt and shorts, he looked like he had just played a round of tennis. With him were two scrawny boys, whom Frank said he was looking after. He told me their father had been a friend of his; a month before, he'd been shot in a drug deal gone bad. To my amazement, Frank said he was the boys' guardian, and that day he had taken them to the park, to video arcades, and to a movie. He ushered them into my office, where I had a picture of Frank and his classmates on Rikers.

'Whatever you do,' Frank told the boys, 'don't end up in jail like your uncle Frankie did. You kids gotta stay in school and obey the law.'

Maybe this is good for him, I thought. Now he has a responsibility, something that might keep him off heroin.

That fall our agency moved to the South Bronx and I was afraid we'd lose touch with Frank. I tried calling the number of the chop shop he gave me (and where he lived on occasion), but the phone just rang and rang. It was a gray afternoon in November when a knock on the window startled me. Our office was previously a retail establishment and had a large storefront window that faced the street. I looked up from my work and saw Frank on the other side.

'Oh my God,' said my colleague. 'Is that Frank?' Rachel and I had worked together for two years and she knew the Frank saga well.

I was afraid to stand too close him when he entered. He was strung out on heroin, gaunt, unshaven, and filthy. His hair and face were greasy; he smelled like he'd spent the night in a garbage bin.

He'd heard on the street we'd moved, he said. 'I need to go to detox,' he mumbled through lips with open sores. He was too embarrassed to look at us when he spoke.

'Oh, Frank,' I said. 'What happened?' He looked so beaten down, so different from his tennis-pro image just months before. We found a drug counselor to speak with him, and thirty minutes later the counselor had a bed for Frank in a seven-day detox center. The big question was whether he'd take the counselor's advice and go straight from detox into long-term treatment. He said he'd let us know.

As the week went by, I thought of him often and hoped he'd call to say he'd enrolled in a program. On the tenth day I gave up, figuring he'd try one more time to do it on his own.

About two weeks later, one of the boys Frank had brought to my office the summer before appeared outside the window. I waved for him to come in, and then from behind the boy emerged Frank in a beautiful olive-green suit, striped tie, and clean white shirt. The boy handed me a bouquet of roses from behind his back. Frank winked and asked if he could give the boy my phone number. 'I'm going away for a while,' he said. 'I was hoping you could be there for him if he needs help.'

Frank said he was tired and wanted to change. 'Being a criminal and a dope fiend is all I seem to know how to do.' He felt his luck was running out; he was sick of the dope and didn't even get high from it anymore. He said he was ashamed of himself and never understood why I cared about him. And then the tears came.

'I wanna be a good person, I wanna get off the drugs and the streets and make somethin' out of my life. I want to be a counselor someday for people like me. . . .'

I looked at his crazy face and believed him. For that moment, I did. I saw into the future, Frank in his olive suit, the synapses in his brain somehow repaired, holding forth with a group of men like him, telling them about his broken life and how he put the pieces back together.

It is people like Frank who keep me going back to Rikers. Frank's story is a real one, and his journey out of the gutter, one step backward for every two steps forward, is how it occurs in the real world. Recovery from drug addiction and criminality rarely happens tidily. It takes years to change behaviors; it is a process of stops and starts and relapses and returns.

I admire the Franks of this world, and as I travel home from Rikers Island, noticing how the city gets cleaner and whiter with each mile closer to Manhattan, I ask myself how they do it, how they live such wretched lives in the richest city on earth, mired in the underclass yet still finding it in their hearts to take care of little boys without fathers and bring flowers to their teachers, when most people – certainly me, I know – would have given up long ago, or been too embittered to care.

Eight months later I got a call from Frank. He was still in the drug-treatment program and had accepted his counselor's advice to stay the full year. Unlike residential programs in the city, which my students say are as crowded and chaotic as jail, Project Renewal offers a program on a quiet farm about an hour and a half north of Manhattan. As part of the treatment, recovering addicts work outside, planting flowers and vegetable gardens and selling their produce at Green Markets in the city.

'I know you're busy,' Frank said when I answered. 'But I have something for you. I can be there in ten minutes.'

This should be interesting, I thought.

When he stepped through the door, I barely recognized him. His eyes were bright; he'd put on weight and muscles. His smile was irrepressible. He handed me a bouquet of sweet Williams, a bushel of cherry tomatoes, and little bundles of exotic herbs: red basil, cilantro, lemon rosemary. 'I didn't steal 'em,' he said. 'No more shortcuts. I planted these myself.'

On the day of his graduation, I traveled by bus to Goshen, New York, a forested hamlet about an hour and a half from the city. It was sunny and warm and my spirits were high. Every time I opened the newspaper, I found myself gazing out of the window, remembering all that had transpired with Frank since I'd met him two years before.

I remembered a Thanksgiving on Rikers, when the students in the cooking class were furloughed – yes, freed – for the day to deliver 100 turkey dinners they'd made to soup kitchens, a battered women's shelter, and a hospice for people with AIDS. For several years now, Fresh Start has worked this bit of magic. Barbara Margolis persuaded the correction officials to let us use the jail kitchen overnight to cook the turkeys and stuffing. To this day, New York City restaurateur Michael Weinstein donates 100 twenty-pound turkeys for the project. The department provides canned goods and bread for the stuffing. The male teens in 'junior' Fresh Start bake and decorate 500 cookies.

For two nights we'd be up, defrosting, basting, and cooking the turkeys, letting them cool on the massive steel tables. It was eerie driving onto Rikers at one o'clock in the morning – the entire island still and enshrouded in mist, the busy roads suddenly desolate, a guard dozing off in his booth. In the jail, the corridors were empty save for an inmate porter buffing the floor.

In the kitchen, however, the Fresh Start cooks worked furiously, sweating from the heat of so many ovens, taping and stacking a hundred cardboard boxes for delivery. I remember trying to stir the stuffing in a steel vat that was deep enough for me to stand in, and how Frank laughed at the look on my face when he handed me the 'oar' to mix it with. The next morning, exhausted and pie-eyed, we rode into Manhattan in a bus with NYC DEPARTMENT OF CORRECTION painted on the side. I remember noticing Frank, lost in thought, as he stared out the window at the line of people by the church awaiting their turkeys from Rikers. One of the men recognized a friend; I wondered if Frank had stood in that line himself.

When I arrived at Project Renewal's drug treatment facility, Frank gave me a tour of the grounds and showed me the fields where he grew the flowers and vegetables he sold at the Green Market. He was bursting with excitement.

'See these?' he said, pointing to a cluster of lilies. 'I won a blue ribbon in the county fair for them.' He breathed deeply and said he'd never known air so fresh. 'Except for those little animals, whaddayou call 'em? The ones that stink?'

Frank was almost forty before he saw his first skunk.

The landscaped grounds were dotted here and there with wooden planters of flowers. On them the residents had painted familiar NA slogans: COMMITMENT, EASY DOES IT, COMPASSION, HALT. We walked through the old stone building that housed the drug program. Coincidentally, it was formerly a women's prison. Frank took me to the basement and I saw the medieval-like cells with their crumbling stone walls and iron bars. He said it was a good reminder of where he'd end up if he quit the program.

High on the hill stood another stone building, unaffiliated with Project Renewal, known as Camp La Guardia. Frank explained that the 'residents' of this camp weren't Fresh Air Fund kids but 800 homeless men from the city. Sure enough, there was the blue and orange Housing Authority sign. I marveled at the irony – Manhattan's eyesores transported to bucolic Goshen.

Frank introduced me to a counselor, who explained that Camp La Guardia is a shelter for the 'hard-core homeless, the ones who can't make it in city shelters.' Since the men hadn't been convicted of any crimes, he said, they could leave if they wanted to on buses that departed daily for Port Authority. However, most of the residents stayed. If they got the urge to travel, they'd wander into the village, where they'd sometimes 'expose themselves,' the counselor said, or urinate in public. During the outdoor ceremony I saw a couple of residents wandering the fields. One tried to climb a tree.

There was something strange about Camp La Guardia, but stranger still was meeting two homeless men at the WBAI radio station in Manhattan a year later. A Fresh Start graduate and I had been on the air talking about the program. The men were the next two guests, and the subject they were addressing was Camp La Guardia.

To David Wilson and Tony Albert, Camp La Guardia is no paradise. It's punishment, they said, the jail of the shelter system. I spoke with them for fifteen minutes, and they didn't seem disorganized or 'hard core' in the least. Well-groomed and neatly dressed, they explained that the harassment began when they teamed up with a man who was producing a documentary on conditions in the city shelters.

Shortly thereafter, a counselor at the Bellevue shelter, where they'd been living, told them they were being shipped off to Camp La Guardia. When they refused, they were ousted from Bellevue 'for noncompliance' and banned from the shelter system altogether. 'They took our IDs,' David said. They told their story on the radio that morning.

Camp La Guardia, it seems, performs the same magic trick as Rikers: It disappears the city's undesirables.

Over a lunch of grilled hamburgers and salad greens from the farm, Frank and I spent several hours talking. He said he'd decided not to go back to the South Bronx, to the chop shop he'd called home and office while he bounced in and out of jail.

'I remember calling there looking for you,' I said, and how a Spanish-speaking man would answer in a cryptic tone and then yell outside for him.

'I'd be on the corner,' Frank said, 'rubbernecking and watching for victims like a vulture, like Dracula!' (Even drug free, Frank had a way with words.) 'Your phone call would come out of nowhere, out of heaven, like you was an angel.'

If he went back to the Bronx, he said, the temptation to make a quick buck or get high would likely be irresistible. The 'good news' was that he'd landed a job at a supermarket in town unloading boxes off trucks. 'They hired me in five minutes flat.' Best of all, he said, he found a room in a boardinghouse. 'For the first time in my life I'll have a room of my own.' Given what I knew about his past, I wondered how he'd adjust to his quiet new life.

In the literature on drugs and crime, a study by anthropologist Edward Preble, author of *Taking Care of Business,* describes the

FROM THE BELLY OF THE BEAST TO THE NEW YORK STREETS

frenetic lifestyle of heroin users. Based on interviews with hundreds of addicts in the streets of New York City, the article was considered groundbreaking because it defied the popular notion that heroin addicts were passive and retreatist. Dr. Barry Spunt of National Development and Research Institutes, Inc., says it remains as relevant today as it was then.

Their behavior is anything but an escape from life. They are actively engaged in meaningful activities and relationships seven days a week. The brief moments of euphoria after each administration of a small amount of heroin constitute a small fraction of their daily lives. The rest of the time they are aggressively pursuing a career that is exacting, challenging, adventurous, and rewarding. They are always on the move and must be alert, flexible, and resourceful. The surest way to identify heroin users in a slum neighborhood is to observe the way people walk. The heroin user walks with a fast, purposeful stride, as if he is late for an important appointment – indeed, he is. He is hustling (robbing or stealing), trying to sell stolen goods, avoiding the police, looking for a heroin dealer with a good bag (the street retail unit of heroin) coming back from copping (buying heroin), looking for a safe place to take the drug, or looking for someone who beat (cheated) him – among other things. He is, in short, *taking care of business*.

Frank had used heroin on and off for seventeen years. 'The way I look at it is, compared to my friends who've died or are doing heavy time, I'm lucky,' he said. 'I crossed that bridge to Rikers Island when I was sixteen years old and I never left. It took Fresh Start and High Impact to stop me from goin' back. . . .

'Maybe I'm maturing, but I really think it's the positive environment, hanging out with doers and achievers instead of muggers and thieves.'

In addition to his sixteen 'skid bids' (inmate slang for short stays in jail) on Rikers, Frank served time in several state prisons: Elmira, Coxsackie, Fishkill. He estimated that he'd spent approximately

47

twenty of his thirty-nine years behind bars – about half his life. Recent research has identified prison itself as a criminogenic factor, meaning that the experience of incarceration, measured as an independent variable, is positively correlated to repeat criminal behavior.

'It is undeniable that the experience of going to prison increases recidivism,' writes Elliott Currie in *Crime and Punishment in America*. 'Indeed, the tendency for incarceration to make some criminals worse is one of the best-established findings in criminology.'

People like Frank who grew up behind bars are handicapped not only by their record, making them employers' choice of last resort, but also by the psychological, social, and intellectual toll that years in prison have taken on them. Each year locked up is a year out of work and a year out of school, a period in which nearly every social encounter is with either a convicted felon or a cynical CO. Every year behind bars deepens prisoners' dependency on the system to meet their most basic needs, infantilizing them in the process. As Eddie Ellis, a prison activist who spent over two decades on the inside, commented, 'They tell you when to go to bed, but they supply the cot. They tell you when to eat, but they supply the food. They tell you what to wear, but they supply the uniform.'

Thus, prisoners emerge way behind the curve, with outdated skills, antisocial tendencies, hatred for authority, and sagging self-esteem. In fact, 'the negative effect of incarceration can move the prisoner to a more serious level of criminality,' observes criminologist Alfred Blumstein.

'For a while after I got out of prison,' Frank said, 'life was looking a little brighter for me. I was doing pretty well, I was in the Neighborhood Work Project, a program for ex-offenders. You get a stipend of twenty-five dollars a day and go around the neighborhood and renovate buildings. But the program only lasts six months. They say they help ex-offenders find work, but there wasn't no follow-through. . . . Everybody expects these revolutionary programs to rehabilitate people, but a majority of times they don't work 'cause there's no follow-through, and so what happens is you figure that the only way to make money is going back to crime.'

He told me about a burglary he committed soon after he was released:

'I got three reliable guys from around the way and broke into a warehouse. Once we were inside, I told 'em, you gotta watch carefully, figure out where the eyes are at, you know, the electronic beams. My plan was to hijack one of the trucks full of meat and drive out the gate.'

Instead, they found a safe in the office. Applying the skills he learned in prison, Frank picked the lock in thirty seconds flat. Inside was $7,000. 'I felt like a millionaire!' he said. 'I had so much money I couldn't believe it. There's nothin' in the world like scoring big when you don't expect it!'

I asked him what he did with the money.

'The first thing I did . . . well, like a dummy I went to cop heroin. I bought me like five or six bags so I could sniff it – I just sniff, you know,' meaning he doesn't inject.

'So, Frank,' I said, 'let me get this straight. You did this right after you got out of prison?'

'Yeah, yes, right after prison.'

'So obviously prison didn't scare you.'

'No, of course not, are you crazy? I had a great time in prison.'

'Do you want me to quote that? That you had a great time in prison?'

'Sure,' he said, taking ahold of my tape recorder. 'Let me explain.

'I had a great time in prison because prison was a learning experience. That's where the old-timers, the three-time losers, and the lifers teach the younger individuals like me all about crime. Our discussions are all about crime and how to commit crime, and how, when we get released, to actually carry out those crimes. That's where I learned how to pick locks, how to watch out for the Man, how to wear a mask, why I should go from armed robbery to burglary.

'See, burglars don't carry weapons, so that way you avoid confrontation. And when you don't use a weapon you don't get hit with heavy time.'

Another graduate joined us. Frank told him I was writing a book and handed him the tape recorder. 'Here. Tell her why people like us end up in places like this.'

The man, a healthy-looking African American from Brooklyn who looked to be in his late thirties, straightened his tie, cleared his throat, and held the tape recorder like a microphone. 'We have to give the people something in the community they can latch on to,' he said. 'When you place someone in an environment where there's no growth, they're just going to wallow in it and get caught up in it. Drugs are *everywhere*. It's outta control. It's hard to *stay* away from it when you can't *get* away from it.'

He held up his certificate, and I took a picture of him and Frank. 'This is my certificate,' he said, 'but it's not one of completion. This place here – man, it's a protective environment. This is where treatment begins, but recovery happens when I go back into my community.'

Several months later Frank was in the city 'on some business' and offered to give me a tour of his old neighborhood in the South Bronx. He seemed pleased that I was writing about him and wanted me to see where he grew up – when he wasn't incarcerated, that is. We met in the city and boarded the Number 4 train to 170th Street.

On the subway, Frank told me he was bored at his job in the supermarket and wanted to be a truck driver. 'I talk to those truckers where I work. They say the pay is great and you get to see the country for free.' His plan was to get his commercial driver's license and then apply to trucking schools. He'd paid off his traffic violations and recently got his first 'real' driver's license. 'It's one of the greatest accomplishments in my life!' he said. 'Here – check this out.'

I offered to get him some information on trucking schools off the Internet but mentioned that his record (he had two felonies and sixteen misdemeanors) might present a few problems. 'No, they hire ex-cons!' he protested. 'Lots of them drivers I know are ex-cons. And if you write me a reference letter' – he winked – 'I bet they'll take me.' His optimism was beginning to depress me.

More depressing was seeing that the prolonged bull market on Wall Street, just twelve stops south on the Number 4 train, hadn't made a dent in Frank's community. The 1999 unemployment rate in the South Bronx was an astounding 50 percent, according to *The New York Times*. Nearly half the families there have incomes

below $15,000. The per capita income of the borough at large –
$10,514 – is the lowest in the city.

It was a steamy July day, and the neighborhood teemed with children playing in pools of fire-hydrant water. Adults sat on their
stoops, fanning themselves, while salsa music echoed in the alleys.
Hispanic men played dice on tables made of milk crates. As we
walked along, not a Starbucks or a Gap (or a white person) in sight,
Frank pointed out various landmarks, most of them grim.

'See that lot there? That's where I saw my first dead body. I was
eight. I think the guy OD'd.' We stopped in one of the many bodegas, which Frank said was a front for a thriving drug business. He
introduced me to the owner and they exchanged a few words in
Spanish. 'I had to tell him you weren't a cop,' he explained.

Everyone in the neighborhood seemed to know Frank and like
him. 'Hey! Frankie G! Where you been, man? You're lookin' good.
Lookin' good!'

At the chop shop he introduced me to the man who'd answered
the phone when I called. *Buenas tardes, amiga*, he said cheerfully. I
smiled and shook his hand.

Inside, the place was jam-packed with junk: old tires, tools, dirty
clothes, empty beer cans, stolen goods.

'Here, wanna camera?' Frank laughed, tossing me a disposable
camera with the price tag still on it.

'You still haven't gotten rid of this yet?' he asked the Spanish
fellow and pointed to a laptop computer.

'*Esta rota*,' the man said, and grimaced, indicating that it was
broken. The only sign of color in the place was two large parrots
squawking in a cage.

'You *lived* here, Frank?'

'Yeah, there's a cot in the back. And a bathroom too – you gotta
use the bathroom?'

I didn't, but I wanted to see it. The sink was coated with grease.
The toilet lacked a seat. 'Where did you shower?'

'I took bird baths. Like I did in the joint.'

Outside on Webster Avenue, a gust of hot wind blew trash across
the cracked sidewalk. Piles of garbage scaled the fence surrounding
a vacant lot. Most of the buildings were condemned, boarded, and

covered with graffiti. Curtain shreds flapped in gaping windows. The scene, I thought, could be a billboard for the 'broken windows' theory of crime control.

In a now-classic article published in *The Atlantic Monthly*, James Q. Wilson and George Kelling describe the link between crime and neighborhood disorder, arguing that a broken window left unrepaired inevitably leads to more broken windows. They wrote:

> A piece of property is abandoned, weeds grow up, a window is smashed. Adults stop scolding rowdy children; the children, emboldened, become more rowdy. Families move out. . . . Many residents will think that crime, especially violent crime, is on the rise, and they will modify their behavior accordingly. They will use the streets less often, and when on the streets will stay apart from their fellows. . . . It is more likely that here, rather than in places where people are confident they can regulate public behavior by informal controls, drugs will change hands, prostitutes will solicit, and cars will be stripped.

'That's where I went to school,' Frank said, pointing to a massive brick building that looked more like a jail house than a school. At PS 147, 84 percent of the students qualify for a free school lunch, according to *The New York Times*. Ninety-two percent failed to meet performance standards on the city's recent round of testing. In a rating of middle-school student performance, it ranked 247 out of 249.

Not surprisingly, Frank's most vivid school memory wasn't about a teacher, a friend, or a science project. 'This is where I got my first JO,' he said as we stood outside the entrance. (JO is a criminal charge received by a juvenile offender).

'For what?'

'I shot a kid in the eye.'

'You shot a kid in the eye?'

'Well, it wasn't really that. We were just in the school shooting wildly in the staircase. I was shooting up and he happened to be looking down. I was fourteen years old. I used to put a sawed-off shotgun in my locker.'

Frank rattled off the details so casually my head spun.

'Didn't you have security in the school? How'd you get in a gun?'

'We didn't have metal detectors then. We had security but they were rent-a-cops. Them guys didn't care. They were drunks.'

For shooting his classmate, Frank was sent to Spofford, at the time considered one of the roughest juvenile detention centers in the country. 'The most notorious kids in the city were there. I loved it. I felt camaraderie. I was among my peers; we got to smoke and play pool all day. To me it was like camp.'

'So what was your second JO?'

'I burned down the school.'

I vaguely recalled Frank talking about arson when he interviewed for Fresh Start. But when you hear about the criminal activities of ten men in an hour, the stories begin to blur. I guess we hadn't probed enough, because if I had known then what he was about to tell me, we probably would have turned him away. He took hold of my tape recorder and said:

'I knocked down seventeen buildings. No one was in 'em so it wasn't like we were hurting anyone and the money was great. Them landlords, you know, the rich Jews, they paid us big time, two thousand dollars a building. For a kid like me, growin' up in the streets, that was good money.'

He spoke about the hazards of his occupation as an arsonist, and the incident that landed him in prison on a 'three-to-nine.'

'Me and this guy – he was like my assistant – went into this apartment, spread gasoline, and lit the place up. The problem was we couldn't get out. The fuckin' door was locked! Gasoline's all over the place and the smoke is choking me. So we had to jump out of the window. I took out the twenty-five automatic I had on me and pointed it at my partner – you first, I told him. He landed fine and ran like hell, but when I jumped, it was like Humpty Dumpty. By the time I got up the cops was rollin' up on me and started shooting at me. I shot back, runnin' with the gun under my arm. That's when I got caught – they hit me with a B Felony, fifteen to life, but I played crazy. I fought the case for a year until they got tired of me. I ended up with a three-to-nine.'

In the ensuing months, Frank pursued his dream job of truck driver. He followed up on the leads I sent him and filled out applications for various trucking schools. Barbara Margolis and I wrote letters of reference; he studied for the commercial driver's license exam and picked up some tips from the truckers at his job. He'd call me every so often with an update on his progress. Once, in a fit of excitement, he mistook a letter from a school saying they had received his application as a letter of acceptance.

In the end, he was rejected. The seriousness of his rap sheet eliminated him. I was afraid that a relapse to heroin was imminent; he was still working in the warehouse and hated it. He was bored and lonely and started talking about moving back to the Bronx. 'It's so quiet up here and I really don't have any friends. Nobody knows about my past. They'd think I was some kind of thug from the city if I told 'em.'

Several weeks later, he got an amazingly lucky break. He had applied for a part-time maintenance job at Camp La Guardia on the weekends ('I was goin' crazy starin' at these four walls') and told the interviewer he was a graduate of Project Renewal. 'I didn't tell her I was a crook, just a drug addict,' he said. 'I didn't want to scare her. . . . She loved me! I told her I was comfortable working around the homeless men, how I used to talk to them for hours.' The woman told Frank she thought he'd make a better counselor than maintenance man and offered him a full-time position.

'They even sent me to training,' Frank said to me over the phone. 'They call me *Team Member* Garcia! Can you believe it? *Team Member Garcia!*' I'd never heard him so elated. 'I'm counseling people, helping people. There's this old man, I listen to him for hours.'

An image of Frank from two years before, when he stood in our office in his olive-green suit, came back to me: 'I want to be a good person,' he'd said. 'I want to get off drugs, off the streets, and someday be a counselor for people like me.' And there he was.

Christmas Eve, 1999: Frank drove his new (used) car into the city. 'Now I even have insurance!' he said. We planned a lunch to celebrate his job, the holidays, and the encroaching millennium. 'I got a feeling the year 2000 is gonna be my year,' he said. 'I turn forty this year, you know.' He wanted to tell me about his new life for my book. 'The chapter on me is gonna have a real happy ending, huh?'

When he arrived at my apartment, he handed me a bouquet of peach-colored roses and two wrapped gifts: a bottle of wine and a black leather handbag from Coach. The three ties I gave him paled in comparison to what I knew was an expensive (and beautiful) handbag. The scene was vintage Norman Rockwell: Christmas carols playing on the radio, Frank holding forth with the details of his new life, as if he couldn't believe the existence he described was his own: 'I have a beautiful apartment, a car, insurance, and a job that I get up early for. . . . I actually commute to work. I have a job as a counselor. I'll have benefits soon.'

We had lunch in a restaurant and then walked along the Brooklyn Heights Promenade with its world-famous views of Manhattan. He had a disposable camera and asked someone to take our picture. Even the cold wind blowing off the East River couldn't dampen our spirits.

In the late afternoon, he drove me to Grand Central. I was going to my parents' house in Connecticut and he was off to see a girl-friend in White Plains. It was one of the happiest Christmas Eve's I remember.

It would be easy – and some might say logical – to end Frank's story here. As a writer, you can do these things. Who would know if I left out the rest? And who could cast blame? As I said to Frank the day he called me from jail, 'You just ruined the best part of my book.'

The first call came from his girlfriend, telling me that Frank was back in jail but she didn't know why. 'He won't tell me,' she said. 'But I think he'll tell you. He wanted me to ask you if he could call you collect. He doesn't have any money in his commissary.'

And then came the call from Frank. With very little prodding, he spilled out his story, every incredible detail. I'd like to think it was cathartic for him.

'It was New Year's Day,' he said, 'I'd been drinking champagne all night. I wasn't thinking clearly. I got busted. I was numb.'

'Busted for what, Frank? What did you do?' I figured it was something minor, a singular screwup – a DUI or maybe a bar fight – which, combined with his rap sheet, had landed him temporarily in jail. I was wrong.

Frank had driven into a public parking garage, parked his car, and broken into another car. 'There were no workers; no one was around,' he said. And then came the part that stunned me: 'See, I have a pattern: I take a long piece of metal, hook it inside the door lock, and when the alarm goes off I open the hood and disconnect it.' Every time he visited his girlfriend, he said, he'd 'hit the garage.'

'I had a laptop and a couple hundred CDs in my trunk. The plan was that I was going to retire in 2000 'cause I didn't wanna lose my job. I loved that job. The night before, I made a resolution to stop. I was gonna sell the stuff and that would be it. I'd have two thousand dollars in my pocket and say, "Yeah, I won!" But something drove me to that garage. I had to do it one more time. I just don't get it. I don't know what came over me. The Devil, I think. I dunno – maybe subconsciously I wanted to get caught. They caught me leaving the garage.'

At first I was sure he'd relapsed and was 'hitting the garage' to feed his drug habit. But he told me repeatedly that he hadn't picked up. In fact, he couldn't have been happier with his life at the time: 'I was chasing the American Dream and for a brief moment I had it. I felt like a human being. But I still had that get-over mentality.' It wasn't drugs, he said. 'I suffer from a unique disorder: suicidal stupidity.'

The more I thought about it, the more clearly I realized that the ferocity and duration of his drug addiction would likely make being a functional user impossible at this point. The downfall would be too fast and all-encompassing. If he were using, chances were strong he wouldn't have been able to get and hold down a job. What depressed me was the undeniable realization that he was a thief, plain and simple. There was no drug habit to feed; poverty wasn't an issue. He stole because it made him feel good. 'I was into the money,' he said. 'I felt like a big shot.'

He described in detail how 'taking something and getting over' is 'the most exhilarating feeling in the world. It's like winning the lottery. I'd tell myself, Don't steal; you got money. Did I listen? Hell, no. I just got this euphoric feeling in me. I thought I was invincible. It was like flying.'

In *Seductions of Crime: Moral and Sensual Attractions of Doing Evil,* Jack Katz reports that the major reward of stealing and vandalism is the thrill they produce and that 'after the scene of risk has been successfully exited . . . the euphoria of being thrilled' is realized.

'Jennifer,' Frank said, 'I was like a serial killer. I'd put all my proceeds in the trunk. When I came to see you on Christmas Eve and you got in my car, I wanted to open the trunk and show you all the stuff, show you the prize. I should have, 'cause you woulda said, "Frank, you're a fuckin' loser and a failure." Maybe I woulda listened.'

I thought about the leather handbag he gave me (how would Frank know to buy Coach?) and the expensive-looking bottle of wine. 'Frank, don't tell me you stole the presents you gave me.'

He paused for a moment. 'I bought the flowers.'

When the police put Frank in jail on New Year's Day, 'it was so quiet,' he said. 'No one else was locked up there but me. When I was in that cell I thought about hanging up [killing himself]. I'm too old; I don't got another bid in me.' After a while, it dawned on him that he had ruined his greatest chance.

'I thought the new millennium would be my decade. I transplanted myself to another environment. I was happy for the first time in my life. But I was living two lives. The good Frank was looking at life and everything was in harmony. I won ribbons at the county fair. I'd get into my car, eager to get to work helping other people. I commuted to work! I'd pull up in my car and they'd say, "Good morning, Mr. Garcia." Can you imagine? *Mr. Garcia. Team Member Garcia.* I was a somebody, Jennifer. For the first time in my life, I was a somebody.'

His last words struck me: *'I live in the best fuckin' country in the world and I keep asking myself, Why can't I make it?'*

A few weeks later Frank sent me a letter from jail. It's reprinted here as he wrote it, save for a few spelling errors.

Hello Jennifer,

Time plus pleasure have given me no greater opportunity now than to correspond with you. But first, I send my most sincere respects to you and your family.

As for me, I am fine mentally as well as physically. Who doesn't have a sad story to tell?

First of all, I am both ashamed and embarrassed to be writing to you from the joint. Thank God I have someone 'safe' to write to because you know how emotionally vulnerable I am in here. You are the only person who has helped me examine and understand the traumatic experiences in my life and what a blessing it is. I love to talk to you because you unearthed the hurt I buried as a little boy. My feelings weren't understood or respected. Thank you, Jennifer, for it takes courage to shine a light into the dark corners of my life, the last place I ever wanted to look.

But I guess that pain is information and it does have a purpose. I think it will open me up to a deeper and wiser understanding.

I feel like a deeply disturbed child, really a sad and lonely boy who was taught, as all boys in here are taught, not to tell the truth about fear, not attend to my wounds. This made me psychologically fragile and the desire for retaliation has enslaved me. It ultimately pushed me over the edge. I constructed a wall around my heart, blocking wisdom and love. It was making me ill.

Shit, I only had one career in my life and it was breaking and entering people's homes and businesses and cars and taking as much of their property as I could carry. I only had one criterion in choosing my hits or targets: I only took from those who could well afford to lose it. Please understand that the adrenaline rush that accompanies each job is absolutely unique.

As you know, a good many of my 39 years have been spent in assorted medium- and maximum-security prisons in New York. I have two felony convictions and they hang around my neck like blocks of granite. Years have been carved out of my life, important years, and I can't do nothing to change that now.

I wonder again for the hundredth time why I continued with my criminal activities. It certainly wasn't worth it. I had $300 in my pocket when I was arrested. I live simply, and I give away

*much of the proceeds from my hits. 'Wealth redistribution' is what
I call it.*

*But Jennifer, in answer to your question as to why I continued to
steal . . . perhaps it was only to show that I could.*

Your devoted friend,
Frankie G.

That semester I was taking a class called 'The Treatment and
Rehabilitation of the Offender.' Every lecture held me nearly spell-
bound, because I was still searching for an answer to Frank's
question: 'I live in the best fuckin' country in the world – why can't
I make it?' One night, Professor Charles Bahn, a renowned criminal
psychologist, commented:

'Among the poor, there is a value attached to "getting over" on
society. . . . You see it in their participation in the underground
economy, in activities such as selling food stamps in the street, lying
to welfare.' Even if they make it out of poverty, he said, many continue 'to attach a value to getting over on the system.'

I began to see that nearly every criminological theory I was studying applied to Frank: Merton's theory of anomie, Akers' theory of
social learning, Gottfredson and Hirschi's theory of low self-control.
Nearly every precursor to crime and deviance and repeat offending – impulsivity, parental violence, poverty, poor education,
prisonization, and drug addiction – were present in Frank's life.
Not just one or two circumstances or variables existed, as was true
with some of my students, but *all*. Even the 'high' he experienced
when stealing has been borne out in recent studies.

'Difficult, risky behavior activates the same endogenous reward
system activated by cocaine and similar drugs, and as a consequence, for some individuals such behaviors produce a
physiological high,' wrote Wood et al. in their study of career criminals. 'Inmates reported that when performing crime . . . they felt
intensely alive and had a sense of accomplishment.' There is, they
emphasized, a 'neurophysiological high,' unrelated to drug use,
that 'is sustained partly through the positive sensations those
crimes activate within the offender.' The findings of their study
'suggest that the experience of committing crime is intrinsically

rewarding and tends to reinforce such behavior among habitual criminals.'

Frank's return to criminality could be easily misconstrued as an argument against rehabilitation. It is important to understand, however, that the longest amount of time he ever spent in the free world – almost three years – was achieved only *after* he had completed Fresh Start and Project Renewal. It is still quite extraordinary that just one year of treatment was able to alter the course of his life at all, even if temporarily. I wonder how Frank's life would have unfolded if his early days at Spofford and subsequent years in prison had offered similar opportunities for rehabilitation, how much money taxpayers would have saved and how many fewer crimes he would have committed.

'It is likely that the period of incarceration will change post-release behavior,' writes Alfred Blumstein in a sad commentary on the American penal system. 'It could do so in pro-social terms through the mechanism of rehabilitation, although this has largely disappeared from the stated purpose of incarceration in the U.S. criminal justice system.'

Frank's two decades in prison did not deter him, correct him, or rehabilitate him. One might say, in fact, that they ruined him. But they didn't. They simply did what prisons have always done, since the first American penitentiary was opened in Philadelphia in 1821: They gave a person who entered prison with problems many more.

MIKE

Mike is the kind of person you don't expect to find on Rikers Island. First, he is white, and whites account for only about 5 percent of the inmate population. He was raised in a middle-class family in the suburbs and completed several semesters of college. He is an expert computer technician and graphic artist.

Men like Mike have the hardest time on Rikers. They see their less-fortunate peers in greens and realize how far they've fallen and how few excuses they have. Until recently, they couldn't even use the phone – the blacks in the dorms controlled one phone; the Hispanics controlled the other. Inmates like Mike can't blame poverty or discrimination for their descent into hell. In fact, the only thing Mike had in common with the other inmates was a ten-year addiction to crack.

We usually don't choose men like Mike for the program; they tend to be overqualified. It's hard to justify filling the few spaces we have with inmates who, by virtue of birth, race, and education, have a better chance at making it. But Mike was irresistible. Instead of waiting to answer our questions during the interview, he took charge of the conversation and sold himself. He pitched his skills as a graphic artist and said he'd design the *Rikers Review,* saving us the money we'd pay an outside professional. He devoted his writing sample to how he learned the Japanese art of origami while in solitary confinement in prison upstate. To maintain his sanity, he said, he taught himself how to fold paper into intricate figures – frogs, birds, and flowers – and color them with wax he'd scrape off the floor of his cell. When we told him it looked like he could contribute more to Fresh Start than the program could to him, he assured us he'd need all the help he could get when he was released. Truer words were never said.

On the first day of the program, Mike showed none of the enthusiasm he had at the interview. He dragged himself into class, eyeing his peers suspiciously. His long black hair fell in his face; his greens hung off his thin frame. Like most white men in the general jail population, he had to earn respect from his fellow cons either by wit or by force. Now that he'd spend virtually every hour with the same group of inmates for the next three months, he'd have to figure out how to be one of the boys.

I started with an exercise. 'Write a characteristic you admire in other people and would like to develop in yourself on the inside flap of your folder.' I know it sounds corny, but the students say these 'reminders' help them focus on specific behaviors they want to change. I asked if anyone wanted to share his word with the group and, as usual, most of them did. 'Unstoppable,' one said. 'Honest,' said another. 'Responsible.'

I called on Mike to get him involved.

'Pass.'

I interpreted this as 'I dare you to confront me' and tried again. 'You're saying you'll pass?'

'You got it.'

'Not allowed,' I said, remembering the advice of my mentor. Start out tough, she said. You can always go from firm to nice but not the other way around.

I waited. Mike glowered at me. One of the inmates started humming the tune to *Jeopardy*. The other guys found that funny (so did I, actually) and started laughing. Finally, Mike blurted that his self-esteem was 'so low' that nothing came to mind except for how he saw himself: 'A loser,' he said. 'You guys satisfied?' Whoa . . .

That got his classmates' attention. His authenticity impressed them. In jail, 'frontin'' by inmates is as common as it is despised.

'If you was a loser, man,' one of them said, 'you wouldn't be sittin' in this classroom. You'd be kickin' the Willie Bobo [jail slang for shooting the breeze] in the dorm.'

'Yeah, man,' said another. 'And talkin' about the dorms, look what you done in there. That ain't no sign of a loser.' The origami artist had brightened the dorm with mobiles of colorful birds, tropical fish, and airplanes. The CO in charge must have appreciated the bit of fantasy and let it go.

After some coaching from the students, Mike wrote the word *Perseverance* on the flap of his folder.

Over the next couple of months, Mike motivated his teammates and encouraged them to write. 'I can make this the best magazine Fresh Start's ever produced but that doesn't mean squat unless you guys gimme some articles to lay out.' He coaxed their stories out of them and laid out the copy according to their specifications. He made the other inmates feel as if he worked for *them*. He proved to be a fine editor as well, skillfully editing their articles without engendering resentment. He saved me hours of work by editing and designing the magazine. All I had to do was proofread the growing pile of articles he'd have for me each week. He assured me that we would meet our deadline and the issue would be ready by graduation.

Several weeks later, the program director informed me that Mike was in serious trouble. He would likely be kicked out of the program, she said, and advised me to find another way to get the magazine published. I panicked. How would I get the magazine produced in two weeks and how could our star student be facing termination?

As it turned out, Mike had been operating a thriving jail business back in the dorms. He made long-stemmed origami roses and sold them for seven cigarettes apiece (about a dollar in jail). He'd been doing it for several months on the 'down-low,' as the inmates say, but when the orders started flowing in he increased his output and enhanced his product line. He recruited, hired, and trained several inmate 'employees' to help fill the orders. He sold his roses by the dozen, in bouquets tied with shoelaces, packaged in top-opening boxes that once held ten rolls of toilet paper. He had Tommy Girl perfume smuggled in to scent the paper flowers. Soon his customer base expanded from inmates to correction officers, and that's when the ax fell. A captain discovered the operation and wrote him up for running a business in jail. Mike also received the more serious charge of 'possession of contraband.' A CO had brought in the perfume for Mike, in exchange for a dozen roses.

From the first day of the program, we tell the students that if they get an infraction (a ticket for breaking a jail rule), we won't help them fight it. It's an agreement we have with correction officials and it's not unreasonable. It's their jail – they make the rules; the inmates know them and know how to live with them. We also try to teach consequential thinking, considering outcomes before acting on impulses. If Mike was found guilty at the disposition hearing, he'd not only be kicked out of Fresh Start but would likely spend a week in the 'Bing,' a jail within the jail where inmates live in single cells twenty-four/seven except for an hour of court-mandated recreation.

I have no idea what Mike said in the hearing, but it must have been good. He beat all of the charges and promised to shut down his business and stay out of trouble. He got back to work on the magazine and, true to his word, produced the best-looking issue I'd seen. For the first time in the twenty-year history of the *Rikers Review*, the magazine the men unveiled at graduation was produced entirely on the inside. As Mike walked to the podium to accept his diploma, the audience of inmates, family members, counselors, and correction officials gave him a standing ovation. Not bad, I thought: from 'loser' to luminary in three short months. I said I'd take him to lunch when he got out to thank him for his work. Before the ceremony was over, he gave me the names of a few places he said he'd like to go.

So I was surprised when I didn't hear from him. His counselor said he planned to go straight into a drug program his first day out, and the fact that none of us had heard from him wasn't a good sign. About a week later, Mike called me. He was back in jail.

Whenever I get a call like this I know I shouldn't be surprised, but I always am.

'I'm sorry,' he said. 'I'm really sorry I let you down. I don't know what to do. I can't seem to live out there and not get high.' He said he'd be released in a few weeks, a month, tops.

I asked him what he was planning to do when he got out, hoping he'd say he'd enroll in a drug-treatment program.

'I'm not going to lie to you. I wish I could tell you this was the wake-up call I needed, that I'm not getting high again and learned my lesson. But I can't. I know I'll get high when I leave here.' His voice started to tremble. 'I'm afraid of myself. Do you know how it feels to not be able to trust yourself, to know *every fucked-up thing* that's going to happen but not be able to stop yourself?'

I knew the feeling but avoided the question. I told him I knew a lot of addicts, Fresh Start graduates I thought would never go straight but somehow did. 'Try to turn off the committee of maniacs in your head and keep telling yourself you'll stop using. "Fake it 'til you make it." Isn't that what they say in NA?'

'I don't know if I can make it 'til I see the judge without losing my mind. What's *wrong* with me?' he groaned, slamming the phone against the wall. 'Why am I like this?'

Truthfully, I didn't know why and I didn't know what to say. I wasn't a recovering addict. I wasn't a substance-abuse counselor and didn't know the healing words they whisper to their strung-out clients. But I remembered the pride Mike took in his work on the magazine and how having a job, whether designing the *Rikers Review* or selling roses in the dorms, made him feel better about himself.

'Mike, how about this: Get a pen and paper and write about what happened and what drives you. Write the truth and I bet you'll learn something about yourself. I'd be interested to read it when you get out.'

I doubted he'd do it but having a project seemed to pick up his spirits. 'Okay. I'll call you when I'm out.'

When Mike was released, I took him to lunch at a trendy diner near my office I knew he'd like. 'I did that assignment you gave me,' he said, removing ten worn sheets of paper from his coat pocket. The penciled words were faded and smudged from his travels in the belly of the beast. Thankfully, he could still read it, which he did right there in the restaurant.

In jail, if I had been wearing civilian clothes instead of greens, people would have thought I was a counselor. I projected togetherness, a quiet confidence and was always alert. The eight months on Rikers wasn't a loss at all. In fact, it was productive and enlightening. I was involved as much as anyone could possibly be. People looked up to me. I was commended and rewarded for the computer work I did in Fresh Start. I did a lot of thinking about the mess I had made of my life and myself and was ready to once again begin the arduous journey of repairing things. I had an appointment lined up at an outpatient drug program for the Monday following my release, which came on a Friday, at three-thirty in the morning. I had lots of support, inside and out. I had all the resources necessary to start a new life.

Let me pause right here to make sure I'm not giving you some bullshit. I exude bullshit from every pore in my body. I carry myself as if everything is just fine, even when I was homeless, hungry and strung out on crack. So to tell you the truth I was not fine before I left Rikers. On more than one occasion I had smoked a joint in the yard. Not a big deal, I thought. I'd chill out before release so I wouldn't totally fuck up when I got out.

It was about a week or two before I was released that I took an incredibly wrong turn. No – it wasn't when I took a quarter ounce of some really great 'hydro' and rolled it for a buddy that altered my course. It wasn't when I smoked a joint of it that I was totally doomed. It wasn't the two shots of Bacardi with the guys, which I figured must be okay since I'd just smoked the joint. The turning point came when my boy got several bottles of prescription drugs and asked me to identify them. Yes, that was it, when I examined each pill, showed him which were the Percocet, which were Valium, and sampled them just to make sure. It was then that I knew the addict in me was fully alive and reeling to get out and get what I really wanted: crack.

My conscience tore at me, pleaded and begged for attention, but I was like an armed warhead. There would be no reconciliation now. The only reply my brain offered was that fuckin' universal lie: 'Don't worry. We're gonna only do one and everything will be okay.' Sucker ass me.

So my big day comes. I'm well rested and ready, very well rested considering that the Percocet had me in a languid slumber for two days and nights before my release. I had some leftover origami paper on me and in the bullpen a guy asked me to make him a rose. Then another guy wanted some, so I made him three for $5. A wave of pride went through me as he handed me his money. Another guy bought three for $5. More pride. By this time, a small audience had gathered around me, watching me as I sat on the bullpen floor quietly folding the last of my colored paper. With my well-earned money, I couldn't wait to get out there to play out my script of self-destruction.

I stood on the subway platform in Queens Plaza waiting for the train to take me to Washington Heights. The scene was thoroughly familiar. Ripples of excitement and fear washed over me, and at this point reality gave way to a surreal recognition that this was precisely where I was standing before I got arrested the last time. I was even wearing the same Levi's and flannel shirt. It was as if the eight months on Rikers never happened.

I got out at 145th Street, hoping the drug spot hadn't changed. I stopped at a bodega and asked for 'ahs-ah-bah.' The guy looked at me quizzically, wondering how I knew this magic word, then handed me a bag containing a crack stem and a lighter. I paid and off I went, round the corner, up the avenue, then round the corner and down the block. I paused to pick up the vibe, which is something you always do before entering a drug spot. It was crisp and energetic. It said 'go.'

Up to the drug spot I went. Number 507. If you know this number you're in as deep as I am. If you know this number, you're fucked.

The next few days brought me to the subways, where I do the MetroCard scam, and back and forth to the drug spot like a mouse in a maze. [Mike collected discarded MetroCards and bent and folded them like origami art, which somehow reactivated them at full-price fares. He'd accumulate a stack and sell them to the token booth clerk or to straphangers looking for a deal. He could make $100 in an hour or so.]

After four days, I couldn't stay up any longer and I absolutely refused to sleep in a park or on the subway because that would feel pathetic. So I dragged my worn-out, strung-out ass to Bellevue Hospital, where I knew I could get a bed, and maybe another 'Fresh Start.'

When I arrived and told the nurse I needed help, she sent me to see the social worker. While waiting for her, I broke down and sobbed. The drugs had worn off and the pain poured out. I couldn't believe I'd reached this point again.

The next day I left. They suggested a program to me, but I told them and myself that since it was now Monday I would go back to my original plan and go to the program I had found while on Rikers. But when I stepped outside, it was strange. The intense pain that I felt just the night before was forgotten. I felt rested and ready for the day. I did my MetroCard thing and made eighty dollars in about two hours.

It was that day I ran into Cassie. I remembered her from NA meetings I went to about eight years ago. Back then, she was gorgeous – blond, blue-eyed, tall and thin and always smiling. She easily could have been in a Guess or Tommy Hilfiger ad. But now she's an addict and a hooker. Most of the hookers I know at least go downtown to find dates. They have their little places they feel comfortable with. But Cassie didn't bother. She stayed right up there in Washington Heights close to the dope spot. We hung out that day and night and later went our separate, twisted ways to make our money.

I got off the train at a station where I figured I could easily sell the five MetroCards I had in my pocket, worth seventeen dollars a piece. I noticed a cop outside the station and decided to smoke a cigarette to kill a few minutes. The cop wasn't going anywhere so I figured I'd better get back on the train and go to a different station. But the cop came down and stopped me. He told me he had just cut me a break three weeks ago and he was tired of seeing me. I thought it was a joke at first, but he actually believed I was someone else. Then he cuffed me and said he was going to run a warrant check. 'No problem,' I said. I'd just gotten out of jail. There was no way I could have any warrants. But instead he tells me the impossible – I had a warrant and he was taking me in. Now that he could arrest me, he had reason enough to search me. He found the crack stem. Another charge. No! Not again! my brain screamed. And then the denial set in: I'll be out tomorrow.

Ever since the moment on Queens Plaza, when my mind had somehow obscured the entire eight months I'd spent at Rikers, the façade was alive and well. But now it was as if a fault line had opened. Reality came crashing through as I stood in Central Booking with scores of people pushing up on me – from nasty, fetid-smelling street scum to well-dressed drug dealers.

Off to the Tombs I went, feeling sorry once again for my stupid ass. I turned down the judge's offer of thirty days because if I held out, I wouldn't get sent back to Rikers until I got sentenced. Going back to Rikers was my biggest fear. That would be the most humiliating thing that could happen to me.

About a week later I went back to court and the offer was down to twenty days. I figured I'd better take it. Maybe I'd get released from the Tombs before they transferred me to the Rock. No such luck. They awakened me at five in the morning the next day and packed me up. Lumps in my throat and knots in my belly told me that a new misery awaited.

As soon as I set foot in the C-76 receiving room, there was Hector in the outgoing bullpen on my left and Ed in the 'Why Me' pen on my right. [The 'Why Me' pen is a large kennel-like cage where inmates are held for up to eight hours for violating jail rules. Inmates and correction officers alike use the moniker.]

'What the fuck, Mike?' they asked in near unison. The nightmare had begun.

It is in my nature to be truthful, but something told me that a lie would make things easier. The truth of how I got arrested, in the most ridiculous way, was too embarrassing. So I told them I got caught up in a drug sweep and sentenced to sixty days. An hour or so later I arrived in the reception dorm, One Upper, land of the misfits. I felt like a dog that had been beaten, punished, and locked in the cellar for the night.

The next morning they awakened me at 8 A.M. to go to orien-motherfucking-tation. Sitting there in the chapel watching that stupid movie about how to conduct yourself in jail, played by really bad actors, I felt *totally pissed off at myself. Orientation in C-76 was a grim landmark on the cycle of my sorry existence, telling me I had just made a full revolution on the funhouse ride of my life. And then in walked Kenneth Johnson, my Fresh Start counselor.* [Kenny graduated from Fresh Start three years ago. After he completed a year of drug treatment, the Osborne Association hired him as a counselor. He's one of the best in the program.]

I seriously considered hiding. I couldn't walk out – this was jail. I thought about lying on the floor under a pew, but inmates lined both sides of me and there wasn't room. I folded my head in my arms on the back of the pew in front of me and tucked my ponytail down my shirt so Kenny wouldn't recognize me. For the next ten minutes, I thought I was safe. He didn't see me, or so I thought. But I knew he was in there somewhere.

I remembered all the times Kenny got on my ass, how he more than anyone was able to cut through my bullshit like a barber's razor through warm butter, how he'd look into my eyes with his mean, tough face and ask me: 'So whatcha gonna do, Mr. Mike? Do you got what it takes or are you a pussy?' His forceful way, dramatic and intense, combined with his hardness from years on the street and in the joint, not to mention his size and countenance, make Kenneth Johnson one of the few people I'm uncomfortable around. Kenny also knows the truth inside me, even when I don't.

And then I heard his voice. He had launched into one of his powerful monologues, and I could feel the inmates around me shifting and sitting up to listen. I heard my name. My full name. Again and again. In a mocking voice he called out, 'Hey, everybody! There's Mike. My old buddy Mike. You don't need to see no movie about jail, you can just ask Mike. He's been here plenty of times. He can tell you everything you wanna know about Rikers.'

He went on and on about why the inmates should think seriously about changing before they ended up like me.

The lowest point was still ahead. I returned to the place I called 'home' for eight months, Six Lower, and when I got to the gate I called out for the steady officer. He knew me real well and we had a good rapport, almost like a father-son thing. I wanted to see him, but he wouldn't even greet me. He just opened the gate and stared somewhere over my head. I stood, speechless, as the other inmates piled up on the second gate and gaped at me as if they were viewing a freak of nature. A wave of disorientation washed over me. I felt dizzy. When a dorm full of convicted criminals and junkies are ashamed of you, what the fuck else is there?

I walked, zombie-like, into the dorm. The inmates circled me, eyes wide, mouths open. I was the one who should have made it. I was the one they were rooting for. I was the origami artist, the Fresh Start graduate, the computer whiz. But there I was, feeling like I'd mutated into an alien creature, half-human, half-insect. Sheepishly I asked if anyone had a cigarette.

Angelo, the one who used to get all the weed for us, brought me a pack of cigarettes, a couple bags of coffee, a Danish, chips, and some soup mix. I was embarrassed to take it, but I did. I spent the next hour telling them how I'd gone out, gotten high, and ended up back in the joint. Most of them were disgusted; a few were sympathetic. I left with my bag of goods, feeling as if I'd stolen from friends.

Later that night as I lay on my bunk, I promised myself for the millionth time I would never get high again. Every time I make this declaration it scares me, because I've been in this same spot and made it so many times before. I know that at any moment a new seed can grow in my brain, igniting yet another episode. I feel like a walking time bomb.

Now my bid is almost over. Every day I pray that the insanity won't repeat itself. I tell myself that the person I was out in the streets is not really me. It's not who I was supposed to be, it's not the person who lives deep inside. No. I don't want to live like a freak anymore; I don't want to be a junkie on the street.

Many aspects of Mike's story intrigued me. In particular, I marveled at the ease with which he was able to get high while incarcerated. He obtained marijuana, prescription drugs, and Bacardi rum in jail, one of the most controlled environments in the world (or which should be, given the money we spend on prisons). With cameras and round-the-clock correction officers, pat frisks and cell searches, and even the new 'Boss' chairs that can detect contraband in body cavities, Rikers should be squeaky clean. Yet drugs are available there and in most prisons and jails throughout the country. A 1995 *New York Times* investigation, for example, found that 'evidence of the prison drug trade abounds' all over the country. In the first half of the 1990s, twenty-six correction officers on Rikers were charged with drug smuggling. Just the other day, in fact, one of my students, twenty-one-year-old Michael from Brownsville, New York, told me that he could get any drug he wanted on Rikers, including heroin and crack.

When I worked at *Prison Life* magazine, our executive editor took a trip to the Oklahoma State Reformatory in Granite. We were doing a cover story on drugs in prison, and there, *in solitary confinement,* our editor bought marijuana from a prisoner. Chris Cozzone also took a picture of a prisoner shooting up (with a needle) in his cell, which we featured on the magazine's cover. Before Chris left, he told Warden Jack Cowley he'd scored drugs in his pen and that he saw an inmate shooting up dope.

'Prison is a microcosm of the streets,' Cowley said in his blithe southern drawl. 'Whatever's out there is gonna be in here – the drugs, the violence. Generally, all the bad characteristics of what's in the streets is also right in here.'

A prisoner who wore his hair in neat corn rows and called himself Snake Hill commented, 'There ain't nothin' you can't get in here. I just smoke my weed, lie in my cell, and look at the TV. Fuckit – I ain't hurtin' nobody.'

The assistant regional director of the Oklahoma Department of Corrections, Justin Jones, told us that a prisoner on death row recently overdosed on drugs the night before he was scheduled to be executed. 'They had to revive him so they could kill him,' he said. 'The point is, somebody got the drugs in, even in maximum security, even on death row. Nobody in their right mind would say their prison is drug free.'

I am not blaming the Correction Department for Mike's drug use. He could have 'just said no' to the joint, the rum, and the Percocet he was offered. Nonetheless, it's disturbing to know that when taxpayers spend $175 a day to lock someone up, particularly nonviolent drug addicts like Mike, we still can't provide a drug-free environment.

At the restaurant, Mike said he'd been drug free for 'well over a month' (thirty days in jail plus a few days on the outside) and was happier than he'd been in a long time. 'I got my hair cut today,' he said. 'I cut all the jail out. I walked down the street and a woman actually smiled at me instead of scowling.'

The best news, he said, was that he found a place to live. 'I got a room for a week and money in my pocket. God works in mysterious ways, huh?'

Very mysterious, I thought. 'How'd you get the money, Mike?'

'I never lied to you before, I don't wanna start now.'

'Please don't tell me you did the MetroCard scam.'

'Okay, I won't tell you.'

'Mike!' I shouted. 'Are you an idiot? Do you know how easy it is to get arrested these days? I have friends who are cops and I'll tell you – they are *desperate* to make arrests. Desperate. I guarantee you, you *will* get caught. And getting clean doesn't include stealing . . . even from the Transit Authority,' I added.

'What am I supposed to do? I don't have a job. I know I'll get one, but I won't see a paycheck for two weeks, at least. How am I supposed to live until then?'

'Go to a drug-treatment program. Go to a shelter.'

'That's so goddamn depressing it would make me wanna get high. Look, I have money in my pocket and a roof over my head for a week. I'll go to an NA meeting.'

'You know, you were lucky,' I said. 'But I bet you anything that if you do it again you'll get caught.'

'Great. You've jinxed me now.'

'Good. Maybe you'll thank me one of these days.'

As the weeks went by, I knew Mike was struggling. He'd show up at my office occasionally to use the phone or work on his résumé. He looked beaten down and sad but swore he hadn't gotten high since he'd been out. I believed him and called my friend Paul, who had hired Fresh Start graduates in the past, to see if he had any work for Mike. Paul said he could give him a couple hours of work and pay him twenty dollars. It wasn't much, but Mike seemed pleased to have a place to go where someone needed him.

That weekend, he called and asked if I had any spare time. 'I'm sick of staring at the walls,' he said. 'I spend most of my time in NA meetings and coming back here.'

I could tell he was lonely and agreed to go to a movie with him. I knew from other graduates that going straight was a lonely process. They don't have many friends who aren't getting high or stealing. It reminded me of Jose, a classmate of Mike's who'd been released a few weeks before. 'I don't got no friends,' he said and asked if I'd go to the planetarium with him.

When Mike and I met, he handed me a large shopping bag. 'This is for you,' he said. Immediately I felt uneasy. I was touched, but I remembered what I'd learned from Frank. The gift, I saw, wasn't stolen or even purchased. Inside were prize pieces from his origami collection, the art he created in solitary confinement to keep from going mad. From the bag he carefully removed a pink seahorse with a long tail of intricately folded triangles, then a horse with a little jockey perched in the saddle. Next came a blue car with axles made of coiled magazine paper and wheels that turned. 'See, it actually works,' he said, pushing it across the floor. 'But this is the best. . . .'

In his hand was a fairy princes, about six inches high. She wore a dress of glossy red paper; her tiny hand was curled around a wand topped with a perfectly folded, five-pointed star.

'That's you,' he said. 'You wave your wand and my problems disappear.'

In this line of work, there are no better words than these.

Several weeks later, Mike and I had lunch. He'd been calling every other day, but I could speak with him only briefly. I was swamped with work and had recently entered a doctoral program at John Jay. Given his computer skills, I couldn't understand how it was that he still hadn't found a job.

Distracted as I was when we met, his relapse was undeniable. His clothes hung off his body; his eyes looked hollow and avoided me when he spoke. Over lunch, he showed me the journal he'd been keeping since I gave him the writing assignment in jail. He'd filled the entire notebook. 'Writing and NA meetings are the only things keeping me from getting high,' he told me.

I knew he was lying and considered confronting him. I looked at my watch. I had to be at a meeting in fifteen minutes. I spoke about how the first three months are the hardest and suggested that he call Kenny Johnson. He said he would, and I breathed a sigh of relief. Kenny could work miracles; if anyone could get through to Mike, it was Kenny. Maybe, just maybe, Kenny could persuade Mike to go to a drug program.

As I watched him cross the street – head bowed, hands deep in his pockets, his birdlike shoulders hunched against the cold February wind – I wondered how soon it would be before he'd crack.

That evening he called me. 'I wanted to tell you this at lunch,' he said. 'I can't keep lying to you. I've gotten high three times in the past couple of weeks,' he blurted. 'I haven't talked about it in the meetings. I feel like such a failure.'

He went on and on, saying how he was lonely and depressed and afraid he was going to be re-arrested. He admitted he'd been doing the MetroCard fraud and now a Transit worker was in on it with him. I urged him to check into a program, but he refused.

'I can do this on my own. I haven't gotten high now in five days. If I can just keep it up . . .'

Several times a week he'd call with an update on his progress. He was now nearing a month clean and I was beginning to have hope. One of our volunteer instructors, an executive recruiter and author, was thinking about paying him a handsome sum of money to set up a database he needed. But things didn't quite pan out.

Mike was on the phone and sounded miserable. When I asked him what was wrong, he insisted he was okay.

'Mike, you're not okay. I can hear it. I have time to listen if you want to talk.'

'I'm fine. I mean I'm not fine, but it's not your problem.'

I tried again. He didn't want to talk and hung up.

Two minutes later he called back. 'I'm not going to burden you with my problems. There's nothing you can do about it anyway.'

We went on like this for a few minutes, but he still wouldn't talk about what was wrong.

'I guess there's nothing I can do, then,' I said. 'Actually, I have a meeting. . . .'

His voice started shaking. 'Did you read the *Daily News* two days ago? Did you see "yours truly" featured in the fuckin' *News*?' By now he was shouting.

Apparently, the *Daily News* had run a two-page story on the city's top ten MetroCard thieves. I logged onto the Web site and found it. SCAMMERS TAKING SYSTEM FOR A RIDE shouted the headline. A sidebar featured Mike's name and his entire rap sheet. (It was longer than I thought.)

'My landlord saw it,' he said, his voice beginning to crack. 'She recognized my name and told me to pack my bags and leave. I freaked out. I started pulling money out of my pocket and throwing it on the counter. I offered to pay her ten dollars more for the room but she wouldn't take it. She told me to pack my stuff and get out. I've been on the street for two days now.'

And then he started to cry. The screech of an oncoming subway and his gulping sobs choked the line.

'I didn't get high,' he said. 'I want you to know that. I haven't gotten high in almost a month. I'm so close but I can't because I know if I do, I might as well kill myself. I tried every SRO [single-room-occupancy hotel] in this fuckin' city but I can't get a room.'

'Mike, go home,' I said. 'If your parents will take you back, you should go.'

He hadn't seen his parents for a while, and he dreaded facing them. They'd paid for several stints in drug rehabs and seen him through numerous jail terms. They were getting old and he wasn't getting any better.

'It's your choice. It's that or a shelter. Or a drug program, which is really what you should do but I know you won't. You can't live on the street. It's winter. Go home. Take a shower, get some sleep. Collect your thoughts.'

When I got home that night there was message on my machine. 'I'm at my mother's house. I took a hot bath. We had dinner together. I'm glad I'm here. Thank you for helping me. I don't know why you do.'

I was starting to wonder that myself.

The next time I heard from Mike – it was several weeks later – the noise in the background told me he was back in jail.

'It's worse than that,' he said. 'I fractured my collarbone and two ribs.' He went on to say how he was arrested in the subway station, how the cop who handcuffed him told him to sit on a bench while he filled out the paperwork. Already the story wasn't making sense.

'I saw a train coming,' he continued. 'One of those slow-moving service trains. I couldn't go back to jail again. I was desperate. I tried to jump onto the train, but I missed.'

While I listened to him drone on, a strange feeling of relief washed over me. His voice was a hammer driving home the point that there was nothing I could do for him. I knew I would no longer accept his collect phone calls from jail; I knew I would stop imploring him to get help for his addiction. As his voice faded into the background, I remembered something he once said to me: The only way to help certain addicts is to pull all the stops. Desert them. Let them self-destruct. Turn your back and walk away. Then maybe, just maybe, they'll get better.

'I have to go, Mike,' I said, and hung up.

Sometimes when I think about Mike (and I think of him often – his origami still decorates my office) I wonder what his story must look like to a foreigner, to someone from Australia, say, Great Britain or Switzerland, where drug addicts are treated medically, not criminally; to someone other than a jaded New Yorker inured to the dysfunctional nature of the city's criminal-justice system.

Obviously, Mike has a ferocious crack addiction. And his addiction demands criminality. Whether he's on the street or in jail, he will find and use drugs. Given that, how could judge after judge look at his rap sheet, revealing ten arrests in eighteen months (and for twelve of those months he was locked up), and ignore the obvious addiction? Ten times he was sent to Rikers for the same two crimes: drug possession and the MetroCard scam. Eight of those arrests netted him jail terms of a week or less.

Statewide, New York's criminal-justice system handles more than a million cases a day, according to Stanley Sklar, president of the New York State Association of Justices. Fully 75 percent of New York City's cases are drug related. The cost to incarcerate an inmate in the city system adds up to $68,000 per year. In-patient drug treatment costs $17,000 a year. A ten-year-old can do the math.

Mike's time on Rikers, excluding things like court fees and police time, cost taxpayers about $75,000. For $75,000 he could have spent two years in the best private drug treatment program in the country. Instead, he went to jail, got high, and left with the same addiction he had before the criminal-justice system intervened, and taxpayers foot the bill.

'Most intelligent people now agree that treating drug addicts is more effective than locking them up,' writes Sheryl McCarthy in *Newsday*. 'Everybody from Brooklyn District Attorney Joe Hynes to the American Bar Association has called for a move in that direction.' Ironically, had Mike been arrested one borough over, in Brooklyn instead of Manhattan, he would have had a much better shot at treatment. DA Hynes has managed to circumvent the state's harsh drug laws through an effective drug court that diverts non-violent offenders into treatment instead of prison. 'If they successfully complete the program,' *Newsday* reports, 'their charges are dismissed. Otherwise, they go to prison.' According to Dr. Mitchell Rosenthal, president of Phoenix House, the residential program where drug offenders stay for twelve to eighteen months, about 70 percent of those who complete at least a year of the program have tested drug-free up to five years later. Hynes estimates that his office, via the drug court, has saved taxpayers $13 million.

Had Mike had been arrested in Arizona, he would have been *mandated* to drug treatment. Arizonans recently looked at the high price of operating prisons, in which 75 percent of inmates are substance abusers, and decided that diverting nonviolent offenders from prison into treatment made more sense. Under a bold new law, drug treatment is provided for any substance abuser convicted of a nonviolent crime. And there's no way around the law: People with first or second drug offenses are required to get treatment rather than go to prison. An evaluation conducted by the Supreme Court of the State of Arizona found that the recidivism rates of participants was low, and that Arizona taxpayers saved vast amounts of money.

Indeed, in drug-treatment courts throughout America, fully 70 percent of the people sentenced to treatment instead of jail successfully complete the program, according to the General Accounting Office of Congress. On the other hand, 'People who are sent to prison

77

instead of treatment are four times as likely to commit another drug crime within five years of release,' reports *The New York Times*. And treatment instead of prison saves about $20,000 per person a year, according to a study by the National Center on Addiction and Substance Abuse at Columbia University. The study also says that 70 percent to 85 percent of state prison inmates need some level of substance-abuse treatment, but only 13 percent of inmates received any kind of treatment in 1996.

Unfortunately, America battles its drug problem by imprisoning addicts and spending billions of dollars on a drug war that even the four-star general in charge of it admits is a failure. 'The much-trumpeted war on drugs ... has hugely misfired,' said General Barry McCaffrey, the national drug czar in 1999. 'We have a failed social policy and it has to be re-evaluated.'

When President Richard Nixon first used the phrase 'War on Drugs' in 1971, the federal budget to fight the drug war was $101 million. By the year 2000, it had grown to $17.8 billion. From $101 million to $17.8 billion in less than thirty years – that's a sentence worth re-reading.

Former police chief Joseph McNamara is one of the most impassioned and articulate critics of America's drug war. People listen to him because he fought on the front lines for thirty-five years, starting as a beat cop in New York City, then serving as police chief in Kansas City and San Jose. Today he's a Research Fellow at Stanford University. In November 1999, at a presentation in New York City, he revealed in layman's terms just how much the country's war on drugs is costing.

'I try to explain it to people in a way they can understand,' he says. 'In 1972, the average monthly Social Security check was $177. If those benefits had increased at the same rate that drug war spending had increased, the average Social Security check today would be $30,444 a month. The average weekly salary of $114 would be $19,000 a week, and if you had a mortgage of $408 a month in 1972 and it had increased at the same rate, your mortgage today would be over $60,000 a month.'

What did we get for our $17.8 billion war on drugs? Not much. Drugs are cheaper, purer, and 'more available today than they were a decade ago,' says McCaffrey. 'More than 85 percent of high school seniors say they have tried an illegal drug,' says McNamara, 'and 85 percent of high school seniors say that it is easier to get marijuana than to get beer.' Despite enormous expenditures and enormous imprisonment, he adds, 'we have not been able to reduce foreign production of drugs, we have not been able to seize any more of the drugs coming into America. America – indeed the world – is awash in illegal drugs and illegal drug money.'

A key point in understanding the current state of affairs is how anti-drug money is allocated. When Nixon first declared the 'War on Drugs,' he directed about two-thirds of all federal funding at treatment and prevention. Compare this to the Clinton Administration's drug-fighting budget, which at $18 billion is the biggest in history: Nearly two-thirds of the money went to law enforcement and interdiction of drugs, 'a proportion unchanged since the Reagan Administration,' reported *The New York Times*.

Conceptually, the war metaphor used by politicians suggests that we're up against a foreign enemy, and many people blame America's drug problem on those 'foreigners' who import drugs. But the problem isn't 'out there'; it's right here – in our own huge appetite for drugs and in the ineffective policies we use to deal with it.

3

KEEPERS OF THE KEPT

The essential relationship inside a prison is the one between a guard and an inmate. Any true progress in the workings of a prison ought to be measurable in changes in the tenor of that relationship. The guard is mainstream society's last representative; the inmate, its most marginal man. The guard, it is thought, wields all the power, but in truth the inmate has power too. How will they meet, with mutual respect or mutual disdain? Will they talk? Will they joke? Will they look each other in the eye?

– Ted Conover, *Newjack: Guarding Sing Sing*, 2000

Of the many things I liked about the new captain, what I liked most was that he broke the rules. Not major ones, just some of the hundreds of small, annoying rules that make working on Rikers exhausting, like having to walk across a huge parking lot and through the Control Building to turn in your pass instead of simply handing it to the guard in the booth as you drive out. When the new captain would drive me off the Rock in his flashy red sports car, he'd roll down the window, stick out his beefy forearm, and wave my pass at the guard. 'Hey buddy,' he'd say. 'Do me a favor . . . turn this in for me.' The guard would seem pleased to help. 'You got it, Cap,' he'd reply.

The new captain knew how to get things done. His efficiency reminded me of my businessmen friends on the outside. He was charismatic and upbeat. He didn't have the corrections slouch.

I met him shortly after I became the program director at Fresh Start. I'd been there less than a month and was already overwhelmed by the red tape, the clearances that failed to be at the gate for our guest instructors, and having to solve the same problems day after day. 'It's part and parcel of working in jail,' the former director told me before she left. 'Just don't expect things to go smoothly and you'll never be disappointed.' An inspiring orientation.

In all honesty, I didn't expect much when I'd heard there'd been a change in captains. One barrel-chested 'white shirt' would be as steely and uncooperative as the next, I thought. Behind bars, the relationship between correction officials and civilians, particularly volunteers, teachers, and counselors, is usually one of weary tolerance. From their perspective – and sometimes they're right – free-world teachers, psychologists, and volunteers are easily manipulated by inmates and fail to follow security measures, like leaving their names and addresses on magazines instead of crossing them out. Many 'do-gooders,' as we're known, see correction officers as power-hungry oppressors. That was my mind-set when I started working on Rikers in 1994.

HARRY

My first change of heart came when I met the pleasant and retiring Harry. Because of Barbara Margolis's heralded status in the jails (in addition to being a former city commissioner she also serves on the Board of Correction, the watchdog agency over conditions on Rikers), Fresh Start enjoyed the services of an 'escort officer' in the early years of the program, before the budget cuts. A CO would actually drive a Department car into the city to pick up volunteer chefs for our cooking classes, and after they were done would swing by Queens Plaza to pick me up on his way back to Rikers. Perhaps because we spent more time in the free world than in the jail, Harry was the only CO who introduced himself to me by his first name instead of his last. And, just like the first prisoner I met on Rikers, he defied my stereotypes of people who live and work behind bars.

Three afternoons a week, Harry would wait for me in the Department's old black station wagon, wedged between buses idling on Queens Plaza or parked alongside a hotdog stand. Sometimes I'd arrive ten or fifteen minutes late, convinced he'd be gone, but he was always there, smoking and listening to the radio. He'd lean across the ripped seat to open the door and pretend not to notice the box of doughnuts I'd bought for the inmates and pushed under the seat.

In the beginning, I'd pepper him with questions about his work as a guard, about inmates he'd known or the latest scandal in the jails. 'Same old, same old,' Harry would say between cigarettes, switching the subject to one that interested him more: an upcoming motor-cycle trip, a video he'd rented, a late night of drinking at a bar. The countdown to the weekend – 'just two more days' or 'tomorrow's over-the-hump day' – was a staple in our weekly exchanges. And then we'd be over the bridge.

There were only two prison stories Harry told me, and I remem-ber them well. I remember exactly where we were on our drive to the Rock when he started speaking, how he pulled more intently on his cigarette as he spoke and seemed to drive a little more slowly. It wasn't so much his stories that held me transfixed, but a feeling that I was being given a glimpse into the secret world of prison.

The first story was about an escape, a tragedy and a romance really, and it's one of my favorite prison stories. According to Harry, a male guard in the women's jail fell in love with an inmate. He was so in love that he decided he would risk his freedom to grant her hers and they could share freedom together. He brought in a dress, ladies' shoes, makeup, and a wig. He 'guarded' the door while she transformed herself from a lowly inmate into a pretty civilian. He then gave her a visitor's pass so she could leave the island with ease.

Once she was over the bridge, she waited for him in his car, which he'd left unlocked in the visitors' parking lot. Shortly after, he arrived. They'd made it! Or so they thought, until the love-stricken guard realized that he'd left his keys, of all things, on his desk. On the ring were the keys to his car, his house, his life. He panicked and decided to go back. Before he made it over the bridge, the authori-ties found his stowaway crouched behind the seat of the car.

The whole time Harry was telling me the story, I kept envision-ing him as the guard. He was in his early forties, blond and blue-eyed, with a boyish grin and dimples. I knew he lived alone; sometimes we'd talk about the singles scene in the city. 'Did you ever work in the women's house, Harry?'

He could see where I was going and chuckled. 'Nope, but I worked in the death house.'

'You worked in the death house?'

'Yeah, it was years ago.' In fact, New York closed death row in 1976. After the Supreme Court ruled in *Furman v. Georgia* that the death penalty constituted cruel and unusual punishment, the New York State Legislature abolished the death penalty and shut down death row.

'It was up in Greenhaven,' he said, a maximum-security prison about two hours north of the city. I imagined a row of darkened cells filled with terrible people, and lit a cigarette myself in anticipation of what I hoped would be an even better story.

'What was it like? Why did you work there? Were you scared of the prisoners?' The questions came spilling out.

Harry inhaled deeply, and then seemed to disappear for a moment. 'Nah,' he said, shaking his head. 'It was quiet up there. Real quiet.'

Just several months before, New York's Governor George Pataki had reinstated the death penalty. The first person sent to death row, Darrel Smith, was one of New York's Boldest: a CO from Rikers. Pumped up on cocaine and alcohol, he had shot his girlfriend at a nightclub. 'He just flipped,' Harry said. A few years before, the officer had received a medal of valor from the Department. And now he was the newest arrival in the newly named death house at Clinton Correctional Facility in Dannemora, New York: the Unit for Condemned Persons.

How odd, I thought as we pulled in to the parking lot outside the jail. Both of his stories ended with COs in prison.

THE CAPTAIN

Unlike the reticent Harry, the new captain would talk to me for hours about his life on the Rock. Given who he was, and what he told me, it was strange that we became friends.

I'd heard the rumors shortly after we met, and today I see references to the special unit he worked in for seven years in nearly every book or journal article I read on prison violence. The professor of a corrections class I was taking at the time devoted an entire two hours to the headline story unfolding in Rikers' most dreaded unit: CPSU, otherwise known as 'the Bing.'

Opened in 1988, the Central Punitive Segregation Unit is housed in a maximum-security jail on Rikers. Like all supermax units, it is a prison within a prison, a disciplinary lockdown unit where inmates are sent for additional punishment. They are confined to their cells more than twenty-one hours a day; cannot watch TV, have radios or watches; and are limited to one phone call a week. Despite these restrictions, 'the place was a jungle,' the captain said of his first year there in 1989. 'It was a jungle ruled by the inmates.'

Before CPSU, the captain worked in the jail for adolescents (sixteen-to-twenty-one-year-olds), one of the roughest jails on the island. An assistant deputy warden approached him about a transfer. 'He said he needed help in the Bing. The directive from the top was to restore order by any means possible,' the captain recalled. He added that he didn't know whether he was hand-picked for the job or not, but I imagine that his training in the Marine Corps and the fifty or so uses of force he'd racked up in ARDC (the Adolescent Reception and Detention Center) didn't hurt.

He was told the assignment would last eighteen months, and then he'd be given the post (work area) and schedule of his choice. To correction officers, a steady assignment on the 'day tour' (from 7:00 A.M. to 3 P.M.) and weekends off is a gift from the gods. But the prison brass pulled a bait and switch. 'We wanted to get out, but we couldn't,' the captain said. 'No one was willing to take our place.'

In most solitary-confinement units for sentenced prisoners, inmates never leave their cells except for an hour of court-mandated recreation in a dog-pen-like cage attached to the back of the cell. Meals, reading materials, and counseling services are delivered through the bars so the inmate never leaves: a CO's dream come true. Unlike solitary confinement for sentenced prisoners, however, the inmates in CPSU were 'detainees,' meaning that they were charged with but not yet convicted of a crime. Because of this, they are legally entitled to an hour of outdoor recreation, an hour in the law library, daily religious services, showers, and even 'visits to the fucking barbershop,' noted the captain. So part of the problem with CPSU was logistical. The inmates' legally required time out of the cell was time when they could attack other inmates and officers. And that they did.

'It was a nightmare,' he told me. 'The inmates would slash each other – or an officer – in a heartbeat.' They'd light fires in their cells and flood the galleries by jamming the toilets. 'You'd see feces floating down the corridor. I saw officers with their faces cut, with feces thrown on them. I saw an officer slashed with a sharpened chicken bone.'

Inmates who end up in the Bing tend to have an 'I-don't-give-a-fuck' attitude and 'the heart' to sink a shank (prison-made knife) deep into the flesh of a warm body to get what they want: usually respect or protection. A veteran CO described the inmates in CPSU as follows: 'Out of a population of twenty thousand assholes, they are the biggest assholes.' In more eloquent terms, *New York* magazine wrote: 'On an island filled with thousands of murderers, rapists, armed robbers, drug dealers, arsonists and muggers,' CPSU houses 'the city's least reconstructible miscreants.'

The charges that most often landed inmates in the Bing were slashing or stabbing another inmate or guard, or smuggling in drugs, razor blades, or knives. For these offenses, inmates would be given thirty to ninety days in the Bing, though some inmates racked up over a thousand days for multiple slashings or particularly heinous acts. Today, as part of the violence reduction strategy, detainees who assault other inmates or officers, or who are found with a weapon, are arrested in jail and sent to prison, just as if they'd assaulted someone on the outside or were caught with an illegal weapon.

Another reality, which is true on Rikers and in most prisons across the country, is that the inmates who end up in solitary confinement are the hot potatoes of the jails, the inmates nobody wants or knows how to handle, the walking time bombs who, for a variety of reasons, are unable to control their behavior. Many are mentally ill. One expert on prison control units, Stuart Grassian, M.D., described the situation this way:

There is a notion in the popular mind that people who end up in solitary confinement are the most ruthless kind of James Cagneys of the prison system. In fact what you often see there is exactly the antithesis: they are very often the wretched of the earth, people who are mentally ill, illiterate, and cognitively impaired, people with neurological difficulties, people who just really can't manage to contain their behavior at times. The prison system tends to respond to this by punishment. Punishment tends to make their conditions worse and they tend to get into these vicious cycles where they continue to commit this disruptive behavior and they continue to go deeper and deeper into the belly of the prison system and get sicker and sicker. Solitary confinement itself can cause a very specific kind of psychiatric syndrome, which, in its worst stages, can lead to an agitated, hallucinatory, confusional psychotic state often involving random violence and self-mutilation, suicidal behavior, a lot of real agitated, fearful and confusional kinds of symptoms.

Some nights after work the captain would see me waiting for the route bus and offer me a ride home. My feet would ache from standing all day, and the prospect of the hour-long trip home on public transportation – the route bus to the Control Room to turn in my pass, the twenty-minute wait for the bus over the bridge to Queens Plaza, standing on the desolate subway platform to catch the N train to Manhattan – filled me with gloom. In the beginning I'd decline the captain's offer because I knew he lived thirty minutes in the opposite direction. 'You can just drop me off at Queens Plaza,' I'd say. 'I'll get the subway from there.'

'C'mon, get in. I'll drive you home. Really – it's no problem.'

Over the next two years that we worked together, those three words ('It's no problem') were how I came to define the captain. No matter what I asked of him – Could he escort a Fresh Start inmate to the clinic so he could see a doctor faster? Would he mind driving a volunteer chef off the island to spare him the bus trip? Could he stay with me and the inmates in the jail kitchen overnight while we cooked turkeys for our Thanksgiving project? – his response was always the same: 'It's no problem.'

As we drove into the city, we'd review various jail issues: which dorm officers weren't letting the inmates out on time for class; the upcoming graduation that needed to be coordinated; how the spiral-bound notebooks I gave to the inmates were contraband. He'd educate me about security issues and the inner workings of the Department. He'd explain who had power and who didn't and how to navigate the sea of red tape. He helped me in more ways than I can remember.

During one of our rides, I brought up the subject of CPSU. I'd been following the accounts in the papers and had heard the gossip in the jails. In a class-action lawsuit filed by the Legal Aid Society, eleven correction officers had been charged with planning concerted attacks on inmates and falsifying reports to cover up the abuses. Thirty-three inmates sustained perforated or ruptured eardrums during uses of force by correction officers. In one year alone, forty inmates suffered head injuries while they were handcuffed, sometimes behind the back. According to Legal Aid lawyer John Boston, Department officials had been alerted to the unusually high number of injuries soon after CPSU opened but failed to stop guard misconduct. (Several years later I met John Boston and asked him what he thought about my friend the captain. 'That man is a sadist,' he spat.)

I thought the captain would clam up when I asked him about CPSU, but he didn't. In fact, the more I'd ask, the more he'd tell me. 'It feels good to get it off my chest,' he said. 'It's nice to have someone who'll listen.' Like most of his friends from CPSU, his marriage was over by the time he got out.

'My divorce had a lot to do with CPSU. When things are so fucked up, so incredibly violent and you're doing so much overtime, it's impossible to just *leave it* at the job, or even *leave* the job, for that matter.' There were times he'd get home at 1 A.M. and receive a call to report back to work at 5 A.M. He once worked thirty-six hours straight.

'Being in CPSU took your personal life on a roller-coaster ride,' he said. 'A lot of us got divorces, a lot of the officers started drinking because the only people who could understand what they were going through were other officers. They'd clock out at midnight, go to a bar, and drink til five in the morning.'

Sometimes the captain and I would stop for dinner at a Vietnamese restaurant near my apartment on the Upper West Side. Over spicy prawns and sesame noodles he'd tell me things that made my stomach turn. 'I had my first use of force five minutes into the job,' he said one night. 'I was making a tour in a housing area. An inmate slashed another inmate and refused to give up the weapon. So I turned around, beat the shit out of him, and took the razor.'

The captain wasn't tall, but he was brawny. His hands looked like they could crush walnuts. He was intensely alert (his eyes continuously scanned his surroundings), and he possessed an almost robot-like ability to focus on whatever issue was at hand.

The beleaguered guards in CPSU welcomed his new style of management. After his first inmate beat-down, he said, 'one of the officers looked up to the sky, put his hands together, and said, "Thank you, Jesus! Finally we got someone here who knows what he's doing." By the end of the tour,' he added, stabbing a prawn for emphasis, '*everyone* knew who I was.'

He recounted another incident that occurred his first week on the job. An inmate had slashed an officer in the face with a razor, and for that the COs nearly killed him.

'Now to assault an officer with your fist is one thing,' the captain noted, 'but to *cut* an officer is a complete violation.' He described the retribution as 'one of the worst beatings' he'd seen. 'They beat the inmate so bad the doctor had to drill a hole in his skull to relieve the pressure. It looked like there was a grapefruit mounted to his forehead when they were done with him. I didn't know whether he'd live or die.'

'So what happened to the officers?' I asked. 'Didn't they, uh, like, get into trouble or something?' Despite my best efforts at nonchalance, his stories had me stammering. I feared that if he knew how horrified I was, he might clam up.

I tried again. 'So what I have trouble understanding is how they could almost kill an inmate and get away with it. Don't you have to write a report after a use of force? Aren't questions raised when an inmate is beaten so badly he's sent to an outside hospital?'

'Back then it was different,' he said. 'If there was proof that an officer was injured, like in this case, if there were puncture wounds, slash wounds, whatever, then IAD [the Internal Affairs Division] would just close out the case. You could practically *kill* an inmate and you'd never even be questioned about it.'

'So the reports, essentially, were lies,' I commented. 'Hmmm. How does that work?'

'Listen, there's always time after an incident where you can sit down and think of what to say. You gotta be able to explain why an inmate has blood gushin' outta his fuckin' ears and make it sound plausible. Sure we used to make up the reports. We'd write whatever we could think of.'

The bill would come, and more often than not he'd insist on paying. 'Please, lemme get this. Really, it's no problem.' He'd stand up from the table and hold out my coat for me. He'd smooth his black leather jacket neatly over his gun. (For protection against ex-cons they may meet on the street, COs are allowed to carry guns.) 'I'm sorry if I spoiled your appetite. Let's get outta here.'

An hour or so later, we'd still be in his car talking. He'd add a new detail to the story, I'd ask another question, and we'd be off to the races. I was simultaneously fascinated, outraged, and confused by what he would tell me. The fascination and outrage I could understand. It was like covering my eyes at a bullfight I once saw in Mexico but peeking every so often to see if I could stand it. Reconciling the captain's past with his present, however, challenged my conscience on a regular basis. One night he'd be telling me about inmate beat-downs, or 'tune-ups' as they're sometimes called; the next day I'd see him slip a piece of birthday cake to the inmate-porter who worked in his office. If an inmate had a personal problem he didn't want the men in his dorm to know about, the captain would take him to the social services office to use a phone in private. More than once I saw him escort an inmate to the commissary or the barbershop even though it wasn't the inmate's scheduled day. 'The man's gotta go to court tomorrow. He should have a haircut,' he'd say if I teased him that he was getting soft.

At the time when we became friends, I wasn't writing a book. But the more the captain told me, the more I wanted to get his account down on paper. He was giving me information that rarely escapes the blue wall of silence, so one night I asked if I could tape our conversations for possible publication in a magazine, journal article, or maybe a book. 'It's no problem,' he said. 'Just don't write anything until I'm retired. And don't use my name.'

The captain's accounts of life in the Bing sounded like hazardous duty in Vietnam. 'We were responding to eight alarms a tour, approximately one every hour,' he recalled. Alarms signify emergencies that the COs can't handle alone. A special team of helmeted, baton-wielding officers in army fatigues storms the jail and provides backup muscle. They are officially known as the ERU (Emergency Response Unit), but the inmates call them the Goon Squad. I've also heard 'Ninja Turtles.'

'I knew the inmates could kill me if they wanted to,' he said. 'And I was ready to die. So fear was out of the question. I'd go into the cells of the cop killers, the six-four meanest motherfuckers you can imagine and sit there and talk to them, hang with them for hours. They respected me for that.'

He described the correction staff in CPSU as 'the most cohesive unit, the closest thing to a special force unit' he'd seen since the military. They ruled the Bing with iron fists and operated on four assumptions, which the captain enumerated for me. They were so engrained in his mind it sounded like he was reading from a script:

'One, the inmate is always wrong; two, never turn in another officer; three, always come to an officer's aid; and four, always keep your mouth shut.

'Until you had your first use of force,' he added, 'none of the other officers would trust you. You had to show you were prepared to help if it was needed. Good officers always have to watch each other's back.

'I'd tell the officers if there's a problem and you don't watch my back, if you're not there when I need you, well, then' – he laughed – 'you better hope that inmate kills me 'cause I'll hold you down and beat *you* fucking senseless. Hell, I'll have the *inmates* hold you down while *I* beat you senseless – you'll *wish* you were dead.'

I commented that the whole thing sounded absurd. 'Didn't the Department give you any training? Didn't you have Mace or something?'

'I got no training whatsoever,' he said. 'And there wasn't any gas [pepper spray] back then like there is today. The Department didn't care what was going on – they just wanted us to get the place under control. Their message to me was "handle it," so I did it the best way I knew how.' He likened the assignment to 'the opening statement of Mission Impossible: Get the job done by any means necessary and we will disavow all knowledge of your actions.' He gave me an example:

'A captain I know got slashed from his back to his gut. He got forty stitches and was back on the job two days later. Of course he had a vengeance for the inmates. Of course he was bitter. The warden knew what happened to him but he let him come back to work forty-eight hours later. In fact, they kept him in CPSU another three years. If I was him I woulda sued the fuckin' Department.'

I asked the captain how he coped. 'I just dealt with it.' He shrugged. 'I didn't question myself. And I never took the same way home after work.'

'Because you were afraid of inmates who'd been released?'

'Hell yeah. And I taught my family that if we were ever in the city and I told them to move, not to question me, just do it. I've run into inmates on the street before, but, thank God, I never had a problem.'

The day before Thanksgiving in 1996, New York restaurateur Michael Weinstein delivered 100 twenty-pound turkeys to Rikers for Fresh Start's Thanksgiving project. The inmates in the culinary arts class would cook them during the night and deliver them to soup kitchens in the city the next morning as they'd done for the past several years. It's a challenging project to pull off under any circumstances, but in jail we're at the mercy of correction officials to make it happen. Cooking turkeys wasn't high on their list of priorities, so I was more than relieved when the captain offered to help.

Shortly after midnight, he picked me up at my apartment. We stopped at a twenty-four-hour store to buy pancake mix, eggs, and orange juice so the inmates could have a breakfast other than cereal when they finished. 'Here – I bet they'd like this,' the captain said, tossing in a package of bacon.

Later that night, as the inmates and I unpacked the shipment of turkeys, we noticed that four of them were missing. I figured it was an oversight on the part of the restaurant and there wasn't much we could do about it. The captain wouldn't hear of it. 'Where were they stored? Was the refrigerator locked? Count 'em again!' he growled.

'What's up his ass?' one of the guys muttered under his breath as we set about counting.

'Just be quiet,' I said. 'You really don't want to get him mad.'

We recounted the turkeys and still came up short. The captain grabbed the phone and dialed the Control Room, clenching and unclenching his fists while he spoke. I imagined his shiny gold rings popping off from the force, zinging around the room for an inmate to find and slip into his pocket.

'Who was on duty in the mess hall?' he shouted. 'Yeah? Uh-huh. And when was that? Right.'

He slammed down the receiver. 'Un-fucking-believable! They'd steal from their own goddamn mothers.'

He found our four turkeys in a CO's trunk.

Around six in the morning, an hour before we were scheduled to load the truck and leave for the city, the inmates had finished the job. They'd cooked, boxed, and stacked 100 turkeys. They'd made vats of stuffing and sealed portions in aluminum trays. They'd separated the canned goods that the captain had collected from storehouses around the island (where he knew the officers) and transported to our jail in his car. The inmates worked so single-mindedly that he left us alone and slept on a couch in his office while we cooked.

I'd been expecting a night of headaches and breakdowns, delays and disagreements, but the project came together with amazing efficiency. The inmates were proud of themselves, and so was I. One of them found a boom box in the cook's office and carried it out to the kitchen. 'Hey, Cap,' he said. 'Mind if we play some tunes?'

'Yeah, all right. Just keep it down.'

I couldn't believe it. I'd never known a CO, much less a captain, to be so relaxed. The inmate turned to the local hip-hop station and rapped Puff Daddy into a mop handle. '"It's all about the Benjamins [$100 bills] baby,"' he sang. I stifled the urge to dance.

The captain brought in the groceries and unpacked them one by one, laying them out on the long steel table like Christmas presents. 'You got us bacon?' a stunned inmate asked. 'Word!' He raised his hand and high-fived the captain.

While pancakes and bacon hissed on the grill, we collected some milk crates to sit on. 'I never done such easy jail time,' one of the men said, licking syrup off his lips. 'The hours flew by.' Another inmate talked about how doing something good for people in need made him feel better about himself. 'This is one of the best Thanksgivings I can remember, even though I *am* locked up.'

Somewhere after dawn, we opened the massive gates of the loading dock and stood for a while at the edge, letting the cold air wash the kitchen smells from our clothes. A man offered me his coat with D.O.C. INMATE inscribed in big white letters on the back. Another held out a piece of pancake to a seagull that circled overhead. Its cry sounded even more doleful as we beheld the view before us: the Manhattan skyscrapers shimmering in the distance, a pastel pink sky over the landscape of jails, where twenty thousand inmates slept in their beds.

The captain came out, squinting in the sun. 'You guys did a great job,' he said. 'I put aside a turkey and some stuffing for you in the programs office. I made arrangements with the cook to heat it up when you get back.'

During one of our talks I asked the captain if he'd describe himself as 'violent-prone' before he started working in CPSU. 'Absolutely not,' he said. 'But don't get me wrong, I wasn't afraid to use my fists if I needed to.' The prisoners in CPSU, he said, 'were a whole different breed of inmate. They were predators. They used to challenge us all the time.'

Once, he said, an inmate refused to 'lock in,' meaning he wouldn't return to his cell. 'When I got to work, the officers told me what happened and I went to talk to the guy. I said, "Listen, you gotta do what you're told here. You wanna be treated like a human being, then you gotta act like a human being. If not, we'll treat you the way we wanna treat you." With that, the inmate said, "Fuck you." So I say, "Yeah? Fuck me?" Okay, fine.

'As I'm walking down the tier, I heard another inmate say to the guy, "You just earned yourself a trip to the hospital."'

By the early nineties the threat of violence by COs pervaded the Bing. The inmates knew they'd be beaten with fists or batons for disobeying an order and that no one was watching the shop. 'Officials from the Federal Bureau of Prisons did a tour of CPSU,' the captain recalled. 'As they walked down the cell blocks they said they'd never seen such fear on inmates' faces . . . such absolute terror. The inmates wouldn't talk to them because they knew what we'd do to them if they did.'

The captain realized the pendulum had swung too far in the wrong direction when the following incident occurred.

'I was sitting in the captain's office when an officer came in and said, "Listen, I think you better go to the receiving room, you better go – they're trying to murder this guy." I went in and they were tossing the inmate around like a rag doll. His whole face was crushed in.'

'Did you stop them?'

'I stopped them from murdering him if that's what you mean.'

The inmate, he said, had stabbed a captain in the cheek with a pen. The captain had planned to attend a christening that day, but the ragged gash in his cheek landed him in the hospital instead.

'The officers took the inmate into the receiving room and beat him with batons for fifteen minutes,' the captain told me. 'They were playing baseball with his face. Every bone in his face was broken. They did everything but make his brains come out of his ears.' By the time they were finished, he said, 'Everyone was covered with blood. Eight batons were broken. It made Rodney King look like kindergarten.'

In the spring of 1996, I was taking a graduate class in research methods, and the professor cited a study known as the Stanford Prison Experiment conducted in the 1970s by Philip Zimbardo and Craig Haney. (The results of the experiment show how easily the prison environment can turn almost anyone – in this case a group of college students – brutal and mean.) In the study, college students who had been 'authenticated' as psychologically normal were assigned to play the role of either prisoner or guard in a makeshift prison in the basement of a Stanford building. All of the participants knew that the experiment was artificial. 'At the end of six days,' wrote Zimbardo, 'we had to close down our mock prison because what we saw was frightening:'

> It was no longer apparent to most of the subjects (or to us) where reality ended and the roles began. The majority had indeed become prisoners or guards, no longer able to clearly differentiate between role-playing and self. There were dramatic changes in virtually every aspect of their behavior, thinking and feeling. In less than a week the experience of imprisonment undid (temporarily) a lifetime of learning: human values were suspended, self-concepts were challenged and the ugliest, most base, pathological side of human nature surfaced. We were horrified because we saw some boys (guards) treat others as if they were despicable animals, taking pleasure in cruelty, while other boys (prisoners) became servile, dehumanized robots who thought only of escape, of their own individual survival and of their mounting hatred for the guards.

One of the most interesting findings was that 'the worst prisoner treatment came on the night shift and other occasions when the student-guards thought that they could avoid the surveillance and interference of the research team,' write the authors.

When I asked the captain how he could watch the COs 'play baseball' with an inmate's face, his response was straight out of the Stanford Prison Experiment. 'Unfortunately,' he said, 'you get caught up with a lot of things. Even though you may not want to be violent, if everyone around you is and you see so much of it, you become immune to it. It no longer bothers you. You get to the point where you can watch someone's brains run out while you're eating dinner. You become numb. That's what CPSU did to me.'

Still, he was aware that something inside of him had changed, that the darkest aspects of human nature had emerged and taken root. 'The vilest deeds like poison weeds bloom well in prison air,' Oscar Wilde wrote in 'The Ballad of Reading Gaol.'

'Some nights after work another captain and I would go to City Island and sit on his boat and talk 'til three in the morning,' he said. 'We'd look at each other and say "I can't believe what we're doing. I can't believe what we've become." We'd sit there and talk for hours, wondering what happened to us.'

In the early 1990s, stories of guard brutality in CPSU started to trickle out. Ex-inmates, family members, and physicians from the jail and outside hospitals made too many calls for the officials to ignore. The abuses were exposed when the Legal Aid Society filed *Shepard v. Phoenix*. Shepard was an inmate who'd been beaten by CPSU guards; Warden Phoenix was the man in charge. The city launched its own investigation shortly thereafter. The New York City Department of Investigation (DOI) sent confidential informants into the jail and put up electronic surveillance.

'They'd put up cameras and the officers would fuckin' break 'em,' the captain said. 'I'd see cameras eighteen feet high that were shifted. I don't know how they got up there, but whatever had to be done to get the cameras off them, they'd do. And once we knew the investigation was on, mum was the word.'

By 1995, enough evidence was produced to officially charge nearly a dozen COs with assaulting inmates and falsifying reports. Fifteen captains were implicated as ringleaders but none of them were indicted. Several correction officers, however, were. 'The COs who got indicted were the ones who talked in bars,' the captain explained. Because he wasn't a drinker and didn't hang out in bars, by the end of the investigation he had never even been deposed.

'What hurt me the most was the day I came home in 1995 – before I even knew about the extent of the allegations – and got the letter from Corporation Counsel [the legal agency for the city] saying they weren't going to indemnify us.' This meant that if the inmates won the $2 million lawsuit, the correction officers and the captains would foot the bill instead of the city.

'The letter said some shit like "We advise you to seek private counsel because we don't feel your actions were warranted." I got on the phone to the vice president of the union and said what the fuck is this we're not indemnified? We risked our *fuckin'* lives for this Department and they're *turning their backs on us*? "We'll get back to you right away," he said. "Everything's still being negotiated. Don't worry, the union will pick up the tab if the city doesn't.'"

He got off the phone and read the letter again. "'Not acting within the scope of our employment?" I musta read that letter a hundred times.'

Ultimately, the union hired a different law firm for each of the captains. 'They were willing to spend millions of dollars on our defense if it came down to it,' the captain said. Several months later he was transferred to a 'no-inmate-contact' position in the jail. 'I was told I had to get out because I was involved in too many uses of force. . . . I felt like I was being punished, but after I saw what was taking place and how the Department basically disowned us, I was glad they transferred me. Things had gotten so out of hand.'

He recalls going to a wedding around the time when 'charges were being issued right and left.' Some CPSU brass and guards were there and sat at the same table. 'If DOI and Legal Aid want us so bad, they should come here tonight with the daisy chains and round us up. We're all here,' one of the officers joked. 'Then one guy goes "We weren't guards. We were *gods*." That was good,' the captain said. 'We raised our glasses and toasted to that.'

Over the ensuing months, three COs were indicted and sent to prison. 'The investigators tried to get them to turn us in, but they said, "Fuck you. I'll do state time before I snitch." They told the general inspector, "Fuck you. I ain't testifying." He tried to cut them a deal, but they refused. That's how loyal those officers were.'

In the end, the inmates won $1.6 million and the Department – i.e., the taxpayers – paid the bill. 'You know why?' the captain asked. 'Because they *knew* they fucked up. The Department got a pound of flesh from us, but they paid for it in the end.'

'Actually,' I suggested, 'you and I and every other taxpayer in the city paid for it, not to mention the inmates.'

'Hey – equal opportunity,' he laughed.

When a position opened up in one of the calmer jails on the island, where Fresh Start runs its program, the captain took it. He described the transition as being 'like taking a lion out of the jungle and trying to tame him.' Part of him missed the action in the Bing.

'I roamed the halls like a predator looking for someone to pick on. The officers would tell me, "Relax. This is an old-age home."'

Sociologists describe this kind of heightened sensitivity to danger as fear of the symbolic assailant. Observed mostly in police officers patrolling high-crime areas in search of suspected 'perps,' it is particularly common among prison guards who work with convicted felons on a daily basis. As COs often comment, 'There's no guarantee you're going home every day.'

Shortly before he retired, I asked the captain how many uses of force he accrued over his twenty-year career.

'Me? I dunno. Probably somewhere between 350 and 500 are on file. But I was never charged with excessive use of force. The only thing I was ever charged with was failing to conduct a proper investigation and failing to gather sufficient inmate statements.'

I found this astounding. He was involved in over 350 uses of force – and that was only what showed up on paper – and no red flags went up. No official in the Department found that excessive. No official told him to get counseling or get out until independent investigators blew open the case. In fact, it was only several years ago that the Correction Department began tracking uses of force by computer.

When Michael Jacobson took over as commissioner in 1996, he went to work on transforming the infamous Bing. 'The first thing we did was move CPSU from the oldest, most decrepit, dungeon-like jail on the island to one of the newest jails, the Otis Bantum Correctional Center, where it was bright and airy,' he said. He transferred all of the staff to other jails, putting some in non-inmate contact positions, and replaced them with correction officers who went through a week of CPSU-specific training. 'We settled with Legal Aid, and a key agreement was that both Legal Aid and the Department would place internal monitors in the unit to oversee operations.' As with Rikers generally, the violence and chaos that once plagued the Bing have subsided significantly in recent years.

During his last year on the job, the captain moved to the night shift so he could spend his days pursuing various business ventures he hoped would crystallize after he retired. Around the same time, I left Rikers to oversee Fresh Start's new welfare-to-work program in the South Bronx. The captain and I remained friends, and occasionally we meet for dinner. Inevitably, the conversation returns to the past.

'I can't imagine what you must have thought of Fresh Start,' I said the last time I saw him. 'All of us do-gooders running around trying to help the inmates.' It was a warm June evening and we sat outside a restaurant in Brooklyn Heights, where I'd recently moved. Every so often, the wind would kick up and rustle the trees along the Promenade, parting them like curtains over the skyscrapers across the river. I was glad to see the captain again and revisit a part of my life that was still as vivid and strange as a midnight dream.

'You know, I actually started to enjoy helping them,' he said. 'Some of the guys who worked with us in the office, I didn't even think of them as inmates.'

'I remember how you used to take them to the barbershop before court and give them a piece of cake if we were having a party.'

'Yeah,' he laughed. 'I knew I was breaking the rules, giving "contraband to an inmate." . . .'

He looked away for a moment and stared in silence at the street. The jingle of an ice cream truck broke his spell. When he spoke, there was a pensiveness in his voice that I hadn't heard when we worked together on the Rock.

'Working with Fresh Start did me good,' the captain said. 'Considering my past, it did me good.'

I asked him what he'd miss about Rikers. On the top of his list were 'the people, the camaraderie, the laughs, the bullshit.' The insular nature of the work, he explained, makes retirement particularly hard for COs. 'Ninety percent of your friends are in the Department. It's so difficult for outsiders to understand what we do, what we go through, what we see. I mean, how do you go out with people and say, "Yeah, I saw a guy get stabbed to death today," or "There was a riot in the mess hall," or "My best friend got slashed in the face?"

'If you talk about things like that at a party, outsiders are mystified. They look at you like "Wow, you're kidding?" Like you used to do,' he teases me. 'And you wanna say, No, I'm *not* kidding. I'm not telling you a *fuckin'* fairy tale. I'm telling you what really happened.'

His last words stayed with me.

'Listen, I did a lot of bad things in CPSU, things I'm not proud of. It was like I was a drug addict. I was on a ride and I couldn't get off.

'Believe it or not,' he adds, 'I've hired some ex-offenders for a security business I started, guys who've been upstate and had the shit beaten out of them by COs. I told one of them about my past – a guy who just did a decade on a murder charge – how I barely escaped prison myself. "You've done your time," I told him. "You've made your amends to society." I try to help out inmates now when I can.'

Today I have far more respect and sympathy for 'prison cops,' as COs are sometimes called, than I did when I started working in this field. The job of a correction officer is far more difficult than most people realize. A good CO needs to have the street smarts of a cop, the training of a psychologist, the resources of a social worker, and the patience of a saint.

In a small way, I feel I can empathize with some of the downsides of their job. I know, for example, that when I spent most of my time on Rikers working with inmates, I was far more irritable and impatient with them than I am now teaching there one night a week. Because we civilians are prisoners' main line of access to the free world and because their needs are so vast, you find yourself in the position of having to say no every five minutes: No, I can't put money in your commissary. No, I can't bring you in deodorant. No, you can't have a cigarette, my pen, my home phone number. No! I'd sometimes want to shout out of exasperation at the litany of problems they'd hurl at me like hand grenades: 'I cannot fix your whole entire screwed-up life for you. I really wish I could, but I can't.'

For correction officers, denial is the very essence of their job. They are paid by the public to deny prisoners their freedom and keep them safely behind bars. They are expected to show a dismissive and detached demeanor on a daily basis. If not, they're perceived as soft, leaving them subject to manipulation by inmates and scorn from other officers. I've often wondered what it must feel like to be a CO who's on top of the world, say newly in love or in receipt of a prize-winning lottery ticket, who has to leave his happy face at the gate lest an inmate exploit his high spirits.

I've wondered, too, what it feels like to live in fear of physical injury five days a week for twenty long years, or to be doused with a stew of feces and urine in a horrific inmate stunt known as gassing. Only once has an inmate physically threatened me, and the experience wasn't easy to forget. In the most unwise move I've ever made in jail – and I've made quite a few, as the good Officer Gray (who's worked with Fresh Start since the beginning) can attest – I once snatched a newspaper from the hands of an inmate. Despite my friendly requests to put the paper down and pay attention, Danny continued to read, carefully folding back the pages like a Wall Street executive studying the financials. I knew he heard my requests because he briefly lowered the paper and looked at me when I addressed him for the third time. Then, in what my students would call a 'total dis,' Danny raised the paper back over his face and continued reading. I felt the other inmates staring to see what I'd do. Is she soft or not? Can we play her or not?

To this day I am still amazed at how aggressive I acted. I charged up to him and yanked the newspaper from his hands. 'Listen to me when I speak to you!' I yelled.

The next moment was a blur. I remember him kicking over the desk and towering over me with rage etched into his face. (He wasn't muscle-bound, but he was tall and clearly pissed.) I remember his clenched fists and how he shouted in my face, 'Get off my fuckin' back!' Before I had time to get the guard from down the hall, the other students tackled him to the floor.

The jail environment itself tests your patience, particularly in a place like Rikers that's totally cut off from civilization. Despite everything else on the island (a hospital, three schools, a firehouse, a bakery), there are no commercial businesses to speak of aside from a couple hundred vending machines. There are no restaurants, cafés, or bookstores to escape to on your lunch hour. You can't just zip off to Wal-Mart to run a quick errand or, if you're a woman, to pick up a needed feminine product. Like the inmates, you're trapped, at least for eight hours, in a gray and windowless world where every social encounter is with either a 'keeper' or a 'kept.' Punishment pervades the atmosphere and sours your spirit. I never appreciated fresh air and sunlight so much as I did when I worked on Rikers full time. And I was a civilian with transferable skills. I could get another job in the free world with relative ease; I wasn't bound by the golden hand-cuffs of a lifelong retirement package.

Last year, the Correctional Association (where I work today) began exploratory research on the attitudes and morale of New York State correction officers. During our monthly prison inspections, we spend an hour or so with a group of COs. At first they look at us suspiciously, like why in the world do you inmate-sympathizers want to talk to us, or is this some kind of setup from Central Office? We emphasize that no, we're not there to harass them. We want to know about your jobs, we say, why you became a CO, how you feel about the inmates and the Department. In most cases, once the ice is broken, they're just as eager as the inmates to talk, perhaps even more to be understood.

Some describe the job as hour upon hour of tedium punctuated by moments of terror; others use the language of prisoners in portraying their work: 'We're doing time too,' a CO at a maximum-security prison commented. 'When I retire with thirty-seven years on the job, I'll have served a fifteen-year sentence.' Another officer told us: 'If my kid said he wanted to be a CO when he grows up, I'd slap him.' In fact, many COs tell strangers they do something else for a living, like security work, because of the stigma attached to the job.

'It's the dirtiest, most thankless job in law enforcement,' said William West, a former CO who's now the executive vice president of the 21,500-member union representing state correction officers. West and his group are engaged in a multipronged effort to raise the salaries of state COs (currently they start at $23,000) and boost their public image. In their video, *Inside the Walls: The Toughest Beat in New York State,* viewers are treated to images of rioting inmates, a bloodied CO uniform, and a spate of homemade prison weapons. A CO voice-over talks about the toll the work takes on them.

The Department's chief medical officer, Dr. Lester Wright, speaks about the growing number of people with mental illness behind bars, accurately noting that there are twice as many psy-chotic inmates in prison as in mental-health institutions across the state. 'On any given day, there are close to 8,000 people with mental illness in New York's prisons and jails,' writes Heather Barr in *Prisons and Jails: Hospitals of Last Resort*. Nationally, more than 265,000 of the country's mentally ill are in prison, while only 70,000 receive hospital-based care in public facilities. 'The correctional system has become the biggest psychiatric hospital in the world,' comments Robert Davison, executive director of the Mental Health Association in Essex County, New Jersey.

According to West and others familiar with the correctional landscape, COs suffer from a kind of mental illness themselves, feelings of isolation and anomie that freeworlders with more mainstream jobs can never comprehend. He points out that five COs have committed suicide in the first six months of 2000. 'We average about one per month,' he said.

On a recent visit to Great Meadow Correctional Facility, a fortress-style maximum-security prison surrounded by a towering wall, an inmate handed me a clipping from a newspaper when we asked about 'inmate-officer' relations. 'How can it be anything *but* "us against them" with stuff like this around?' he asked. The ad, distributed by the union, parodied the Department's latest recruitment efforts. Union spokesperson Dennis Fitzpatrick called it 'political satire.'

NEW YORK WANTS YOU
SIGN UP NOW TO REPLACE SOMEONE WHO QUIT

Now Accepting Applications for:

Correction Officer Trainee

THE JOB:
- Meet new and different people in a setting where you and they can't get out.
- Get stabbed, kicked, punched, spit on, cursed at, and mentally tortured on a daily basis. Be one of the 1,000 correction officers who are assaulted each year.
- Walk unarmed in a yard full of violent criminals who outnumber you three hundred to one.

- Expose yourself to AIDS, TB and hepatitis on a daily basis so you can have something serious to talk to your doctor about.
- Maximize stress in your life to the point where you will die early – probably before you turn 58.
- Get ready to divorce your spouse and have them take your children away.

THE EMPLOYER:
- The New York State Department of Correctional Services.
- Starting pay ($25,029) is low enough so families of four can qualify for food stamps. Your kids will be able to get subsidized lunches at school along with others at the poverty level.
- You may get suspended indefinitely without pay if a prisoner says something bad about you. The state will believe criminals before they believe you.
- Learn to work without a contract and be ready to be away from your home for at least a year at a time.

One of the most authentic and insightful books on the world of prison guards is Ted Conover's *Newjack: Guarding Sing Sing*. Conover, who's both a journalist and an anthropologist, spent 1997 as a CO in New York's famous maximum-security prison in Ossining, New York. Similar to the liberal who became a Republican upon being mugged, Conover emerged far more sympathetic to guards than he imagined. 'The environment of prison is such that it dehumanizes everyone who comes into contact with it,' he said.

On his first day at the Training Academy, Conover writes, the instructor asked the group, 'What's the first three things you get when you become a CO?' The answer: 'A car. A gun. A divorce.'

Conover's description of his last day on the job shows the kind of cynicism that sets in after a year behind bars with 2,000 prisoners.

Not only was the officer who came to relieve him a half hour late, he was just three days out of the Training Academy, Conover writes. He knew the recruit would be overwhelmed by the encroaching onslaught of inmates returning to the cell block. 'I could have been a great guy and stuck around to help with the impending chaos,' he wrote. 'But my head was about to split open. Fuck it, I thought. And in the true, not-my-problem spirit of Sing Sing, I fled.'

Many miles from New York City, in small rural towns nourished by the prison boom, the job of correction officer is a respectable, even enviable, position. Up near the Canadian border, a $25,000-a-year salary goes a long way in the village of Dannemora, home of Clinton Correctional Facility, where New York's death row is housed. Across the street from the prison is the Breakaway Saloon, where a cheeseburger costs $1.65. Here, COs unwind over beer and a game of pool after eight hours in New York's largest maximum-security prison, in a town that has twice as many inmates as residents. *Village Voice* journalist Jennifer Gonnerman observes that 'prisons are redefining rural communities across the country – not only their landscapes but the most intimate details of people's lives.'

When we interviewed a group of COs at Albion Correctional Facility in the westernmost reaches of the state and asked how they, as prison guards, are perceived in the community, they looked at us funny and explained that they *are* the community. 'When the Lipton tea factory closed down,' one of them said, 'the prison became the number-one employer.' With over 2,000 female prisoners, the majority of whom are from New York City, Albion is the largest women's prison in the state.

In Manhattan, however, where professional jobs and sophisticates abound, saying you're a CO on Rikers is far more likely to be met with bewilderment or pity than envy or nonchalance. In city law-enforcement circles, COs are the forgotten stepchildren. 'People look at us as lower than cops,' a CO from Rikers with a decade on the job told me. New York's Boldest [COs] begrudge New York's Finest [cops] for their higher salaries and more respected status in the public eye. Worse, the dirty nature of their work seems to follow them over the bridge.

'Try going to a bar in Manhattan and picking up women,' the CO said. 'Tell 'em you're a correction officer and watch 'em run. Hell, I even told one woman I was a warden – a fuckin' warden! – and she goes "What? A dog warden?"'

Even if she had understood, I thought, she'd still probably run. How can the chief executive of a jail compete with the tycoons on Wall Street, the publishing powerhouses, the real estate moguls, and the zillion other glitterati of Manhattan?

Despite their public image, COs on the Rock tend to have a more congenial relationship with inmates than their counterparts in prison 'up north.' Many Rikers COs come from the same city neighborhoods as the inmates. As such, they are more aware of the hazards of growing up poor in New York. They know the resilience it takes to resist the profits of the drug trade, to graduate from a dysfunctional high school, to withstand the loss of a parent to addiction, AIDS, or incarceration.

In the thirty-some prisons I've visited upstate, there is a palpable tension between the keepers and the kept that I have rarely felt on Rikers. Clearly, much of the tension stems from the difference in the inmate populations: Most city inmates are misdemeanants; every state prisoner is a convicted felon. Inevitably, the tension stems from another disparity as well – the racial divide between COs and inmates. A mere 5 percent of state COs are black or Hispanic, while 85 percent of the inmates are black or Hispanic. (By contrast, 75 percent of city COs are black or Hispanic, as are 92 percent of the inmates.)

All kinds of racial issues are bound to arise in the face of such skewed numbers. Stereotypes are perpetuated and resentments are solidified – on both sides. White officers from rural, homogeneous communities know blacks and Hispanics mainly as the criminals locked up in their local prison. Their unfamiliarity with the cultural norms and expressions of inner-city minorities heightens their suspicions of the prisoners they watch over. My heart went out to a forty-three-year-old dairy farmer I met at the CO Training Academy outside of Albany. His farm had gone 'belly up,' he said, and he wasn't qualified to do much else. The benefits of a pension upon retirement and health insurance outweighed the downsides of the job. 'I ain't never seen me an inmate before and two weeks from now I'll be surrounded by them,' he said over lunch in the cafeteria, where inmates actually worked. He told me he was scared, and from his perspective I couldn't blame him.

By contrast, more than a few inmates on Rikers Island have relatives or friends who earn their living in the jails. My student Jermaine, 24, has served time on Rikers with his cousin, his twin brother, and his 'foster brother.' His aunt is a correction officer. 'The whole family's here,' he said.

My student Jack recently bumped into an old classmate from high school in jail. Jack was embarrassed when he saw his uniformed friend and wrote about the incident in the *Rikers Review*. Excerpted here, it illustrates the familiarity between some COs and inmates on Rikers, which not all COs would endorse.

MY FRIEND IN BLUE – CHANCE ENCOUNTER

Jack: Yo, Ed! What's up? It's good to see you – even under these circumstances. What you been up to besides bein' a CO?

Ed: Chillin' man.

Jack: I see your ass put on some weight!

Ed: Yeah, about 50 pounds since the last time we saw each other in high school.

Jack: Ed, man, I have to tell ya, when I first saw you I wanted to hide.

Ed: Yeah, I felt bad seeing you too, man. It hurts seeing people you know from the streets in here.

Jack: Do people around the way know you're a CO?

Ed: Yeah, they do and they respect me. They give me my props. So what got you here, Jack?

Jack: Boosting [shoplifting], and let me tell you it's a profitable enterprise. But sooner or later one meets his fate. I've too much to lose and this isn't the place to be. How do you handle the stress?

Ed: I give respect to every individual. Inmates in my house know the rules and know they have to follow 'em. I don't kiss ass, and I don't *kick* ass unless pushed.

Jack: What's next for you, man?

Ed: First things first. I'm gonna bust out my 20 and take it from there.

Sadly, this is the sentiment among many COs, whether employed by the city, the state, or the Federal Bureau of Prisons. They can't seem to 'bust out their 20' fast enough. The most satisfied COs I've met work in boot camps like STEP and High Impact on Rikers or in state prisons like Eastern and Washington, where 'conversation before confrontation' is part of the culture. In correctional facilities such as these, the superintendents not only support but also lobby for programs, which are run by correction officers as well as civilians.

We recently visited Washington Correctional Facility, tucked in the mountains 250 miles north of New York City. It was a radiant fall day, unseasonably warm, which always helps on these grim prison visits. In the medium-security prison, a modern, low-lying facility, the majority of inmates are between ages sixteen and twenty-one. Of the 309 correction staff, just five are black or Hispanic, including the superintendent. Despite the concentration of male prisoners in their violence prone years and the striking racial disparities between the keepers and the kept, the facility is remarkably peaceful. The number of inmate grievances, uses of force, and misbehavior reports are low, indicating it's a well-run prison.

The facility runs a Community Lifestyle Program, where COs function more like counselors and coaches than security staff. Inmates are rated on the cleanliness of their dorms and are required to attend school or in-house drug treatment. 'If I had to do time,' says Superintendent Israel Rivera, 'this is where I'd want to be.'

He tells me he 'loves his job,' and it shows in his enthusiasm as we tour the spotless grounds, stop by a graduation for men who earned their GEDs, and even when we enter 'the hole.' When I ask him, the superintendent translates for a Spanish-speaking inmate who's confused about the charges that landed him in solitary. He explains to another young prisoner that he can have stamps.

It's easy to see whether such demonstrations are more show than substance; when we talk with inmates, they tell us, and they usually have a multitude of grievances to report. At Washington, however, our conversations with over fifty prisoners yielded few complaints. I knew it was an unusual prison when I heard myself ask the Inmate Liaison Committee (an inmate leadership group) if they couldn't 'give us anything better' to raise with the superintendent in our debriefing session at the end of the day.

Despite the warm-and-fuzzy nature of the visit, the sight of so many young men – there are over 1,000 prisoners at Washington – living behind coils of razor ribbon wire is unsettling. I wonder how the superintendent, raised in the projects in Spanish Harlem, must feel seeing so many young men of color locked up inside his prison.

'Doesn't it get to you?' I ask. 'Do you ever feel sad?'

'Sad?' he repeats, raising his dark eyebrows. His tone suggests that words like 'sad' aren't part of the prison vernacular.

'Honestly,' he says, 'most of them are living better in here than they did on the streets.'

And there lies the bitter irony in the work of a prison reformer. My colleagues and I advocate for more humane conditions and better-run prisons, for jewels in the system like Washington, and at the end of the day we're left with words like these – accurate, hard pills to swallow.

The sadness, for me, always comes later, after we've returned to the hotel, debriefed over dinner, and reviewed the agenda for the next day's visit. I take a hot bath and lie in the water, trying to forget the faces: the young man in the hole who couldn't speak English, the smiles of twenty-year-olds holding up their high school diplomas from prison, the man with the prosthetic leg, broken and unrepaired for seventy-five days, the 200-plus inmates on psychotropic medication to 'help them adjust, sleep better at night,' as the nurse said.

4

CONVICTED AT BIRTH

The crime and disorder which flow from hopeless poverty,
unloved children, and drug abuse can't be solved merely by
bottomless prisons, mandatory sentencing minimums, or more
police.

– FBI director Louis J. Freeh

Anyone who's been to prison or who has taught writing behind bars
knows the ugly truth about prison poetry: It tends to be as bad as it
is abundant. The 'beauty lies in the eye of the beholder' theory
might apply in the realm of love, but it doesn't work with prison
poetry. Believe me, I tried.

When the editor of *Prison Life* magazine asked if I'd 'make the
first cut' on the nearly 1,000 submissions we received for our annual
poetry contest, I jumped at the chance. I was certain I'd find gems
of pathos and profundity in the three U.S. Postal Service bags he
dragged into my office.

No need for another cup of coffee, I thought. I'm going deep into
the belly of the beast, where angst and demons live.

I resisted the urge to open the first envelope I pulled from one of
the bags. Instead, I made three large piles on the floor, and from
each pile I extracted the envelopes that bore the return addresses of
the worst prisons I knew: Marion Federal Prison in Illinois, home of
John Gotti; Florence ADX, the 'Alcatraz of the Rockies' where prisoners describe being 'buried alive' in supermax cells underground;
Angola; Attica; even one from death row in California.

Now these, I mused, are the prisons that only poets can survive.

After reading for about an hour, I started to think I'd read the
same poem twice. Not only were they sounding similar, they were

putting me to sleep. Was it me or were stanzas such as 'Here I sit/in my cell/life in prison/is living hell' excruciatingly dull? Maybe sixty poems out of the entire batch departed from the wretched singsong rhyming scheme that only skilled poets can pull off without sounding like amateurs.

I was determined not to let this fate befall my aspiring poets on the Rock.

RICO

The next week, using an exercise from a creative writing book, I asked the men to write a poem about a place, and to impart to that place human characteristics. I gave them some examples of the kind of (non-rhyming) poem I was looking for, and five minutes to do it. 'Don't censor yourself,' I said. 'Just write from your gut.'

'I'm hungry.'

Huh?

When another inmate mouthed the letters 'MO' and pointed at Eduardo, a new student, I understood. In jail, MO is short for Mental Observation Unit, where inmates with varying degrees of mental illness are sent for counseling or medication. Other inmates refer to them as 'MOs.' They're also called 'bugs,' as in 'he bugged out.'

Apparently, Eduardo was a bug.

'Okay, hungry . . . we can work with that,' I said. 'Let's say the feeling of hunger reminds you of a certain place . . . right?'

Eduardo nodded.

'So what I want you to do is write a poem about that place, but pretend the place is actually a person.'

'Like the Statue of Liberty?'

My exercise in abstract thinking was falling apart. I was about to ditch it when one of the men turned to Eduardo.

'I'm feelin' that, man. That's good. Gimme your tired, your poor, your hungry . . . yeah.' He nodded approvingly.

Rico, 19, looked up from his doodling. He pushed back the black curls that fell over his eyes, and I felt like I was seeing him for the first time. Although we were a month into the program and the other men had finished entire articles, Rico hadn't written a thing. He spent every class drawing, head down and silent. I was considering kicking him out when he wrote this poem about the South Bronx. He'd been listening all along and knew exactly what I was looking for.

I AM THE BRONX

I am the Bronx
burnt down
fallen as ashes.
The graffiti walls
in my mouth
shout panic.
These tattooed arms
show danger.
My drug-filled teeth
are stained with stories of horror.
Look deep in my eyes
and see visions of death.
Watch out for what
lurks around my elbows. . . .

I was amazed, not only at the violent imagery, but also at his skillful use of language. I encouraged him to write about growing up in the South Bronx for the *Rikers Review*. He shook his head.

'No way. I can't write about that. There was some wild shit in our 'hood.'

'You've got a lot of talent, Rico. Why don't you just start writing and we'll see what you come up with? We don't have to publish it in the magazine, but you have to start doing some work.'

The next week when he came into class I noticed a new haircut. He talked instead of mumbling. He handed me his notebook and flipped through the pages, all twenty-five of them. He didn't want to read his writing aloud like the others did, but if he could use a pseudonym, he said, he'd like it published in the *Rikers Review*.

I read Rico's story that night on the subway home, quickly, like eating popcorn. When I finished I felt woozy. The sad and simple truth was that it was no surprise that Rico was on Rikers Island. Convicted at birth, he couldn't have been anywhere else. Here is his story:

A True Bronx Tale
By Sombra

Once upon a time in a small borough of New York City called the Bronx, or 'Boogie Down' as we would call it, lived a really big and insane family. The family was so big it took two five-story buildings on Longfellow Avenue. The buildings still stand today, it's just that the family keeps getting smaller due to death or jail.

I was brought into this family when I was two years old. My mother was in love with Mickey Sanchez and bound to get married. They never did get married, but they managed to stay together for sixteen years of my life. By the way, my name is Rico. But everyone calls me 'Sombra.'

Anyway, there I was, a non-English-speaking two-year-old from Puerto Rico and already an alcoholic due to my mother's habit of mixing *Cuarenta y tres* ['43,' a liqueur] in our bottles. She did this to make us sleep or stop us from crying. I got used to the mixture and didn't stop having bottles until I was seven.

From one side of the family I had 21 male *primos* [cousins] and about 8 female *primas* – yup, we all lived together in those two little buildings on Longfellow Ave. We played together in the back yard, an empty lot we called 'No Man's Land.' It was as big as a city block and all it had in it was dirt and bushes and junked-out stolen cars. A big dead tree stood in the middle but someone put barbed wire around it so we couldn't use it to climb onto the roof of the beer factory.

I really don't remember my real father too well but I know I used to go to El Barrio for the weekends to stay with him. He lived on 105th Street and First Avenue in the East River projects with his girlfriend Iris and her three kids, two boys and a girl. I remember playing in the house with one of the boys,

Junior, while our parents got high in the other room. It's funny how all you can remember about the past are the bad things.

I was smoking weed myself by age eight, but nobody knew about it except for my father. Junior and I used to smoke the cigarette butts from the ashtray and one day we took a half a joint, thinking it was a cigarette. I lit it up and took a pull. I coughed like hell. I figured I was coughing because it didn't have a filter on it, so I took another drag. After that I passed it to Junior and he went through the same thing I did, but worse. When it was burning our fingers we put it back into the ashtray. A few minutes later we felt real funny and very hungry. My father noticed we were high because we had a bad case of the giggles, and we were eating like we hadn't eaten in weeks.

'Which one of you was smoking from the ashtray?' he said.

I took the blame because Junior was younger, and his mother Iris used to beat fire out his ass. She couldn't beat me because I wasn't her child and my father wasn't one to hit me. He would rather talk to me and tell me I did wrong instead of beating on me. Anyway, he said if I wanted to get high, I could, but only with him. To punish me, he made me smoke a whole joint by myself. About half a year later, I was about nine I think, I smoked again and I liked it, so I kept on until this day.

I'd smoke weed on the weekends with my father and drink an occasional beer or mixed drink on the weekdays with my stepfather. See, Mickey was an alcoholic and he drank beer every day. If I wanted a beer or a drink I would ask Mickey if I could drink with him, and he'd say, 'Only one – I don't want you getting drunk.'

One day I remember my mother packing everything up and just leaving for Puerto Rico. I figured Mickey had come home drunk and hit her again and she just got sick of it and left. This used to happen almost every weekend. I couldn't do anything about it because I was too little to fight with Mickey, especially when he was drunk, so I held it all inside.

When I was thirteen one of my friends gave me five of his guns to hold: a .380, a .45, a .44, a .357 and a 9-mm. I hid them between the mattress and box spring of my bed until we needed them to solve some beef. Sure enough, that day came.

I got home from school really high. At the time, my little sister was about five. As I walked into the building, I could hear screaming from the hallway. When I put the key into the lock, the screaming stopped. I walked in and my little sister was crying. My mother was sitting in the living room crying, too, and my stepfather was standing in front of her. She immediately sent me to my room, but I saw it. I could see that Mickey had hit her.

I blacked out in anger. I was so furious and drunk I stuck my hand under the mattress and pulled out the first gun I could feel. Funny thing, it was my favorite – the .45. She was a beauty: nickel-plated steel with two fluorescent green dots on the front and one on the top. In the dark, the glowing dots formed a triangle. Whatever was in the triangle, if you knew how to use the gun, you'd definitely hit your target.

I went back to the living room and they were still arguing. My little sister was crying but I couldn't hear a word they were saying until I smacked Mickey across the head with the .45. Then all I could hear was screaming and crying and my mom telling me to stop. By now my sister was hysterical and Mickey was on the floor.

I cocked back the .45 and put it to his face. I felt total control when he pissed in his pants.

There he was, kneeling in a puddle of his own damn piss, begging me not to kill him. 'Please, please . . . don't,' he said. He started to cry and I felt like I was in a scene from the movie *Scarface,* the part where he's going to kill Frank for setting him up. Mickey was one pussy-whipped motherfucker.

I didn't kill him, but my mother still called the cops – on me or on him I don't know. All I knew was I had to get the guns out before they came.

As I was leaving the building, the cops were coming in. I thought they were going to grab me right then and there, take me to the precinct and lock me up. I was with my favorite *primo,* Pito; we opened the door for them, they nodded and went straight in.

I hopped on the train to my grandmother's apartment in Spanish Harlem. I didn't know what to expect when I walked in. I put my ear to the door to see if the police were inside. They weren't, so I knocked, and my grandma told me that if I had any guns to throw them down the garbage chute. I told her I already got rid of them and she let me in.

After a while my mother called. She told me to come by in the morning and pick up my things. She said I'd have to stay with my father for a while. She was leaving that pussy-whipped, jealous bastard. She was going to Puerto Rico and would come back for me and my little sister when she could.

Rico continued to write, filling page after page in his black-and-white composition book about his teenage years bouncing back and forth between the South Bronx and El Barrio. Every week he'd write a new chapter and give me his notebook to read. After sixty pages he stopped writing – he'd made it to the present – and asked me to hold on to it. He didn't know where he'd be living when he left Rikers Island and wanted to make sure his notebook was safe.

'Maybe I'll publish my memoirs one day,' he said.

After reading what he wrote, I can understand why he never wanted to read aloud in class and why he selected the chapter he did to publish in the *Rikers Review*. Compared to the rest, it was mild.

At age ten, he wrote, he 'was devirginalized by a fifteen-year-old girl in Pito's house.' He described his first sexual experience as follows:

Renée was one of the youngest girls Pito knew and we were getting high and he made her take my virginity from me. She was very good-looking and wanted to break my ruff-neck ass up. She was very willing to fuck me if you know what I mean. After I was broken in, I was scared to fuck again. I was afraid I was going to bleed again from my uncircumcised dick.

By junior high he was 'already cutting classes and going to hooky parties.' Every day, he said, he 'was getting high on weed and drinking forties [of beer] just as often.' It was at one of the 'hooky parties' that he met Keyla and 'for the first time really made love to a girl.' The scene he depicted, spanning four pages, would make a pornographer blush.

At fourteen, after his mother left, he 'was making a little cash doing stickups with Pito.' They would 'do a fast little stickup and pick up Keyla afterwards to go out. It just so happens that the money wasn't enough,' he wrote, and that's when he started selling drugs.

The 'little cash' Rico made wasn't for 'extras' like movies or CDs, the ways middle-class kids spend allowances they get from their parents. Essentially, Rico didn't have any parents. His father was an addict whose idea of quality time with his son was 'get[ing] high on the weekends' before Rico was even a teenager. His mother fled the country when he was thirteen hoping he'd be able to fend for himself and that various relatives, also in financial ruins, would provide him a couch to sleep on. The money Rico made from stickups and drug dealing put food in his stomach and clothes on his back. And entering the drug trade was as easy as it was lucrative.

'Cocaine and crack, in particular during the mid-1980s and through the early 1990s, have been the fastest growing – if not the only – equal opportunity employers of men in Harlem,' writes anthropologist Philippe Bourgois in his acclaimed book, *In Search of Respect: Selling Crack in El Barrio*. Rico describes his foray into the drug trade as follows:

Roland and Chino were talking about selling drugs and how much money they were making on the block. I jumped in and asked Chino if I could sell with him and he said, "yeah." I told Keyla about it and I started selling the next day after school. So this meant I couldn't have sex with her or go out that day.

Anyway, I took her to the spot with me. She stood by the whole time I was selling. Chino had given me three bundles [of crack] to start. It was amazing to see how fast I could push them off. I sold them all in two hours. After three days of this I got addicted to the money and caught on pretty fast. By the end of the school year I had $2,000 hidden in my uncle's house where nobody would find it. I had about four girlfriends but Keyla was my steady and none of them knew about the others until I got locked up.

So there I was, a couple days before my fifteenth birthday, headed for Spofford Correctional Facility, looking at a one-to-three. This was the first time I'd ever done time but it wasn't the first time I got arrested. I had my run-ins with the cops since I was eleven. The first time was for breaking and entry, then came everything from assaults to weapon possession and so forth. . . .

Essentially, kids like Rico are angry, says Professor David Brotherton, a national expert on gangs and head of the Center on Violence at John Jay College, but their ability to articulate their hatred of the system is limited. Where does that anger go? 'It goes inward,' he says. 'It implodes. They don't have the wherewithal or the support of a political system to channel their anger. Many use drugs to escape their feelings of anger and powerlessness, and some say shared drug use also creates a sense of affiliation with one's peer group; it bonds them. They get high to feel more connected. They get high to feel motivated and empowered. They get high to cope with their feelings of being society's least-wanted citizens.'

Rico continued selling drugs and wrote vivid accounts about his life 'in the game' and the violent code of the street. 'The more inner-city youths choose this route in life, the more normative the code of the street becomes in the neighborhood,' writes ethnographer Elijah Anderson. Even after rival crack dealers beat Rico with a bat and left him for dead, he stayed in the game. 'I laugh when I think about it now,' he says.

I've been shot at, stabbed and thrown out of a third-floor window tied to a chair. A lot of things happen to people over drugs and you know that if you're in the life. I've seen people close to me die or get killed right next to me, people like my *primo*, Pito. . . .

We were walking down Southern Boulevard in the Bronx at about 11:30 on a Friday night when three guys approached us. It was a set-up. They knew how much money we had. One guy asked me for the time, and the other two pulled out guns before I could even answer – and I had a tell-time watch on. They kept telling us to give up the cash but me and Pito weren't about to, and they knew it.

It took no more than three minutes before the one who asked me what time it was pulled out a sawed-off shotgun and shot Pito in the head. Almost everything that was in Pito's head was now on my face, shoulder and chest. I froze. All I could see was Pito falling and the three guys running off. When the cops came, I was still standing there in the same spot, in the same mess. I couldn't even answer their questions.

In the summer of 1998 Rico left Rikers Island – a disaster waiting to happen. When I think about him now I feel guilty. We never should have let him join the program; his needs were too vast for our tiny staff to handle. The job developer had quit, the psychologist had outgrown the budget and I was interviewing for a new job. What in the world could we do for Rico?

At age twenty he had no work history, no academic credentials besides the GED he earned in jail, a rap sheet, and a drug problem. Not to mention an unforgivably rotten upbringing.

He also had a new daughter, born while he was incarcerated, but his 'baby's mother' didn't want to see him anymore, he said. He'd been planning to live with her when he was released, but she replaced him before he got out. His first order of business was to 'go to church and light a candle' for Pito.

'Then I'm just gonna get a job, make some legal money, and be a good father to my baby,' he told me, making it sound as easy as brushing his teeth.

We encouraged him to get stabilized and enroll in a drug-treatment program. He agreed and stayed in the program for a couple of weeks but was kicked out after a dirty urine test for marijuana. Occasionally he'd call me drunk or high and talk about how he was trying to find a job and how his baby's mother didn't love him anymore. He'd moved back in with his 'moms.'

I didn't think I'd hear from Rico again, and, horrible as it sounds, I was relieved. I'd started a new job and things at Fresh Start were in turmoil. Getting attached to kids like Rico with such messed-up lives is a painful ordeal.

But several months later he called, sounding happy and confident.

'I gotta job,' he said. 'I'm selling mortgages to people. And I got my own place. It's in the basement of a building, kinda dark but not too bad.'

I said I was thrilled and asked him how he found the job.

'Some guy I know hooked me up. He got mad dough and has these buildings and we go around and try to get people to buy apartments and shit.'

It sounded strange but I hoped it was true. He and his baby's mother were still fighting, he said, and he couldn't see his daughter as much as he'd like. But overall, the tone in his voice suggested that maybe some luck had come his way, or maybe I was just hearing what I wanted to believe.

'I'm not getting high anymore, either,' he said. 'Just a few drinks on the weekends.'

'That's great, Rico. You're really doing great. Keep in touch, okay?' I gave him my new number at work.

A year passed before we spoke again. I'd tried calling the beeper number he gave me, but it was disconnected. One night while going through some files I found a letter he'd sent me from jail. At the bottom was his mother's phone number. (She'd moved back to New York when Rico was sixteen.) I figured she'd know if he was dead, alive, or back on the Rock.

When I called, I could barely make out her voice over the blaring TV. I said I was a former teacher of Rico's and asked if she knew how to reach him.

'He's here,' she groaned, as if describing the presence of toxic waste in her apartment. 'I doubt he wants to talk to you. Seems like he don't wanna do *nuthin'* but drink me outta house and home.'

She started yelling, launching into a stream of curses in Spanish. I stifled the urge to shout back – *Maybe if you hadn't laced his bottle with liqueur you wouldn't have an alcoholic for a son* – and asked if she'd try to get him on the line.

She screamed out his name, not bothering to cover the receiver.

Finally the TV lowered and Rico picked up. He said he was 'a little drunk' but wanted to talk anyway. He told me he lost his job. Apparently the manager wanted to sleep with him, but he refused and was fired.

'The last six months were rough,' he said. 'I tried to kill myself, you know.' He said he 'took every pill in the medicine cabinet' and washed them down with a bottle of rum. 'I just said fuck it. . . . I'm ending this miserable life.'

What 'really hurt' was waking up in the hospital with his father at his bedside glaring at him. 'You know what that bastard told me? He said, "You stupid motherfucker. You can't even kill yourself without fucking it up."'

By age twenty-one Rico had been stabbed, shot at, and seen his cousin murdered. He'd been incarcerated, had a baby, and attempted suicide. I have no idea where he is today and wouldn't be surprised if he were dead. But his notebook is still in my desk – just in case.

May 5, 1999: It's a humid spring evening on Queens Plaza. I notice how little has changed since I stood at this bus stop five years ago waiting for the bus to Rikers Island. Despite the mayor's quality-of-life campaign, the trash cans still overflow with garbage and spill onto the street. The same debris from an abandoned construction site rots under the elevated subway platform.

The smells of pizza, Chinese take-out, and doughnuts mingle with bus fumes. Everyone on the plaza is bedraggled and sweaty, rushing to somewhere or lounging on the corner outside the Brothers & Son deli. As the clock in Twin Donuts approaches six P.M., women and children congregate at the bus stop.

A large woman yanks the wrist of her child. 'Gimme your fuckin' hand or I'll break your wrist.' When the boy cries, she shouts, 'Shut up!'

I want to scream back at her, but she scares me.

They board the bus in front of me and I sit next to the boy. He falls asleep and his head grazes my arm. I start to smile, and the woman slaps him, telling him to sit up straight.

I look at my fellow travelers to the Rock and notice that just about everyone is overweight and eating junk food. It reminds of when I worked in the South Bronx, when I gained ten pounds in a year and doubled my nicotine intake. I was the director of a new welfare-to-work program, funded by three city agencies, and the stress of having to train and find jobs for 100 welfare clients in twelve months, coupled with the ugliness of my new surroundings, had me gobbling packs of M&M's while waiting for the subway, eating mayo-drenched tuna sandwiches for lunch, which I gladly washed down with Coke – the real stuff. No salad or sushi bars flanked the streets like in Manhattan; there were no models or fashion plates to compete with or aspire to. At the one bodega within walking distance of the office, the owner spoke only Spanish. I asked for a yogurt one day and he pointed to a dusty can of condensed milk.

'People eat for comfort,' a psychologist on Rikers told me. 'That's why food is so coveted in prison and in poor communities where ordinary comforts don't exist or are unaffordable.' I think about all the comfort the women on the Q101 need and about how it must feel to be broke with a baby to care for and a man behind bars, to return from a four-hour visit on Rikers to a roach-infested apartment, to live in a neighborhood where the delis stink like rat poison and the playgrounds are bereft of equipment.

Later that night I'm on the phone with my sister and she tells me that her two-year-old daughter is driving her crazy. She lives in a four-bedroom house on a tree-lined street in Connecticut. She has child care, a good husband, and a career she enjoys.

When I tell her about the woman and boy on Queens Plaza, she says: 'If I were in her position, I'd be a child abuser – easy. If I had no job, no car, no air-conditioning, a husband in jail, and my kid is screaming because she didn't get her Barney cup, I'd lose it.'

My boss at the Correctional Association, Robert Gangi, is often quoted in the press. Not only because he's always ready with the latest prison or drug law statistic, but because he knows how to show in human terms the implications of misguided policy.

Before I met Bob, I remember reading an article in *New York* magazine about his work to improve conditions in the city's court pens, where people who've been arrested are held before arraignment. Mainly because of the agency and Bob's relentless advocacy

(The commissioner at the time referred to him as a 'royal pain in the ass,' to which Bob replied, 'I take that as high praise.'), the arrest-to-arraignment time dropped from three days to one, every cell has a working pay phone, and emergency medical technicians are on site, twenty-four/seven, to attend to sick detainees.

Explaining to the magazine reporter why people deserve better treatment – besides the fact that they haven't been convicted of a crime – Bob quoted the poet Auden to the effect that schoolchildren who are treated evilly 'do evil in return.'

I had just started teaching 'schoolchildren' on Rikers when I read the article in which Bob was featured. As the weeks went by and I came to know my students better, Auden's words replayed through my mind like a ticker tape.

Opened in 1985, the Austin H. MacCormick–Island Academy was the first high school in the country to be located within a correctional facility. Under the auspices of the Alternative High School Division of the New York City Board of Education, it serves males sixteen to twenty-two years of age. The principal of the jail school, Tim Lisante (now the deputy superintendent of alternative high schools in New York City), is known as one of the most dedicated and creative 'correctional educators' in the Northeast.

It was under Tim, for example, that the school received computers; that vocational classes in printing, barbering, auto mechanics, and food service came to life; and that parent-teacher conferences were put on the schedule. Tim even created a basketball league for Rikers inmates to compete against players from alternative high schools in the city who were bused onto the Rock. 'Talk about a home advantage,' he joked.

Once during parents' day a father remarked to Tim, 'This is the best school my son's ever been in. I wish my other son could be here.' If public schools in the inner city weren't such a wreck, I thought, his son probably wouldn't be in jail the first place.

The school is also blessed with some outstanding and compassionate correction officers. Officer Simpson, Officer Beasley, Officer Miller, and Officer Garlick come to mind. For many of the adolescents, these men in blue are the fathers they never had.

'I've seen approximately two generations grow up on Rikers Island,' said Officer Herman Simpson in an interview with one of my students. Anibal was writing a profile of Officer Simpson for the *Rikers Review*.

'It's depressing when you see the same adolescents in beige uniforms today and then in green uniforms a year or two later as adults.' (Both adult and adolescent inmates attend school in Island Academy, but they wear different-colored uniforms.)

It was depressing, too, when I'd find my students in beige, unlike my students in green who'd be reading quietly when I came in, riding the backs of their chairs like cowboys or flopped over tables and desks. And it was depressing – maybe 'troubling' is a better word – when they threatened to 'bash' each other's 'face in' at the slightest 'dis,' or laughed when I threatened to call the CO. It was moments like these when Auden's lines came back to me.

The testosterone in the room was palpable, and it almost made me quit. Being young and female was not an asset when working with teenage boys. I was relieved when the beloved librarian, Paul Auerbach, offered to co-teach the class.

With help from him and pointers from the officers, the adolescents shaped up considerably. They produced their own issue of the *Rikers Review* that was as chockfull of stories and poems as the issue published by the adults.

Maybe because they were the only adolescents I taught, or maybe because they tried my patience more than the adults, I remember each of them well. Over the years I've forgotten some of my adult students, but each of these adolescents I remember. Bright-eyed and wired like most teenage boys, I never really saw them as inmates. They just looked too young to be in jail, as if their jail uniforms were regular school uniforms and when the bell rang at the end of the day they'd be going home.

And there lay the root of the problem: home.

I remember Will, the lanky, alert, narrow-eyed Will, who was seething with anger the first day of class, serving a year for assault. Of course he was bitter and saw most adults as betrayers. His father died of AIDS when he was ten, his mother died shortly thereafter.

'I was twelve when my mother passed away on Christmas,' he wrote in the *Rikers Review*. 'I was real depressed. I felt I had nobody. I was so shocked I couldn't even cry. That Christmas morning I sat with my baby sister and opened the presents my mother bought us before she died.'

Will was shuffled between foster parents who worked the system like a racket and sent him to school in rags. 'One lady would take our money and buy herself two-hundred-dollar pocketbooks,' he said. He had nowhere to go when he was released, homeless at age sixteen. He called me the day he got out. 'I'm living in a crack house,' he said and never called again.

I remember Shanduke, all muscles and cool, with the kind of scowl that empties subway cars in Manhattan. He, too, grew up fatherless and poor ('We was broke!') and wrote about how he felt safer in jail than in his neighborhood.

'I feel safer in here than on the streets because at least while I'm here I know I won't get killed. I might catch a cut on my face, but I won't die. If I was out in the world right now, I'd be ducking bullets or shooting my gun instead of writing this.'

His other piece in the *Rikers Review*, 'Snitches Get Stitches,' served as a warning to his inmate peers and defined his life's motto in unvarnished terms: Be bad or be had. 'You got nice eyes,' he said as he sauntered into class.

I remember the sweet-natured Anibal from Spanish Harlem, who raised his hand when he spoke and couldn't write a complete sentence in English at age seventeen. He wanted to be a CO on Rikers when he grew up, he stated in his bio in the magazine.

And then there was Lorenzo, vibrant and gifted, whose smile brightened the classroom and mellowed the bullies, who had 'cut his own record label – Baby Entertainment' and produced two children by age seventeen. He was shot for his cell phone when he got out and died a few days later.

There was Fred, thank God, who put pen to paper and never stopped writing, who left Rikers Island and never returned. He went on to college and became editor of the literary journal.

And who could forget Darrell? Funny, silly, happy-go-lucky Darrell, raised by a single mother in Brooklyn, doing eight months on Rikers for stealing a car. We hired him at *Prison Life* when he got out, and for a while he did well.

One Saturday he joined me on a sixty-mile bike ride to raise money for multiple sclerosis. A post-race picture of us, smiling and sweaty, still sits on my desk. But after a while he started smoking 'blunts' (super-size joints wrapped in cigar paper), and it was downhill from there. He left a window open in the office one night; naturally, it rained. A computer was destroyed and Darrell was fired. I didn't hear from him for over a year, then one day he stopped by Fresh Start. I wasn't there, but he left me a note. 'I've been in a drug program for six months,' he wrote. 'I'm learning about my addiction. I want to tell you sorry for the past. Please forgive me. I want you to be a part of my life, bike riding and all that good stuff. Please think it over.'

Aside from being teenagers with criminal records, none of these boys grew up with a father. Researchers have long suspected a connection between father absence and crime, but few have had access to the kind of large and nationally representative database that's needed to rule out other theories. That changed when a demographer from the University of California and a professor from Princeton conducted a longitudinal study to see how family structure affects criminal activity.

The researchers followed 6,403 boys who were between the ages of fourteen and twenty-two in 1979 up through their early thirties. They controlled for family-background variables such as mother's educational level, race, family income, and number of siblings. They controlled for neighborhood variables like the proportion of female-headed families, unemployment rates, and median income. In 1999 *The Wall Street Journal* published their findings. Here is what they discovered:

> Boys raised outside of intact marriages are, on average, more than twice as likely as other boys to end up jailed, even after controlling for other demographic factors. . . . A child born to an unwed mother is about 2½ times as likely to end up imprisoned, while a boy whose parents split during his teenage years was about 1½ times as likely to be imprisoned.

Growing up without a father spawns other problems as well. Children raised by single mothers are five times more likely to live in poverty, compared with children who live with both parents, reports *Corrections Digest*. 'Children who do not live with their fathers are three times more likely to fail at school or to quit.'

The burgeoning imprisonment rate over the past three decades has compounded the problem as more fathers are incarcerated and more children are left behind. According to the Bureau of Justice Statistics, almost 1.5 million minors had a mother or father in prison in the year 2000, an increase of more than 500,000 since 1991. What's more, children of offenders are six times more likely than their peers to end up in prison.

NAPOLEON

And then there was Napoleon. His name alone was worth noticing. His tenacity bordered on annoying. He wasn't in the class but he'd catch me in the hall on my way out of jail.

'I'm getting released soon,' he'd say. 'Can you help me get a job when I'm out?'

I'd tell him that, unfortunately, we could only work with Fresh Start graduates, but he'd plow through the party line.

'You must know people who can get me a job.'

His broad smile and Haitian accent drew me in. I handed him my card with the guilty hope that he would be too disorganized or apprehensive to call.

But call he did, several times in fact. He was living with an uncle in Jamaica, Queens, a dirt-poor pocket of the borough. His mother died the year before; his uncle had taken him in. (I noticed he never even mentioned a father.) We planned to meet at Twin Donuts the following week on my way back from Rikers.

I was fifteen minutes late but he was still there. Unlike some of my adult clients, he looked better on the street than in jail: He had closely cropped hair, smooth caramel skin, and the athletic build of a sixteen-year-old. I offered to buy him lunch.

'Thank you very much but I'm not hungry.' He was so polite it hurt.

I told him I was starved and was ordering a cheeseburger.

He glanced at the ninety-nine-cent special: a cup of coffee and a doughnut. 'That would be fine, thank you very much.'

'Napoleon, I know you're hungry. C'mon, let me buy you lunch since I kept you waiting.'

With a little cajoling he ordered a cheeseburger, well done, with fries. I noticed he even ate the wilted lettuce on the side.

He met me at my office a few days later to drop off his résumé. I'd promised to circulate it among some ex-con-friendly employers I knew. He said he'd been to an employment agency for ex-offenders, and they'd typed him the résumé he handed me.

I was wondering why he hadn't found a job when I noticed the misspelled words and typos, the nonsensical job descriptions that even he couldn't explain when I attempted a mock interview. He stared at me blankly when I asked what 'adjusted thermostat controls to refulate temperature of ovens,' meant, not realizing that the word was supposed to be 'regulate.'

Like this kid doesn't have enough strikes against him, I thought, and retyped his résumé on my lunch hour, pounding the keys more out of anger than altruism.

A few weeks later Napoleon found a job on his own, stacking frozen goods in a refrigerated warehouse in the outer reaches of Queens. 'It's so cold,' he said when we spoke. 'But that's okay. I'm glad to be working.'

The following Saturday was Halloween, and I invited him to Connecticut with me. My sister and nieces were carving pumpkins; I thought he might enjoy a fall day in the country. Then again, he'd just turned seventeen and pumpkin carving with preschoolers might not be his idea of fun. But he said he'd love to go, and luckily my sister had no qualms about having him.

'What was his charge?' was all she asked.

In all honesty, I'd forgotten. As I've said before, the stories of so many prisoners have a way of blending together.

'I think it was a drug sale,' I said. 'But don't worry, he's sweet as can be. You'll love him, and so will the girls. He worked as a youth counselor for two summers before he got locked up.'

On the bus ride out of the city, Napoleon reminded me that it was actually a gun charge – possession, he said, not 'shooting' – that landed him in jail.

Great, I thought, envisioning my sister tied to a chair with a gun to her head, my nieces . . . 'Napoleon,' I said, 'Sorry to ask you this but, um, you're not carrying a gun on you now, right?'

'C'mon, Jennifer. I wasn't even carrying one then.'

Apparently, the gun belonged to his cousin. It was under the passenger seat of his van when the police pulled them over. There'd been a shooting in the park and they fit the profile. When the officers spotted the gun, both Napoleon and his cousin were charged with possession. The shooters were later found.

The public defender called it an 'open-and-shut case.' Just do the eight months and forget it, he said, as if eight months on Rikers were a walk in the park, or the record they'd have wouldn't all but seal their fate as two young black men with gun charges.

Luckily, it was a sunny fall afternoon, and Napoleon said it was the first time in weeks he felt warm. My sister and I stood on the deck and watched him play in a pile of leaves with my nieces. He'd scoop up an armful, throw them over his head – 'I am the leaf man!' he'd say – and they'd giggle and run so he'd chase them. He played with them for several hours and my sister considered paying him. 'He's more attentive than my best baby-sitter,' she said.

Instead, her husband loaded him down with sweaters to keep him warm on the job and threw in a few silk ties. We cooked steaks on the grill and ate outside listening to the crickets.

Napoleon never did shoot my sister or me. In fact, we still keep in touch, and he's still hanging in there. I called him the other day for an update before I finished his story. He's no longer cold – he works as a cashier now at Pathmark – and next week he's meeting with a counselor to see about community college.

Today when I visit prisons in the wildernesses of upstate New York, I see many young men like Napoleon and Rico. Several months ago I was in the keep-lock unit at Attica, where inmates who have violated prison rules are confined in darkened cells twenty-three hours a day. As I walked down the cell block in the bowels of the prison, I came across a young man from the school on Rikers

Island. 'Aren't you the lady from Fresh Start?' he asked, squinting at me through the bars. He wasn't in my class but his 'homies' were, and sometimes he'd stop by when the period was over.

In the three years since I'd seen him on Rikers, he'd been sent to Coxsackie Correctional Facility, a maximum-security prison that houses mostly felons in their late teens and early twenties, known by correction officers as 'gladiator school.' He'd gotten into a fight with an inmate there and pulled out a razor blade, earning him six months in 'the hole.' But the disciplinary cell block at Coxsackie was full, so the officials transferred him to Attica, where, at nineteen, he was housed with the state's most violent offenders.

Nowhere have I seen such fear on prisoners' faces as in the keep-lock unit at Attica. A few of them didn't want to speak with us for fear of retribution from the officers, who were said to be members of a rogue group of guards known as the Black Leather Glove gang. Some of them, the inmates said, were sons of COs killed in the 1971 riot. They wore black gloves made of Kevlar to signify that they were a unit and 'wouldn't take shit' from the prisoners. When we asked the officers why they wore the gloves, which were special-order items that cost thirty-five dollars a pair, they said it was to avoid being pricked by a needle or sliced with a razor blade when pat-frisking inmates or searching cells for contraband. The Department of Correctional Services has since banned the gloves (they replaced them with state-issued blue ones), but I saw a few when I was there dangling from the back pockets of officers.

Nevertheless, the teenager from Rikers, brave and young and not yet broken by the iron fist of the prison, said he wanted to talk. He lit a cigarette and sat at the foot of his cot. In his six-by-eight-foot cell, the end of the bed nearly reached the bars. I kneeled so we could speak eye to eye and the guards couldn't overhear us. 'He's a slasher,' a beefy CO said as he passed, nodding at the inmate, and then to me: 'Better back up.'

I thanked him and stayed where I was.

Between deep pulls on his cigarette, the boy spoke insightfully about the irony of the prison system: Coxsackie was a rough place, he said. To survive it, you needed a weapon. But a weapon is mean-ingless if you don't have 'the heart' to use it. Only 'pussies' went to the officers for help. Even if you asked for protective custody, getting there could take days, and by then word would be out that you 'snitched.' And as every prisoner knows (and I learned from my student Shanduke), 'snitches get stitches.'

So he ended up in the hole, in Attica of all places, with nothing to do but stare at the walls for six months, and then he'd be back on the bus to Coxsackie, where nothing will have changed. 'I might never find my way outta here,' he said, grinding his cigarette on the concrete floor.

At times like these, it is a passage from Norman Mailer's *In the Belly of the Beast* that I think of more than the poem by Auden:

There is a paradox at the core of penology, and from it derives the thousand ills and afflictions of the prison system. It is that not only the worst of the young are sent to prison but the best – that is the proudest, the bravest, the most daring, the most enterprising, and the most undefeated of the poor. There starts the horror.

HILTON

I came to understand my students' life circumstances through my colleague and friend, Hilton Cooper. Hilton runs City Challenge, a state-funded program for juvenile offenders in Bedford-Stuyvesant, Brooklyn. Each year, for crimes such as robbery, drug sale, and assault, approximately 250 young men receive the good fortune of being diverted from juvenile detention to a unique boot camp known as the Youth Leadership Academy (YLA) in the Catskill Mountains.

Designed and overseen by a former military colonel, the YLA departs from the traditionally punitive, in-your-face style of boot-camp instruction. Through a curriculum known as The Magic Within, the teenage felons, or 'cadets' as they're called, learn the core values of self-discipline, affiliation, self-esteem, and self-worth. If they graduate from the boot camp, they finish the last five to twelve months of their sentence at City Challenge, an 'intensive supervision aftercare program' within commuting or walking distance of their homes.

The name City Challenge is fitting. It is, most definitely, a challenge for teenage felons to return to the projects every evening, to walk by their friends who are still in the drug game, to ignore their shiny gold chains, Polo jackets, and 'fly chicks,' to turn a blind eye to their Lexuses and Jeeps and report back to the 'limited secure detention facility' the next day. If they violate curfew, get in a fight, or produce a less-than-sparkling urine sample, they're sent back to boot camp if they're lucky. Some go straight to Rikers, or to adult prison if they're over sixteen.

America is strange. At age sixteen you're old enough to be imprisoned with adults. At eighteen you're old enough to purchase a gun but too young to buy a drink.

'We teach them to use the core values to survive in their neighborhood,' Hilton says. 'We teach them that they're somebody special, that they don't have to go to prison, that there's magic within. We tell them that their environment isn't going to change, so they have to change.'

The typical City Challenge kid, Hilton says, 'has been raised by one parent, most often a mother or grandmother.' Usually there are 'signs of drug abuse, physical abuse, or sexual abuse' from a relative. Many have 'a family member dying of AIDS; the majority have a father, cousin, brother, or uncle in prison.' From an early age, he says, 'they have been hanging out in the street 'til two or three in the morning. They sort of raise themselves.'

Many join gangs because 'it's the only sense of family available to them.' They get into criminal activity and it becomes a way of life. 'We're charged with changing the criminal behavior they've been used to for ten years in eighteen months and showing them there's a different way of life.'

The Fresh Start program on Rikers and the YLA–City Challenge program have several commonalities. Both deal with a relatively small number of offenders and are sufficiently financed. Both programs address the needs of the whole individual rather than a single criminogenic factor through academic instruction, vocational training, substance-abuse treatment, and individualized counseling. Most important, both programs continue after incarceration to help ease the transition from prison to society.

In 1994, City Challenge contracted with Fresh Start to replicate its Rikers Island cooking program at the Brooklyn-based facility, and that was how I came to know Hilton Cooper. Appropriately, the instructor we sent him was a charismatic ex-con and Fresh Start graduate. Since he'd left Rikers several years before, Lynwood had worked at Fresh Start training ex-inmates as prep cooks for our fledgling microenterprise, Catering with Conviction.

In addition to these qualifications, Lynwood had a serious rap sheet and twelve years of prison under his belt. Convincing state officials at the Office of Children and Family Services to let Lynwood teach in their facility took weeks of negotiation. Lynwood, we argued, would be an ideal role model for the City Challenge kids. The years he spent in prison, the mother he saw murdered, and his recovery from two decades of crack addiction would engender respect from the teens and forge an instant bond. But it wasn't until Hilton told the state officials that he 'would personally see to it' that the partnership worked that Lynwood was hired. He became one of City Challenge's most popular instructors.

'I'll never forget the day I walked into the kitchen and saw Lynwood, all 270 pounds of him, sitting on the floor, cradling one of the cadets in his arms,' recalls a Fresh Start colleague. Apparently, a fight broke out in the kitchen and the cadet had swung at Lynwood. Instead of calling for a sergeant and having the kid locked up, Lynwood wrestled him to the floor, held his wrists behind his back, and told him over and over that he wasn't giving up on him.

'That kid was me,' Lynwood says. 'I knew his anger and the rage he had inside. I also knew that he was just fifteen years old and a prison bid would finish him.'

'A lot of these kids,' Hilton tells me, 'were born by crack-addicted mothers. We're starting to see the results. They're hyperactive, real angry.'

He describes a typical crack kid in his program. 'Now this is a really nice kid,' he says, 'very intelligent, but he's got a lot of anger.' His mother 'used to take him around while she prostituted herself in hotels. She did a lot of things in front of him.' The boy was seven at the time.

'One day she just left him and his brother in a hotel while she was prostituting herself.'

'For how long?'

'For the *rest of his life*. She just *left* them there. The child-welfare agency had to come get them.'

Today, he says, the boy's mother is off drugs and wants to make amends with her son. 'I was just in a conference with this kid and his mother, and I could see the anger he had. He didn't want to speak with her.'

As he does with most of 'his kids,' Hilton paid the family a home visit to get a sense of the environment.

'It was a disaster waiting to happen,' he recalls. The mother's boyfriend didn't get along with her son. 'I could see that it could get physical so I asked the kid's aunt to take him in.'

He also got the boy into therapy. 'Most of my kids have been neglected and abused by the people who are supposed to take care of them. And unless they can deal with it in therapy, they're going to be angry kids on the street looking to hurt people.'

In addition to the growing number of crack kids, Hilton says, they're 'starting to run into a lot of functionally illiterate fourteen- and fifteen-year-olds' who dropped out of eighth grade and read at fourth- or fifth-grade levels. 'We get them private tutors from the Board of Ed and prepare them for high schools for the functionally illiterate. It was a crisis when we first came across it, but now we know how to deal with it.'

Finally, he adds, the kids in his program are getting younger. 'We have twelve-year-olds up in the Youth Leadership Academy. These are kids who have AWOLed from private agencies or been kicked out. If a twelve-year-old comes to us it means he's been in private agencies, foster care, group homes, you name it, and he's totally out of control. The last alternative is to bring him to us. We're the last stop for a kid.'

The demographics of the City Challenge population resemble those of my teenage students on Rikers and tell the stories of the older ones. A report by the Children's Aid Society on City Challenge notes that all of 'the youngsters come from poor families of color whose parents have a high school education or less. . . .

One-third of the parents receive Public Assistance. . . . All families are Medicaid eligible.' The report then lists a frightening litany of 'psycho-social factors known to predispose youngsters toward delinquency' and which define the City Challenge population:

97 percent have seen people killed or violently attacked;
35 percent have mothers who were addicted to crack/cocaine;
26 percent have suffered severe and verifiable physical abuse at the hands of a parent;
20 percent have mothers who are psychotic;
13 percent have fathers in prison or who served a prison sentence.

Tragedy on this scale is hard to comprehend. Equally hard to comprehend is how, aside from a few exceptions like City Challenge, policymakers have ignored such obvious precursors to crime and spent more money on prisons than prevention. Despite the fact that juvenile crime has been decreasing for the last six years, politicians have capitalized on the fear of their crime-spooked constituents and adopted a 'tough on crime' posture. They demanded penalties for youths commensurate with those given adults, and they got them.

Today, all fifty states have laws on the books that allow juveniles to be tried as adults and incarcerated with them as well.

'How small is too small?' asks a compelling ad by the ACLU. Depends on where you live. In Massachusetts, it's fourteen. In Oregon, it's twelve. In Wisconsin, ten. 'They finally found an answer to overcrowded prisons,' says the ACLU. 'Smaller prisoners.'

It is also hard to understand how political leaders have denied the racial disparities in America's juvenile-justice system for so many years. I imagine this is because most elected officials haven't been inside a juvenile-detention facility or had a child of their own locked up in one. Senator Orrin Hatch of Utah, the Republican chairman of the Senate Judiciary Committee, stated in 1991 that 'the juvenile justice system is colorblind and there's no evidence of discrimination based on race.'

Do these guys read? A meticulously researched study by none other than the U.S. Department of Justice showed that minority youths are more likely than their white counterparts to be arrested, held in jail, convicted, and given longer prison terms.

'In some cases,' noted a front-page article about the study in *The New York Times,* 'the disparities are stunning. . . . Black youths are more than six times as likely as whites to be sentenced by juvenile courts to prison. For those charged with drug offenses, black youths are *48 times* more likely than whites to be sentenced to juvenile prison.'

Critics say that the racial disparities are due to higher rates of crime among minority youths. According to the Justice Department study, however, of the 2.6 million arrests of persons under age eighteen in 1998, 'the majority (71%) of those arrests involved white youths. Minority youths make up one-third of the country's adolescent population but represent two-thirds of youths confined in local jails and state prisons.' 'When you look at this data,' says Mark Soler, president of the Youth Law Center, 'it is undeniable that race is a factor.'

When you look at Hilton Cooper, it is undeniable that he's a dead ringer for Denzel Washington. The second thing you notice is his energy. He can inspire a roomful of bureaucrats one minute and capture the hearts of the city's most cynical teens the next. He can transform teenage felons into college-bound scholars, and the success of his program proves it.

While a mind-boggling 80 percent of juveniles sent to New York detention facilities get re-arrested within a year, the majority of City Challenge graduates have remained in the community and out of trouble since the program's inception in 1992. Former U.S. attorney general Janet Reno recognized YLA–City Challenge as a national model in 1995. A recent study by the federal Office of Juvenile Justice and Delinquency Prevention (OJJDP) found that the program 'produced statistically significant lower recidivism rates than a control group.'

I ask Hilton what his secret is.

'Twenty-five years in the ghetto,' he says. 'That's what drives me to advocate for my kids.'

Although he moved to the suburbs two years ago, Hilton wears his twenty-plus years in the projects like stripes on a uniform. He not only survived the mean streets, he escaped them. His ticket out was basketball; his talent on the court won him a scholarship to the University of Texas, El Paso. He planned on going pro.

'Did you think about anything else growing up?' I ask.

'Nope, just basketball.'

'Nothing else?'

He shakes his head.

If Hilton weren't so sharp, then maybe I'd understand, but he's one of the most successful professionals in the field of juvenile justice. I couldn't believe he had no other aspirations growing up.

'So if someone told you when you were, say, fourteen, that you should be a lawyer or a doctor, what would you think?'

'I'd think it's impossible.'

'Why?'

'Because to go to law school you have to have money, and I knew I couldn't get that kind of money.'

His next comment spoke volumes: 'And when you grow up in the inner city you don't feel you're as smart as other people. You don't think you can get a professional job because those jobs are for brilliant people, and you just don't feel you're all that brilliant. Basketball was the only chance I had to make something out of my life.'

I wondered about all the other kids: the girls, the non-athletes, the students who didn't have the talent to win a scholarship.

In teaching as in writing, the best way to make a point is through showing, not telling. So, like the good teacher he is (or maybe because he was sick of answering my questions), Hilton offered to show me.

On a sweltering August morning in 1999, he picks me up in his black Eddie Bauer Explorer. We're headed for the South Bronx, to his old neighborhood in Mitchell housing projects. He turns up the Ruff Rider CD for added ambience. 'You can take the boy outta the ghetto . . . ,' he jokes.

Along the way we pick up David, a City Challenge graduate who's waiting for us outside his home in the Baruch projects on the Lower East Side. Later we pick up James, also a City Challenge graduate, also from the projects.

David, 19, is Puerto Rican, the youngest of six kids born and raised in Baruch. Until recently, cops called Baruch a 'dead zone' due to its sky-high rate of homicide.

'Before Giuliani, it was drug city,' my colleague and friend NYPD Sergeant Nathaniel Hall says. In the early nineties Hall worked as an undercover narcotics officer in an initiative known as Operation Pressure Point. 'I'd go in there looking to buy crack in what police call a "buy and bust arrest", and a hundred dealers would appear within minutes.'

He recalls a hideous memory: 'We were working on a particular drug case, and an undercover officer got shot in the eye. They shot him in the fuckin' eye!' he practically shouts. 'His radio exploded, blood was everywhere.' It wasn't just the gruesome nature of the murder that haunts him, he says, but that he'd stopped the 'perp' the day before. 'If I'd found something on him, if I'd gotten him locked up, that officer would be alive today. As a cop you think about these things.'

We pull up to the dead zone and David gets into the car. He's built like a heavyweight boxer and still wears his hair in the military crew cut from boot camp.

'What got me into negativity is this neighborhood,' he says, pointing to the towering brick buildings that hug East Side Drive. He describes his family life as 'pretty good,' noting that he had two parents at home and neither was into drugs.

'My father worked in a factory when he could. My mom was on welfare. About ninety percent of the people around my way are on welfare,' he adds.

As he speaks, I can't take my eyes off the thick pink scar that wraps around his head, cuts across his upper ear, and travels down the side of his face. It looks like a seam holding in his brains. He notices that I'm staring and explains:

'See my face? It happened two years ago, up in Jacob Riis [another project]. I was robbed for my chain. Me and another guy were comin' out of a party and a group of Bloods [a black gang] snatched my chain. I didn't want to give it up and I got slashed.'

'With a razor blade?'

'Yeah.'

'How many stitches?'

'Ah, a lot. I didn't bother to ask. I was in the hospital from two in the morning 'til ten the next day, and all that time they was doing my stitches. Look, they got me on my arms, too.'

He holds out his forearms. Ruby-red slashes crisscross the white flesh, making me think of candy canes.

Violence in his project is rampant, he says, and 'it's increasing with the whole gang thing goin' on. A lot of it's coming from the jails.'

I ask if he carries a gun.

'You can't walk around here with a gun because most of the time you're getting searched by the police. And if you're carryin', that's five years upstate. You get stopped all the time.'

'For what?'

'For anything. If you're walkin' down the street, they stop you. If you're just hangin' outside your building, they stop you. If you're doing absolutely nothing, they stop you.'

'Do they give you a reason?'

'Maybe, maybe not. They might say they got a call about a guy with a gun and you happen to fit the description. Other times it's just "You – face forward, hands up against the wall, spread your legs."' He recites the procedure like a mantra. He says he gets searched two or three times a week.

'Doesn't it piss people off?'

He looks at me and laughs. 'Sure it does. And lots of times people resist. But they end up gettin' Maced if they do.'

I imagine how I'd feel about cops if this happened to me twice a week.

As we drive to the Bronx, I ask Hilton if his old neighborhood has improved with zero-tolerance policing and the mayor's quality-of-life campaign. Crime is down since the eighties he says, when Mitchell houses were 'the number-one projects in the country for murder,' but by all other indicators the neighborhood's falling apart.

'When I was growing up, there was a sense of community,' he says. 'Families looked out for each other. Today, it's a jungle. You're always lookin' over your shoulder; you can be robbed at any time; gangs are everywhere.'

'How about guns?'

'When I was growing up getting a gun was a hard thing to do, but now all these kids have guns. They may not be packin' but they sure as hell got 'em. They can buy a gun for fifty dollars from their buddies.'

'About a hundred dollars if it's clean,' David says, turning to me to explain. 'That means it doesn't have bodies on it.'

They both say it would take about ten minutes and a phone call to get their hands on a gun. Given the availability of guns in poor, inner-city neighborhoods, it is not surprising that homicide is the leading cause of death among young black men in America.

'If there were ever a metaphor for a failure of democracy, lack of firearms control may be it,' writes the National Commission on Violence in their June 2000 report. 'The firearms death rate in America is 8 times greater than those of the 25 other wealthy nations *combined*. . . .

'In 1995,' write the authors, 'handguns were used to kill two people in New Zealand, 15 in Japan, 30 in Great Britain, 106 in Canada, 213 in Germany and 9,390 in the United States.'

In fact, the majority of firearms are no longer designed for hunting and target shooting, but are 'high-powered, rapid-firing, easily concealed weapons that have no other logical function than to kill humans.' The availability of such weapons has had devastating consequences, and not only in the inner city. 'Any confused teenager feeling disparaged by fellow students can blow a number of them away,' writes the commission. 'A worker who has problems on the job can put an end to it with a massacre at the office. A litigant who feels wronged by the justice system can set it right by shooting up the courthouse. Most people resolve things in a more reasonable way – but in a nation of 230 million people and 200 million firearms, the law of averages is producing a growing number of massacres.'

Another problem, Hilton says, is that it's harder for kids to find jobs today. Many of the young men have records, and most are exposed to the drug trade before they're old enough to work. Minimum-wage jobs pale in comparison to the money they can make dealing drugs, which also carries more prestige.

'I worked at Burger King when I was young,' he says, 'but today a lot of kids are ashamed to work in a fast-food restaurant. They're dealing with inner-city ego and being teased. They'd rather be caught dead than be seen walkin' into the projects in a Burger King uniform. So most kids join a gang, sell drugs, and rob people.'

Sergeant Nathaniel Hall also grew up poor and black in the inner city. Like Hilton, he's a success story, an exceptionally motivated individual that white people point to and say, 'If he could do it then why can't the rest of them?' The problem, he says, is that 'most of the successful people in the inner cities are drug dealers. Kids growing up in the projects don't see doctors and lawyers and the blacks who made it, because they don't live there anymore. They moved out.'

Not only does the departure of professionals deprive kids of role models, it also deteriorates the quality of life in the community. 'When they lived there,' Hall says, 'the noise on the corner had to be quieted because they had to go to work. But now if nobody in that neighborhood's working, there's no reason to quiet down and not hang out, so that's what you get – a lot of noise and a lot of guys hanging out. The difference between middle-class black neighborhoods and lower-class black neighborhoods is they're quiet at night because people gotta get up and go to work.'

As we enter the South Bronx, I ask Hilton if he'd call it a ghetto. Some liberals say 'ghetto' is a demeaning and politically incorrect term to describe inner-city neighborhoods. I'd recently been criticized for using it and was told that 'marginalized community' or another 'less loaded' word was more appropriate.

'This is *most definitely* the ghetto,' he says. 'A poor inner-city area where the government isn't really trying to help, where there's a lack of opportunity for kids.'

I notice that he omits any reference to race, and I'm reminded of a line in Jonathan Kozol's *Savage Inequalities*, where he talks about racial segregation with a public school principal in the South Bronx. 'More often than not,' he writes, 'they seem reluctant to describe their schools as being "segregated" or, indeed, even to speak of segregation. It is as if they have assimilated racial isolation as a matter so immutable, so absolute, that it no longer forms part of their thinking.'

Hilton laughs when I ask him about the racial issue. 'There *is* no racial issue because you just don't *see* white people. I never interacted with white people until I went to college. The only white people you see here are schoolteachers or cops.'

We pull up to Mitchell projects, which look just like Baruch: tall, ugly, cold. Behind a chain-link fence stand a few scraggly trees. A sparse patch of grass appears to grow from the dust. A sign warning residents to Keep Off the Grass seems like a bad joke.

'Can you believe it?' Hilton says, shaking his head in disgust. 'It's illegal to walk on the grass.'

I think about growing up in Bernardsville, New Jersey, a ninety-minute drive from the Bronx. In a high school of 800 students, there was one black. And you can't *buy* a piece of property unless it's on five acres of grass, much less walk on it.

We walk into one of the buildings. There's not much to see, not there or in any of the projects I've been to since. In fact, my travels to the projects have left me with one realization: The barren grounds, chain-link fences, depressing grays, and battleship green that covers the floors and the walls bear a striking resemblance to the caged city on Rikers Island. Here as in the jail, the first sight upon entering is a uniformed guard tucked safely inside a booth. Concrete blocks form the walls of the hallways and stairwells. No comforting cooking smells – homemade cookies, a pot roast, perhaps – can penetrate the smell of ammonia that smacks you in the face. Behind triple-locked doors families pack five, maybe ten, to an apartment, much as the inmates are crammed into the dorms in the jails. A child raised in such an environment, it seems, is acclimated to prison before he's old enough to commit a crime.

I ask Hilton how old he was when he realized he didn't live as well as other Americans.

'Maybe around twelve or thirteen I pretty much realized it.'

'How? Through things you saw on TV?'

'Hell no,' he laughs. 'It was more obvious than that. I knew we were poor when there was nothin' to eat. When we ate mayonnaise sandwiches, syrup sandwiches, maybe ketchup sandwiches, and then it would dawn on me – God, times was hard. A peanut-butter-and-jelly sandwich with a glass of milk – that was a luxury.'

He recalls 'waiting on the welfare lines' with his mother. 'There was a place you'd go in the projects with your shopping cart. You'd wait on these long-ass lines. They'd give you a big block of cheese, the jumbo cans of peanut butter and jelly.'

David laughs knowingly from the backseat.

We park the jeep and walk a few blocks to a deli for some water and Coke. It's ninety-eight degrees, according to 1010 WINS. We pass the gym where Hilton played basketball, which looks like it's permanently closed. 'I played there every day of my life,' he says, 'that's why I didn't end up in prison.'

The gym is closed temporarily; the city is building a community center and sports arena, he says. A year later, it's still not open.

In the deli, we step over cigarette butts and head to the refrigerator in the back. David points to the big bottles of beer. 'It's actually malt liquor,' he says. 'If you go into Manhattan, you don't see this stuff.'

'Yup, inner-city beer,' says Hilton. 'Forty ounces for a dollar fifty-nine.'

I think of my students on Rikers: Forty ounces and a blunt . . .

'It's really cheap but very effective,' David adds.

We sit at a picnic table by the basketball court across from the projects. A game is in session and just as many adults as kids are there, watching the game, playing on swings, cooling off in a fountain, squeezing what little joy they can from the neighborhood. A lot of people know Hilton and stop by. He and his friend Rod Strickland, an NBA player for the Washington Wizards who also grew up in Mitchell, return and coach basketball when they can. Hilton's been there every weekend that summer. 'When I work with younger people, I see myself,' he says. 'I believe that every person has the chance to be somebody, and that's why I work so hard doing what I do.'

On the drive to James's apartment in Butler projects on 169th Street and Webster Avenue (not far from Frank's chop shop down by Melrose), the level of neighborhood disorganization is hard to miss. Shirtless men walk aimlessly in the street, occasionally in front of cars, some pushing shopping carts piled high with junk. Cars pull out every which way; some plow straight through stop signs. More than once Hilton has to slam on the brakes. Bone-weary women lug grocery bags in one arm and a baby in the other. It's summer in the city, but there's little green here, not like in Manhattan, where I work, or where I live in Brooklyn Heights. Because there aren't any trees, I think. Because there aren't any flowers, because there isn't any grass – just gray, gray, gray.

Sergeant Hall tells me he's frequently asked to speak to kids in inner-city high schools, the majority of whom are black and Hispanic. 'When they ask me what they should do about college, I tell them they should do whatever it takes to go away, because what people in the inner city are doing isn't living, it's surviving. We don't dream, we don't think, we don't have aspirations. But once you get away for a while and you can sit outside, on the grass, get a little sun, where there's more than just concrete, then you can finally start dreaming.'

JAMES

James is a graduate of Lynwood's culinary arts class, and Hilton says he's been cooking all morning for the picnic that afternoon. Today is Old-Timers' Day in the Bronx and we're meeting James's mother and sisters in Crotona Park. Held every August, Old-Timers' Day brings families and residents into the park for cookouts, outdoor concerts, and various festivities.

I'd always be thankful when Lynwood would arrange catering events and appoint James as the head caterer and host. One month we catered three early breakfast meetings at Brooklyn Borough Hall, and James never failed to impress the judges and politicians who attended. Impeccable and proud in his cooking whites and chef hat, he'd introduce himself and talk about City Challenge. He wasn't a bragger by any stretch of the word, but he'd manage to get in how he was invited to serve on Janet Reno's National Youth Network and traveled around the country with Hilton to speak to at-risk teens.

We pull up to Butler Houses, a cluster of buildings made of faded brown brick. Some of the windows are smashed and gaping. A few are boarded with wood. The level of disrepair is among the worst I've seen in the city.

But there is James, standing by himself at a table outside one of the buildings. I haven't seen him for over a year but recognize him immediately. He has the same baby face and few extra pounds he had at age fifteen and looks just as serious – the kind of kid who seems ridiculously wise for his years.

He's prepared four aluminum trays of food for the picnic. They're sealed and stacked on the table in front of him ready to go. What a good kid, I think. My mother couldn't make me clean my room at that age, much less cook.

At first, I think he doesn't see us; he doesn't wave when we pull up to the sidewalk. In fact, he looks distracted. Or is that fear?

And then I see them, about thirty feet away and not much older than James, sitting on the backs of benches, scowling at him and at us. Rap music pounds on a boom box. One of them stands and flicks a lit cigarette. Gold flashes from his teeth.

'Ghetto thugs,' Hilton says, turning up the volume on *his* rap until it echoes in the street and the jeep feels like it's shaking. He kills the AC, opens the door, and steps out. 'Now, they are *definitely* carrying,' he says.

Doo-rags, low-slung pants, tattoos on muscle – I've seen it all day, I've seen it in every borough. I've seen it on men in prison yards upstate. But here in the Bronx, in the heart of the projects, I feel it.

'Slingin' drugs, no doubt,' says David. He steps out and slams the door, then leans against the jeep beside Hilton. Arms flexed, hands visible.

What they're doing, it occurs to me, is making a passage for James. Creating a safety zone with their presence. Hilton motions to him with his head.

James nods in our direction and picks up his trays. A soldier walking onto a battlefield.

'Shouldn't we help him?' I ask. The rap is so loud I have to shout.

'Stay right where you are,' Hilton says. 'He's got it.' He doesn't take his eyes off James. I feel like anything, absolutely anything, could happen in the next thirty seconds.

James starts walking, face forward, head high, carrying the trays like a pro. He's past the dealers now. A few of them laugh, again the flash of gold. Shoulders back, chest out, just like in boot camp, he waddles a little but there's strength in his stride.

Finally, he makes it to the jeep. Hilton reaches out and takes the trays from him. David and James do a shaky high-five. I give him a hug and squeeze my eyes tight. Thankfully, the tears stay put. The situation is beyond sad.

Inner-city kids like David and James 'cannot imagine what it is like to live outside of a violent-tinged milieu,' Professor David Brotherton tells me. As director of the Center on Violence at John Jay, Brotherton is well versed in the subject. 'The discourse, the disposition, and the currency of violence are rife in their communities. It is so difficult for a person who lives with violence, is surrounded by a subculture of violence, and beyond that by a larger culture in which violence is embedded, to ever escape it. They have layers and layers to go through to get into a safe zone.'

Not only do young men like David and James confront 'direct violence' in the murders, assaults, and robberies they experience in their neighborhoods, Professor Brotherton says, 'they also confront what is known as "indirect violence," which is living in a community characterized by denial – a denial of services, a denial of decent schools, public housing buildings that are crawling with rats. They feel utterly dis-invested in. The message they get is that they are not stakeholders.'

We drive the ten minutes to Crotona and find a parking spot on the perimeter of the park. I feel lucky we have a car; more than a few people we passed were wheeling their picnic lunches in shopping carts along the sidewalk. We walk through the park – the trees are leafy but the lawns are a wreck – and after a while find James's mother and sisters on a blanket, fanning themselves to keep cool. They smile when they see James.

He introduces us and tells his mom I'm writing a book. I try to back the conversation up a bit, make some small talk, but she offers me a spot on the blanket. 'You come sit right here,' she says.

'My name is Elizabeth,' she says into my tape recorder. 'Elizabeth Ford, mother of James.' It's clear that he's her pride and joy.

I compliment her on her son, say how great he was in the program.

'Yes, yes, he's a good boy, he's the last one. Raised him myself, me and the good Lord, that is.'

She says she's lived in Butler projects for twenty-six years. 'I raised six kids in that apartment.'

I ask her how Butler has changed over the years, if it's gotten better or worse.

'A lot worse,' she says, but notes a few improvements. For example, the rats are gone. 'They got rid of them a couple of years ago, but before that you be walkin' down the hallway and the rats be walkin' with you!'

More important, the complex isn't awash in drugs like it was five years ago, 'when James was comin' up,' she says. When I tell her about the incident that morning, she says, quite reasonably, 'Those men need jobs.' There are more police, she adds. 'More cops is a good thing; they're doing their job.'

But the playground in the project is barren, she says, and from her perspective it seems intentional.

'In May they came and snatched up all the swings and sliding boards. They said they was gonna exchange them but they ain't bring nothin' back! Now it's almost end of summer. These kids have nothing. No sprinkler to cool themselves in, no sliding board, nothin'.'

Even here in Crotona Park, she points out, the most basic staples are missing. 'See that basketball court over there? How can kids play? There's no hoop.'

I follow her gaze: no hoop, no net, just a pole.

She points to a trash can that's been used but hasn't been emptied; a mound of garbage results. 'Just look at the ground,' she says. 'There's more garbage on it than grass. City don't come and empty the trash cans.'

I shake my head; she does the same. 'Mm-mm-mm . . . seems like the South Bronx needs a little more fixin'. Seems like the city just don't care 'bout where black people live.'

★

Criminologist Andrew Karmen has studied the New York crime scene down to the finest detail. 'A correlation and regression analysis of murder rates and precinct social conditions indicated that the neighborhoods where residents faced the gravest risks in the 1990's tended to be the poorest, most racially and financially segregated sections of the city, inhabited by many female headed households receiving public assistance and by unemployed persons,' he notes. Not surprisingly, 'the safest communities in the city were the most affluent ones.'

Later, James and I sit on a bench and talk. He's been out of City Challenge more than a year and has managed to stay the course. He recently got his GED and landed a full-time job doing medical billing at a local hospital. 'I really admired you this morning,' I say.

'Yeah, well, it's okay.'

The weekends, he says, are more hazardous. During the weekdays, he's out of the complex and at his desk before the dealers are out of bed. Like David, he says the 'negativity' of his environment paved his way into the criminal-justice system. He explains how he ended up at Spofford at age fourteen.

'I had two charges. One was for armed robbery, the second was just robbery. But I was never caught with a weapon. The guy I robbed told the cops I used a weapon, but I didn't.'

'But you had a gun on you –'

'Yes, yes I did.'

'How'd you get it?'

'Well, I actually had two. I got my first gun from a friend. I told him I needed a gun and I gave him a hundred and fifty dollars. It was a .380 semi-automatic, a baby nine-millimeter. My second gun I won from a bet. We were playing dice and the guy who lost didn't have enough to pay. He owed like two hundred fifty dollars, so that's how he paid. It was a Mac 11, held about seventeen shots, an automatic.'

'That's a pretty serious gun.'

'Yeah, it's federal time.'

Remarkable, I think. James knows the difference between state and federal time for various gun charges and he's not even twenty.

I didn't learn these distinctions until I entered a master's program in criminal justice.

'Did you ever use it?'

'I never shot anyone, not directly I mean, but I shot at people, you know, in a shoot-out.'

'Right, a shoot-out,' I say, as if I know exactly what he's talking about. 'So how do these shoot-outs work?'

'Well, it's like this. There's a fall-out on the block, there's two guys and they have a dispute and they decide to shoot. Now if I have my gun I just shoot back. You just shoot at whoever's shootin'. That's the idea: shoot but don't get shot. It's sorta like a game.'

His familiarity with guns reminds me of something Sergeant Hall said to me one night over dinner. 'Some kids talk about the noises in the country – crickets, wind, birds. The kids in the inner city don't know these noises, but they can identify gunshots. They can tell you what kind of gun just went off, whether it was a twenty-two, a twenty-five, whatever.'

James started dealing when he was twelve. Just as with guns, getting into the game was easy, he says.

'How easy?' I ask.

'Put it this way: It was harder to sign up for high school than to get hooked up with a dealer.'

Drug dealers seek out kids like James for several reasons. First, their youth all but ensures that they'll be out of the system, back on the streets, and working within days. Second, they're less likely than their adult counterparts to use drugs themselves, and therefore less tempted to dip into the product they're selling. Finally, they're cheap labor.

James says he made 'approximately two hundred and fifty dollars a week working ten-hour shifts a day.' When I point out he could have made that much working at Burger King, he reminds me that at twelve he couldn't have been hired.

'But it was okay,' he says. 'All my friends were around, we'd be on my block, smokin' weed, drinkin' beer, it wasn't like real work, no manual labor, just hand-to-hand pitchin.'"

Like most bootstrap capitalists, James worked legitimate jobs as well. He packed bags in a supermarket after school and on the weekends. 'I remember getting my first paycheck and going right back to the supermarket to buy food 'cause I knew that's what we needed.'

His mother was on disability, he says, and with no father and six kids to raise 'the bills were barely being met.'

'We were just eating. . . . We had a set budget we had to follow, so if one month the bills got backed up or if something happened, it was like total chaos.'

'How'd you know about bill paying when you were twelve?' I ask.

'I knew about bill paying,' he says, 'for the simple fact that it was mandatory in my house that once you reached twelve bills were a responsibility. Even if it was only donating to a certain bill, you had to provide. You weren't gonna live rent free. That was never an option in my house.'

When he was seven, his brother was shot. 'He got shot right in front of my building. I remember lookin' out the window, seeing my brother lyin' on the ground, and thinking he was dead. You met him while we was walkin' in the the park,' he says. 'Remember? The guy with the limp?'

I did remember, but it was getting late and I was getting tired. The stories and scenery were getting me down. I was relieved when Hilton said it was time to go.

POSTSCRIPT

Two years later, I call Elizabeth to see about James. 'He's still workin',' she says. 'God bless him.' He has a new job at a prestigious hospital and is making more money. He also has a new son. 'Thank the Lord for my James,' she adds.

5

SUCCESSFUL ESCAPES

I come as an old timer and one who knows what he is talking about, as I have been through the mill since childhood: one act of kindness will do more toward reforming a criminal than a thousand acts of cruelty and than all the punishment that you can inflict.

> – L. Richards, 1913, from *Within Prison Walls*,
> by Thomas Mott Osborne

I hadn't heard from Peter for almost a year when he left me a message at my office. 'I hear there's a graduation on Rikers tomorrow. Tell the guys in the cooking class congratulations from a former inmate and give me a call if you can – things are looking up for me. You can reach me at the job, or leave me a message on my cell phone.'

On my cell phone, at the job . . . Amazing, I think, and quickly dial his number.

'Peter! How'd you know there's a graduation tomorrow?'

'You haven't heard I've been back to Rikers?'

Oh God, I thought, not again.

'I got a full-time job as a cook at a nursing home and – check this out – I graduated from the New York Restaurant School a couple months ago. I go back to Rikers as a volunteer and teach the guys in the cooking class. It's good for them to see a graduate who made it.'

It's good for everyone, I think, and thank him for letting me know.

'For the first time in my life I have medical coverage and a week's vacation,' he says. 'I'm making twenty-two thousand dollars a year.'

Peter is in his late thirties, married to a woman he met 'in recovery,' and has a new baby.

'Wow, Peter, that's great,' I say, then wonder if it's really that great after all. I made $22,000 at my first 'real' job, too – thirteen years ago, when I entered the workforce and apartments in the city rented for half the price they do now.

One of the best things about having a job, Peter says, is that now he can help his family. 'My mom's going through a bad time. I was able to give her two thousand dollars, and I really felt good about that.'

Peter was on the Rikers Island merry-go-round (streets, drugs, jail, and back again) for eight years before he joined Fresh Start. The timely convergence of his determination and the program's intervention ended his years of recidivism.

Kenneth Johnson, another Fresh Start graduate, spent fifteen years as an addict and regular Rikers Island resident. Like Peter, he's also back on the Rock, but he's not wearing greens. He's a counselor for Fresh Start; one of the best the program's had.

In 1996, Carlos Colon was on the Rock serving a one-year sentence for drug sale. Today he lives in Manhattan, designs Web sites, and teaches computer skills to at-risk youths. In 1998 he published a book, a guide to Windows 95 in Spanish. We give copies to the Hispanic students in the Rikers computer class. They think I'm joking when I tell them that a graduate wrote their textbook.

'I wrote that book to keep me out of the drug game,' Carlos says. 'I knew if I came home after work and didn't have something to keep me busy I'd be back in the mix.'

Peter, Carlos, and Kenneth are just three of many Fresh Start graduates who have escaped the cycle of crime, drugs, and incarceration. They are living proof that people *can* change and that good programs work. For some of our graduates, Fresh Start was a catalyst; it sparked a desire within them that led to a succession of accomplishments. For others, it was a bridge to the mainstream, providing access to people they wouldn't have otherwise known, and in the end, making the difference between living and surviving. Carlos is a good example.

CARLOS

Actually, I didn't think I'd see Carlos after he left Rikers. He performed well in the program but most of the time he looked bored. He'd sit in the back, arms crossed, legs stretched out in front of him, a study in casual-cool. He'd smirk instead of laugh when his colleagues in greens joked around. His gaze was intense, and he brimmed with machismo. Sometimes I think he scared them. In the drug world, he was a much bigger player than most of my students: not the guy on the street doing hand-to-hand pitching or the one 'getting high on his own supply.' Carlos was a mid-level manager, ordering kilos and calling the shots, hiring and firing the 'street pharmacists' from an apartment he worked out of in Washington Heights. And if he hadn't been so clever when the cops broke down his door, guns drawn, he'd be in state prison today.

I remember interviewing him for the program. Most of the inmates talk about how they want to change their lives and make a 'fresh start,' how they're 'sick and tired of being sick and tired,' or some other 12-step slogan. Not Carlos.

'You say this program offers computer training,' he said. 'So that's it. I'm interested in learning computers and I want to be in your program.' His accent was strong but his English was nearly perfect.

I told him the program wasn't just about computers, that he'd spend much more time in classes like conflict resolution and relapse prevention than typing at the keyboard. 'It's about a lifestyle change,' I said, emphasizing the word 'lifestyle,' hoping to get a reaction.

'So I will,' he said.

'You will what?'

'Attend the other classes . . . and . . . and . . . how do you say? Change my *livestyle*.' He imitated me a little when he said it, and I laughed.

By the end of the program he'd not only mastered word processing but was learning Quark, sophisticated publishing software. He ordered computer books from catalogs and pored over them with the kind of excitement other prisoners reserve for *Penthouse*. A student from his dorm said that sometimes at night he'd see Carlos crouched over a computer book on his cot, flashlight in hand, scanning the text in the dark.

Fortunately, when Carlos came to our office we had just received a new contract and needed an all-around helper. And despite his strong computer skills Carlos still needed a job. 'Five years' experience running a lucrative, mid-size drug operation' wouldn't quite work on a résumé. Because of his success in the drug world, he had no legal work history. Even attempting a résumé would be futile.

So we offered Carlos his first 'legit' job, and it was fun having him around. He wasn't the tough guy that he had been, or needed to be, on Rikers. For six months he helped in the office, doing spreadsheets, organizing the supply room, running errands, even emptying the trash. He was reliable and efficient, but I knew he was bored and the work was beneath him.

One day, with uncharacteristic openness, he said he needed to talk. He closed the door and sat in a chair beside me. The streets were tempting him, he said. He'd been offered a well-paying job by a former connection. He needed the money, it would be a one-shot deal, and chances were strong that he wouldn't get caught. He wasn't asking for advice – that wasn't his style – he was simply presenting his options and weighing the consequences.

But the worry on his face spoke louder than his words. I told him I could see that he was afraid of losing his freedom, and, more important, his self-respect. It mattered to him and to us that he didn't go back to crime. And because of this, these 'informal social controls,' as sociologists call them, his decision was more complicated than a cost-benefit analysis. 'When you know better, God expects better,' the ex-con, basketball legend Pee Wee Kirkland once said to my students on Rikers.

In a moment of insight for which I'm eternally grateful, I called my friend Paul and asked if he had any meaningful work for Carlos. Paul had just launched a newsletter and he's as ex-con friendly as they come. He had hired Fresh Start graduates before and was willing to try again, even though the last man we sent him had relapsed and stolen twenty dollars from him.

'As long as he can work hard, stay late, and learn what he has to learn, I'm happy to give him a chance,' Paul said.

If there were more people like Paul in New York City, I thought, Rikers could close down a jail.

It was a perfect fit. Carlos rose to the challenge and Paul embraced his help. Over the next couple of years, Carlos created a massive database for the newsletter and designed an award-winning Web site. He learned various computer languages and trained other Fresh Start graduates to help him with the mailings. 'I'm so proud of him,' Paul says. 'He's risen so far. There's not a problem he hasn't been able to solve. I don't know what I'd do without him.'

LENNY

Of the twelve inmates in my spring 1998 class, Lenny wasn't one I'd consider 'most likely to succeed.' He was too high-strung and had too many years in the joint and on the streets. Even though he'd spent a year at Howard University before he had a baby, dropped out, and turned to crack (in that order), his decade in and out of Rikers had taken a toll on his psyche. He stammered when he spoke and interrupted the class at odd and frequent intervals. His thick glasses tilted perpetually on his nose. I was afraid he'd appear too eager to please and too scattered to an employer on the outside.

Fond as I was of Lenny, I dreaded working with him when he got out. He's the kind of student who breaks your heart, because the gap between his dreams and his ability to achieve them seems impossibly wide to bridge. Or so I thought until he started writing.

Using a technique known as 'journal therapy,' I give the men a journal and encourage them to document their feelings and insights as they progress through the program. 'You don't have to hand it in,' I tell them, 'but you'll see that writing is cathartic.' Some of them do, some of them don't, but for Lenny it was a lifesaver. After a couple of weeks, he asked me to read what he'd written.

'Like correct it for me,' he said, pushing up his glasses with his nose.

'It's great you're thinking about grammar, Lenny, but what matters is that you're writing. Looks like you're on a roll.'

'Yeah . . . uh-uh . . . I am . . . uh . . . huh . . . I mean, what I'm sayin' is, could you read it and tell me what you think?'

The clarity with which Lenny wrote about his life showed me that he was far more grounded than I'd thought. At first he vomited his feelings, filling page after page with grief and regret, doubts about his ability to make things right again. He poured out his soul in that journal, struggled through his life story, his crimes, the destruction, the people he hurt who would never forgive him, a son he loved but hadn't been there for. I wrote notes in the margins and underlined sentences where he spoke about the future.

We continued like this for the next few months, and by the time he left Rikers it seemed he'd written his way out of jail. Even his stutter abated.

On the day of Lenny's release, a Friday at five in the morning, our offices were closed. He had the weekend free, a dangerous situation. But Lenny followed his counselor's advice: Just make a meeting your first day home. He did, and it tided him over until Monday. He enrolled in La Fluente, an outpatient program the Osborne Association runs in the Bronx. He graduated from the program and stayed an extra month. 'I needed the structure,' he says.

He remembers the day he received the public assistance he'd applied for when he got out. Nothing came for months, and then he had $600. 'My stomach started turning, my bowels loosened. It was a crack craving,' he says. 'I found Lynwood [his counselor] and told him I was scared. I didn't know how to keep my hands off that money. He told me to stay calm, take a cab to my mother's house, and have her hold it for me.'

For a while Lenny volunteered in our office, making copies, running errands, being a pest. 'I stayed around because it was the only safe place I had,' he says. When our job developer, the ebullient Elizabeth Payamps, told him it was time to leave the nest, Lenny was confused. 'You mean I can't work here? I thought you-all was gonna hire me.'

Elizabeth got him an interview for a telemarketing position paying eight dollars an hour, and, despite my earlier misgivings, Lenny got the job. A few months later he was earning seventeen dollars an hour. 'I never made seventeen dollars an hour doing *anything* legal in my life,' he said.

Confidence high, he decided to go back to college. And like the steamrolling journal writer he was on the Rock, he pursued the lead we gave him to CUNY-Catch, a small program that helps ex-offenders gain admission to the City University of New York.

Designed to 'catch' ex-cons before defeat and recidivism set in, the program helps them collect their high school records, fill out applications, and access financial aid. Once everything's in order, the ex-offenders can apply to one of the seventeen colleges under the CUNY umbrella.

Program director John Chiarkas says the retention rate of his 'Catch' students is 50 percent higher than that of regular CUNY students. 'Ex-offenders are more motivated,' he says. 'They've had time to think about their lives and tend to be more mature because they've had more life experiences. For them education is a savior – it's their only way out – they don't want to blow it.' In fact, studies show that inmates with at least two years of college have a 10 per-cent re-arrest rate, compared to a national re-arrest rate of approximately 60 percent.

I remember the first time John came to Rikers to speak to my students. Despite his doctorate degree from Columbia University, he spoke from the heart and 'kept it real,' as the inmates say. 'We're giving you guys a shot at the square life,' he said, 'an alternative to the 'hood, to your homies, to Julio on the corner.' He told them that to qualify for federal aid, they'd have to take twelve hours of class a week, essentially a full-time course load.

'How's a man supposed to live?' one of the inmates asked.

'Easy. You go to work in the day and college at night. And if you do that, I guarantee you won't come back to jail.'

That fall, Lenny entered Brooklyn Community College. 'The first semester was rough,' he says. 'English was really hard for me 'cause I'd been out of school for so long. But then the second semester, man, I blew up the spot! I made dean's list.'

As a Human Services major, he interns at a group home for chil-dren with HIV/AIDS. 'It's so sad,' he says. 'These kids are all messed up and don't have no one to adopt them.' He tells me about a ten-year-old boy who's blind, about a four-year-old girl on crutches. 'I just smile as bright as I can and wrap my arms around them and try to make them laugh.'

Unfortunately, the college tuition assistance Lenny received is no longer available for people like him, individuals convicted of drug offenses. A recent revision to the Higher Education Act has closed college opportunities for students convicted of a drug offense, regardless of how minor. According to the amendment: 'A student who has been convicted of any offense under any Federal or State law involving the possession or sale of a controlled substance shall not be eligible to receive any grant, loan, or work assistance under this title during the period beginning on the date of such conviction and ending after the interval specified in the following table.'

First-time offenders charged with possession are ineligible for a year; for second-time offenders, it's two years; for third-time offenders, it's 'indefinite.' For students charged with drug sale, first offenses postpone eligibility for two years; second offenses, indefinitely.

On the surface, such restrictions might seem appropriately punitive, but a deeper analysis raises important questions. For example, how is it that violent offenders – murderers and rapists – are entitled to financial aid, but somehow nonviolent drug offenders are less deserving? How is it that the major problem on campuses, alcohol abuse, has escaped the reach of the amendment, even though drinking is illegal for most college students, the majority of whom are under twenty-one? How is it that the politicians who crafted the amendment failed to distinguish between casual use and serious abuse? Smoking an occasional joint is no more an indicator of a crippling drug problem than underage drinking is of alcoholism. I know more than a few Wall Street stockbrokers, college professors, and high-powered lawyers who smoke marijuana on occasion.

In practical terms, the amendment hits working families and people of color the hardest. The students who need financial aid are mainly children of working families, not the children of parents with greater economic means. 'Children of the well-to-do need not worry about losing their college opportunities,' says RaiseYourVoice.com, a coalition created to repeal the amendment, and which includes the Association of Big Ten Schools, the United States Students Association, and organizations such as the American Public Health Association and the National Coalition Against Domestic Violence.

'Setbacks such as not being able to raise money for school can set a young ex-offender onto a downward spiral toward failure,' the group says. And in New York, almost 95 percent of prisoners serving time for drug offenses are people of color.

For Lenny, attending college in a field that inspires him helped him stay clean. 'It gave me back my self-esteem,' he says. 'Being in college helped me get a better job. By next year I'll be at the point where I don't need financial aid, but when I first got out of jail, believe me, I did.'

Postponing eligibility for one, two, or any number of years is a recipe for failure. It's the period directly following incarceration when ex-offenders are most at risk of recidivating. They need the structure, contact with positive people, and exposure to a mainstream lifestyle that college affords. For Lenny, who worked five days a week and attended college four nights after work, his jam-packed schedule left him no time to get high or commit a new crime.

March 7, 2000: My early editor at St. Martin's Press, Dana Albarella, is joining me on a visit to Rikers. She's interested in meeting the students, and my aspiring writers are more than eager to meet her. The highlight of the trip is that our 'chauffeur' to the Rock is Lenny. At 5 P.M. sharp, he meets us at my office in his new Ford Taurus. Like the gentleman he is, he opens the door for Dana. 'This is the first car I've owned that I didn't steal!' he announces with glee before I have a chance to introduce him. I'd told Dana that one of our most successful graduates was driving us to Rikers and hoped his outburst hadn't dissuaded her before the journey began.

As we travel over the bridge, the sunset seems unusually beautiful; or maybe it's just the experience, I think, the whir I feel in my stomach as I glance at Lenny behind the wheel, in his white-collared shirt and navy blue blazer, in a car that he bought, with registered license plates and a coveted Gate One pass on the dashboard. Even the officers have to beg for Gate Ones.

Before we enter the classroom, Dana agrees that Lenny should speak first to give her a chance to acclimate to jail and being in a classroom with twenty male inmates. Lenny starts off with a bang: 'I was a compulsive skid-bidder,' he tells the men. (Inmates call short stays on Rikers 'skid bids.') 'I ran the streets for ten years and every year I'd go to jail, get a rest, straighten out, get released, and start all over again.'

Heads nod. Doodling stops.

'It got to the point that when I came back to jail the officers would ask if I wanted the same job back. "Hey, we missed you," the kitchen workers would say.'

A couple of guys laugh knowingly. Dana looks astonished.

'My time in the free world was like a leave of absence. Every time I left, I had the best intentions but then I'd land on Queens Plaza and the welcome committee was right there waiting for me,' he says, referring to the drug dealers. 'I'd get my welfare check and I'd be off to the races. I'd break into cars, creep around at night, steal anything I could get my hands on. Then I'd sell my proceeds to the dealers for crack.'

Eventually he got tired. 'I'd be so sick and strung out that sometimes I'd just cop the fuck out because I didn't wanna be in the street anymore.'

He tells the men about his time in Fresh Start, how he sat in the very same room with the same demons and doubts they have. 'But I had dreams,' he says. And then, as if on cue, he adds: 'I wrote about them in my journal; I still keep a journal today.' When he encourages them to do the same, I want to hug him.

'I never thought I'd be able to go back to college, get a job, stop getting high. Today I have a car, insurance, and a regular paycheck.' He tells them he's a new father and a college student, that he married a woman he met in Narcotics Anonymous. 'I replaced all the negative things I was doing with positive things, and everything I have today I earned. I didn't steal nuthin' from nobody and that feels real good.

'I'm even the *treasurer* of my NA fellowship,' he says. 'People trust *me* with their money!' The guys laugh and give him an applause.

Lenny writes his phone number on the blackboard and tells them to call him when they're home. He promises to come back for their graduation in two months and he does.

A month later, I take the subway up to St. Ann's church in Harlem for the christening of Lenny's new baby, Elizabeth Grace. I recognize the gold script handwriting on the invitation as his, and think of Lenny at his kitchen table, writing the invitations after he's worked a full day, then gone to class, to an NA meeting, or to the group home for children with AIDS. On the subway to 110th Street, it occurs to me that traveling through Manhattan is like witnessing the changing of the seasons. You know exactly when and where the colors will change. At the stop in Brooklyn where I get on, the train is mostly empty save for a few blacks from the central part of the borough. As the subway car makes its way through Manhattan, it fills with white urbanites carrying briefcases or Bloomingdale's bags. By Eighty-sixth Street, only a few Caucasians remain. By 110th Street, the border of Harlem, the passengers are entirely black or Hispanic. Before I worked on Rikers, I never noticed these things.

I walk the three blocks to the church; a breeze blows garbage over my high heels. I pass by vacant lots and darkened bodegas. The church is an oasis among ruins. Inside, Lenny and his family are seated in the front pews.

After the ceremony Lenny introduces me to his son, Leonard IV. At fourteen, he's a miniature of his father. Through thick glasses, his inquisitive eyes stare up at me. I wonder if he knows I met his father in jail. He adjusts his cardigan sweater and tells me he attends a public school around the block. His favorite subject is science, he says.

'So what field do you want to get into when you're finished with school?' I ask clumsily, distracted by thoughts of how his father's decade on Rikers has affected him.

'You mean what do I want to be when I grow up?' he shoots back.

'Right.' I smile. 'Exactly.'

'I want to be a singer. A rap artist.'

A reception follows at a community center on 111th Street, on the ground floor of the building where Lenny lives with his new wife. His mother and father live in the same complex, in the same apartment where they raised Lenny and are now raising Lenny IV. Its attractive gardens and clean grounds are far more inviting than other projects I've been in, yet they have the same institutional feeling: polished linoleum floors, glazed brick, a security guard at the entrance. Another caged city.

Inside, Lenny and his wife have decorated the community room with pink and white paper flowers. Family members pour bags of potato chips and pretzels into aluminum trays, lay out platters of cold cuts, and put cans of soda on ice. Lenny sets up a stereo system in the corner. 'I Believe I Can Fly' comes on, and Lenny IV mouths the words. I marvel at Lenny's parents, watching them as they keep their eyes on all the children, hold the new baby, offer food to the guests. Lenny beams and looks radiant. I comment on his brown cashmere blazer.

'It's Brooks Brothers,' he says. 'I found an outlet in Jersey and got it for fifty dollars.' Images of Lenny in jail greens flash through my mind.

'How long has it been?'

Coincidentally, he says, 'It's exactly two years ago today since I left Rikers.'

I think of all he's accomplished since then, and I am embarrassed to remember how I thought he'd never make it; how, if it had been me conducting interviews the day he applied, I probably wouldn't have chosen him, and what that would have meant. The randomness of it all is frightening.

DWAYNE

Despite the cliché, when Dwayne and I walk down the street we look like an Oreo cookie. At six-four and built like an icebox, Dwayne is a good foot taller and more than a hundred pounds heavier than I am. His skin is dark and shiny, like charcoal. His voice resonates like a bass guitar, or a growl if he's angry, which isn't often. In fact, Dwayne is one of the gentlest men I know.

He laughs when I tell him this. 'I scared your friend,' he says. He'd recently bumped into a woman from my office on the subway. She was reading, he was standing, and when he leaned over to say 'Hi,' she jumped and dropped her paper.

From the day Dwayne left Rikers, he did everything right. And he made it all look simple, which I know, of course, it wasn't. But that's Dwayne: zero ego, iron will.

He'd been going back and forth from Rikers to the streets for many years before he joined Fresh Start at age thirty-eight. Before the drugs took hold, he worked at the Transit Authority as a token clerk. When he was in his late twenties, he started using crack. He completed a residential treatment program but relapsed several months later and never went back. 'I was too embarrassed,' he said, 'so I lived on the streets.'

I could understand his embarrassment. Dwayne's older brother is a lieutenant at NYPD. His sisters have homes, jobs, husbands, and children. His mother is a churchgoing woman and more. In a 'Tribute to Our Mothers' the inmates published in the *Rikers Review,* Dwayne wrote this about his mother:

> My mother was born in Liverpool, England, where she met my father. They came to America with two children when my mom was nineteen. She went on to have many more children, raising half of them on her own. After several years on public assistance, she volunteered for Head Start, where she became a teacher's aide. She then returned to school and managed to graduate from college with a bachelor's degree – all the while being a mother to nine children and a grandmother to eleven. Today she's a teacher for the New York City Board of Education. She teaches children with special needs and continues to work toward her master's degree in special education. My mother is a very special lady, and I look to her for inspiration.

Alongside his tribute was a poem, 'Listen to Your Mother,' which he wrote for the 'younger brothers' on Rikers.

> Here I am in jail
> Should have listened to my mother
> Here I am in jail
> Let me talk to you my brothers.
>
> Thought I was so smooth
> Thought I knew the streets so well
> Didn't listen to her warning
> And now I've slipped and fell.

Momma taught me how to talk
Say 'hello' and 'thank you, please'
Now the only thing I listen for
Is the CO with the keys.

Maybe it's not too late for you
For you have time, you see
Better listen up my brothers
Don't want to be like me.

Better listen up my brothers
Life in here is not a joke
Listen up my brothers –
Before your heart is broke.

Dwayne knew his chances of relapse were strong once he left
Rikers (most of our clients know this, but it's usually not enough to
convince them to go into a drug program directly from jail), but
when Elizabeth offered to meet him at Queens Plaza when he was
released and drive him to a program, Dwayne agreed. He was a
counselor's dream come true.

I was glad he went to the program on East Third Street because
it was close to my office and he'd sometimes stop by. The first
month was rough, he said. After being in jail for a year and living in
a crowded dorm with fifty inmates, the program wasn't much
better. Some of the counselors had only a few years of recovery as
their primary credential and were known to berate the clients. He
could only leave the facility a few hours a week until he made it to
the second month.

On one of those occasions he paid me a visit. He slumped in a
chair in my office and told me he wanted to quit – not that he
would, but he wanted to. A counselor had confronted him in group
that morning. Apparently, he had singled out Dwayne and devoted
the entire session to his faults, dissecting the choices he'd made in
life and the mess he ended up with. Counselors in therapeutic communities sometimes do this to humble an addict, to burst the
balloon of grandiosity and rid them of excuses. It takes training,

practice, and insight to run such a group, plus time to patch up the person once it's over.

Maybe the counselor thought Dwayne needed a bit of humbling. Maybe he mistook him for a slick drug dealer or a thug from the 'hood. But I'd seen Dwayne's rap sheet and knew him well. He was an addict with a record of nonviolent charges, all for drug possession, not sale. The only person Dwayne ever hurt was himself.

But there he sat, a lump of disgrace, bruised on the inside. For a moment I contemplated calling the counselor. Maybe I'd berate *him* for the mess *he* created. But I wasn't a counselor myself, and I didn't have any clinical credentials. What could I really say, *Dwayne needs to be loved, you dope, not socked in the gut?*

As he told me 'how it went down,' how humiliated and misunderstood he felt, I kept wishing Dwayne had the money, or I had the money (or I'd accepted the money Frank offered me two years before), so Dwayne could go to a private facility, the kind of place where fancy people go, where you can sleep in your own room, breathe fresh mountain air, and counselors have credentials and compassion.

'You know, Dwayne,' I said, 'that sucks.'

'Yeah, well, guess I gotta live with it.'

'Let's think about your options.'

'Don't got many. A shelter, maybe, but that would be worse.'

I agreed. 'Dwayne, from what I understand about these places, the first month is usually the hardest, kind of like in jail. A couple of Fresh Start graduates actually went to the same program you're in now and got hooked up with jobs, I think, and even housing and vocational training before they left.'

In fact, Dwayne said that the counselor promised to place him in a computer-repair program if he made it to the second phase. He decided to stick it out.

He not only completed the computer-repair program, but the company that conducted the training hired him as a computer technician a few months later. He now has his A-plus computer certification, and was the only person in his group of recovering addicts to spend eight full Saturdays in school and pass the five-hour test.

In between, we hired him at the Correctional Association for a few hours a week, where he'd help us with mailings, lug water bottles up the stairs, and do whatever jobs that required superhuman strength. Sometimes he and I would go out for coffee and, if the weather was nice, would sit in the park and talk.

One spring afternoon the recent shooting of Patrick Dorismond came up. I remember the conversation well because it was the only time I ever heard fear in Dwayne's voice. He said the incident rattled him. Dorismond, 26, was shot by a police officer in March 2000, the fourth unarmed black man to die by police fire in the previous thirteen months. His death came shortly after the verdict of the Amadou Diallo case, where four police officers were cleared of criminal charges after firing forty-one shots at the unarmed immigrant. Five days after the verdict, plainclothes officers in the Bronx killed Malcolm Ferguson, 23, also unarmed, three blocks from where Diallo was shot. Then in September police shot and killed Richard Watson, who was also unarmed. Watson was shot in the back. All of the victims were black.

What disturbed Dwayne most about the Dorismond killing was that it so easily could have been him, he said. Dorismond worked as a security guard and was minding his own business when a plainclothes police officer approached him and asked if he knew where to buy marijuana. Dorismond said he didn't. The cop pressed him and Dorismond told him to get lost. There was pushing and shoving, and in the ensuing scuffle one of the officer's backups shot Dorismond in the chest. Here was a black man who said no to drugs and got killed for it.

'That could have been me,' Dwayne said. 'I mean, I'm in recovery, I don't wanna have nothin' to do with drugs, and if some guy's in my face and keeps askin' me about drugs, and I don't know he's a police officer 'cause he's wearing street clothes, I just *hope* I'd be able to walk away. He shoulda backed off when Dorismond said no. He shouldn't have provoked him like that, and if he'd identified himself as a police officer, Dorismond wouldn't be dead.'

The following Saturday, 'more than a thousand mourners filled a funeral home in Brooklyn to pay their respects to the 26-year-old father of two,' wrote the *Times*.

As we walked back to the office, Dwayne's comments made clear to me the heavy burden that many ex-cons carry in their hearts: 'I used to think I paid my debt to society, that I done my time,' he said. 'But now I see that no matter how much I do, no matter how far I go, the police can shoot me and get away with it.'

Since Dwayne left Rikers Island two years ago, he's not only stayed off drugs and held down a job, he has quit smoking – cold turkey after ten years – and lost thirty pounds. His counselor found him a small but affordable apartment in Manhattan. 'The streets didn't get me again,' he said. 'I didn't give them time to catch me.'

MALIK

On Malik's thirteenth birthday, at six in the morning, he got a surprise: eight members of NYPD's Tactical Narcotics Team standing over him, guns pointed at his head. A sad irony was at play: When Malik heard the buzzer from the downstairs lobby of his building, he thought it was his father. 'I was thinkin' he remembered it was my birthday and came by to surprise me. Yeah, well, my surprise was TNT busting through my door looking for him.'

Malik's father was wanted for armed robbery and hadn't been home in weeks. 'I knew he was a drug addict,' Malik says, 'but nothing else, and now these big white men with black vests and guns are searching my room, under the bed, in the closet, screaming at me. "Tell us where the fuck he's hiding!"'

Malik sat in his bed while they tore apart his room. He doesn't remember saying anything. He tried not to cry. 'I was the only man in the house. I had to be strong.' But he remembers the rage. 'I thought I was going to snap, go crazy. I wanted to hurt somebody. For the first time in my life – funny how it was the day I became a teenager – I really wanted to hurt somebody.'

That night, Malik celebrated his birthday by getting drunk. His friends took him to a carnival to cheer him up, he says, but the merriment turned ugly. 'I got so wasted. I stood in the street, pulled my pants down, and screamed "Fuck everyone. Kiss my behind." I had so much pain and anger inside I wanted to drink until I died.' His friends brought him home, and he passed out – a thirteen-year-old boy whose mother died when he was four, whose father was on his way to prison.

'I have one memory of my mother,' he tells me one afternoon. He's been home from Rikers for a year and readily agrees to an interview. 'I'm on a Big Wheel and she's standing over me with her hand on my head. She's rubbing my head. I used to cry every night for my mother, because my dad always left me alone.'

Like most of my students, Malik grew up poor. He lived with his father in the slums of Tallahassee. 'My father was never home,' he said. 'I roamed the streets or hung around the local bars waitin' for him. One day I was in the bar with my aunt and she got shot by another woman. I saw the whole thing.' He describes cooking himself pork and beans from a can, finding the syringes that his father used to shoot dope, and a dog that would protect him – from his father – when the drugs kicked in.

'He'd be lookin' all crazy and just start beatin' me for the littlest thing. My dog would pin him against a wall and he'd threaten to kill him if I didn't make him stop. So I'd call off the dog and that's when he'd really beat me, with his belt or a switch from outside.'

When Malik was twelve, his father decided to leave Florida and take Malik to his grandmother's apartment in the Bronx. 'He rented a big U-Haul, and my uncle came down to help with the drive.' His father was behind the wheel – 'I think they were getting high,' he says – and he drove the U-Haul into a swamp. 'I didn't have much clothes to begin with, maybe one suit, I think, and now my clothes are in the swamp. I'm in the swamp, my cats are in the swamp, the whole truck is in the swamp. I'm hanging on to the door, there were big rats crawling on top of my clothes. I was afraid they'd eat my cats.'

They finally made it to the Bronx. 'I thought life coulda gotten better,' he says, 'but it didn't. My father continued to use drugs and my aunt who lived with us was crazy. She was admitted to Bellevue. She was also an addict.'

Given his upbringing, I'm surprised Malik even made it to Rikers at age eighteen.

It was Lenny who told him about Fresh Start. 'Lenny told me I'd learn computers, how to write. I'd seen the *Rikers Review* and knew I could do it. I didn't want to work in the bakery anymore; I wanted to better myself. But when I saw how many people were applying – I was there with Dwayne, he was like an older brother to me – I thought I'd never get in.

'I saw Barbara Margolis sitting at the table, and thought she must hear a million stories. What can I say that will make me different? How can I convince her? So I just looked her straight in the eye and said I wanted to take advantage of this opportunity to change my life and she believed me. When I found out I'd been accepted, man, that was one of the happiest days of my life.'

Malik started selling drugs when he was fourteen; he also had guns. 'I bought my first gun for fifty dollars. White guys from upstate would sell us guns. They were crack heads. They knew they could always sell us guns, and we had the drugs.' At fifteen, he was shot. 'It was just a small bullet,' he says, and rolls up his pant leg to show me the scar on his calf, the shape and color of a tiny eggplant.

Shortly thereafter, a drug sale to an undercover officer resulted in five years' probation. For two years he stayed out of trouble and reported to his probation officer regularly. 'I was in school, playing basketball, my teachers were trying to help me out, get me a basketball scholarship so I could go to college.' And then his girlfriend got pregnant.

'At that point I had to make a decision. I knew I had to get a job. So I went to McDonald's, Kmart, to the unemployment office. Every day I'd get up early, stand on line to get an interview, a factory job, anything, but I never got anything. I guess I just got tired.' He had 'friends who were making fast money,' he says, and 'when you're down, a bad offer isn't necessarily the worst offer.'

He worked as 'a lookout' on Boston Road and Seymour Avenue in the Bronx. The job was easy, he said. 'I'd stand outside for four hours and make two hundred dollars just standing there with the fellas. You get this whole attitude that you're the man, the girls are coming to see you, you're buying a lot of things.'

His next arrest sent him to Rikers. He was in my class, and I remember him as thoughtful and quiet, one of those low-maintenance students you hardly notice; their conscientiousness renders them almost invisible.

Before he got locked up, he'd filled out an application with a state-run group home for people with developmental disabilities. When he got out, he got a job at Kmart, making $5.25 an hour. He attended our Jails Anonymous meetings for support. He stayed in touch with Lenny and Dwayne, and they inspired him. Today, at age twenty, he works as a developmental aide in a group home.

'I just got a raise,' he tells me. 'I'm makin' twenty-five thousand dollars a year and I have full benefits. I don't even *stand* around drug dealers anymore. I know them, say what's up, but I keep it movin'. There's been times where I've been outta money, started to stress, and thought about making a quick buck. But then I ask myself, Are you crazy? Do you remember where you came from? As long as I can remember Rikers,' he says, 'I'll be okay.'

'It's really strange but I'm glad I got locked up. I wouldn't be where I am now if I didn't go to jail. I would have never gotten to know you guys. . . . It stayed with me that I was a Fresh Start graduate. I wanted to come out and show you that I was taking what you gave me and using it to my advantage.'

He's using it to other people's advantage as well. This former felon, who could have so easily ended up in state prison like many of his peers, now works with people with handicaps. 'We call them "consumers,"' he corrects me. 'I've learned CPR, I'm med-certified. I give them their medication. I cook their food. I change and bathe them. I blend their food so they can eat it. I change their beds.'

He's most happy, he says, when he's 'interacting' with his consumers. 'I talk to them, take them outside when I can, maybe to the park or even a restaurant if the cook agrees to blend up their food. All of them are beautiful to me.' His favorite consumer, he tells me with a smile, is an old man who is partially blind and can't speak. 'Every day I pick him up and put him in the recliner. I give him the remote, he really can't move his fingers, but I put his hand on it so he can get the sensation of pressing a button. He could be watchin' snow, but he looks up at me and smiles and I know he understands. It makes me feel so good to be able to help people.'

6

THEY KEEP COMING BACK

Can anyone get out of prison with $50, limited skills, limited education and no hope to get anything more than a minimum wage job, and then be able to support their family, make restitution, pay court costs, and pay a monthly stipend to the parole board for the privilege of being monitored? We set them up to fail and when they recidivate, we act offended. They can't make it under these circumstances and neither could you.
– Dr. H.C. Davis of the Correctional Education Association

Every year, approximately half a million people in the United States leave correctional facilities and return to society. Every *day,* approximately 350 ex-offenders return to New York City from prison or jail. The majority will be back behind bars within three years of their release.

Are so many people that incorrigible, so indelibly criminal, that returning to crime is inevitable? The ex-offenders I know suggest not. For the most part, they are a hopeful but struggling subculture of men, grappling with such questions as whether to tell an employer about their criminal history and risk not being hired; how to live on a minimum-wage salary of $240 a week when some made ten times that amount; how to follow a counselor's advice to break all ties with drug users and dealers, when such advice would eliminate most family members and friends.

'We expect individuals with convictions to reintegrate into society and lead tax-paying, law-abiding lives,' says Anita Marton, deputy director of state policy at the Legal Action Center. 'Yet we have erected an array of legal and practical barriers that bar many ex-offenders from obtaining housing, jobs, public assistance, and school loans.' Invariably, she says, this leads to the question, Are we setting people up to recidivate?

Professor Rick Curtis is an ethnographer who has been studying drug use on the streets of New York City for nearly two decades. He lives in Brownsville, Brooklyn, one of the city's 'dead zones,' where he's come to know many ex-cons. Recently, he tells me, he has detected a trend, a potential crisis he calls the 'Big Brother Crime Wave.'

'My feeling is we're now going to start paying the price for all those people we arrested ten years ago. Big brother's coming back to the city from prison.' In 1999, New York State prisons released nearly 30,000 inmates, approximately 85 percent of whom returned to one of five neighborhoods in the city. 'All of these guys are coming out of prison and there aren't many jobs they're qualified to do,' Curtis says. 'What are they going to do? There's no welfare for them either. There's no housing for them. It's a recipe for disaster.'

Eddie Ellis, who was recently released after serving out a twenty-five-year sentence for murder, agrees with Curtis's theory. 'Around the year 2005, New York is going to see the release of wave after wave of inmates, at the rate of about 30,000 a year, who were incarcerated after 1990.' Now the director of the Community Justice Center, a Harlem-based agency that helps ex-offenders, Eddie was in prison when the state began phasing out an array of vocational and academic programs. A 1998 study by the Correctional Association found that since 1991, the state has cut over 1,200 program staff positions. During that time, the state inmate population shot up from 56,000 to 71,000 prisoners. 'The next wave of inmates coming out,' Ellis says, 'represents a serious influx of people into a few communities that not only will devastate these communities but will have a larger consequence for the whole city.'

My students often speak of the 'conspiracy theory,' an intentional plan by the power brokers of society, meaning white men, to accomplish through imprisonment what was undone by slavery's abolishment: to keep them in check. When the conspiracy conversation comes up, as it does with nearly every group, I try not to refute or confirm my students' beliefs. As a white woman, the conversation for me is uncomfortable enough, and it also tends to be a circular argument that returns to the same bleak reality: that people of color, especially blacks, do have it worse in this country. Countless studies confirm their economic and political disenfranchisement, higher rates of infant mortality, below-average life span, substandard education, and overrepresentation in prison, not to mention on death row. Data from the U.S. Department of Justice show that African Americans are imprisoned at eight times the rate of whites.

In the face of statistics like these, I try to move the conversation to what my students can do about it, using their greater chances of getting caught in the criminal justice system to motivate them to avoid it at all costs. But when they bring up the subject of methadone, particularly the methadone maintenance program on Rikers, it is difficult to ignore their claims.

Methadone is a cheaply produced synthetic opiate used to detoxify heroin addicts. German chemists Isbell and Vogel were studying methadone treatment as early as the 1940s. In a 1949 article published in the *American Journal of Psychiatry*, they described methadone as 'the most satisfactory method of withdrawal' they'd seen, but they also warned of its dangers:

> Methadon [*sic*] is a dangerous addicting drug. . . . The drug in sufficient dosage produces a type of euphoria which is even more pleasant to some morphine addicts than is the euphoria produced by morphine. . . . Addicts like methadone because it produces a long sustained type of euphoria and because it suppresses signs of physical dependence when substituted for morphine. These qualities make methadone a particularly dangerous drug.

Since the 1970s, narcotics addicts entering Rikers have been able to receive heroin detoxification using methadone. Over a one-week period, they detoxed from heroin through gradually lowered dosages of methadone and then served out their sentence methadone-free. The problem came once they were released: Many returned to drugs and crime and back to Rikers again.

When the inmate population surged in the 1980s, fueled largely by drug-related arrests, overcrowding threatened jail stability. Meanwhile, 20 percent of incoming inmates tested positive for heroin, and most addicts injected the drug with needles. (Today, because it is purer, heroin is primarily sniffed.) City officials panicked that HIV/AIDS, spread largely through dirty needles shared by addicts, would reach epidemic levels.

So in 1987, they turned the methadone *detoxification* program into a methadone *maintenance* program. Known as KEEP, for Key Extended Entry Program, it allows addicts to receive methadone throughout their period of incarceration, which averages forty-five days but can be up to a year or even eighteen months. Rikers Island is the only jail system in the United States where addicts can be maintained on methadone for their entire length of stay.

The 'key' of KEEP is that addicts are released with a referral to a specified community methadone program with instructions to report in twenty-four hours. Essentially, the dirty job of detox would be done on the outside, if the person so desired, but while in jail he would be 'maintained.'

Not surprisingly, the program was controversial from the start. Jail administrators feared that giving out the powerful drug would create a black market among inmates who were not in the program, and that violence and extortion would result. There was also a philosophical opposition to methadone, not limited to correction personnel, which questioned the logic of substituting one addicting drug for another. Moreover, thirty years of research showed mixed results with regard to its effectiveness. Even among its proponents, methadone maintenance was heralded as a tool to control drug use, not to cure it.

If administered carefully, methadone can eliminate the craving for narcotics as well as the euphoric effects. Unfortunately, however, methadone is not always carefully administered. Busy jail clinicians don't have time to monitor, adjust, and re-adjust the dosages of some 2,000 inmates on methadone. On the outside, many 'methadonians,' as they're called, often use heroin and cocaine in addition to or in place of methadone. One researcher found that a large enough dose of heroin will override the methadone blockage; two others reported that 'even after significant dosage increases of methadone, clients continued to abuse other opiates.' In a 1972 study of 173 addicts in an outpatient methadone program at the Philadelphia General Hospital, 15 percent were taking methadone purchased from other patients or obtained illegally through physicians' prescriptions and over 84 percent were still using heroin, according to an article in *International Journal of the Addictions*. *Time* magazine warned in 1972 that 'methadone will turn out to be a tremendous national embarrassment.'

More than anything, methadone maintenance was designed as a 'medical lollipop' to lure addicts into treatment and expose them to necessary lifestyle changes. 'Proponents of methadone maintenance have never claimed that it was to be the sole modality for treating drug addicts. It was thought of as a holding action rather than a lifelong proposition,' write Samuel Yochelson and Stanton Samenow in *The Criminal Personality*. Indeed, in an evaluation of KEEP, drug researcher Stephen Magura reports: 'The original concept of KEEP also involved making a full range of long-term drug treatment modalities available to KEEP participants at release.' Magura's findings were published in the *Journal of Drug Issues*, in 1993, and they reveal a number of flaws with the program.

The only thing I knew about KEEP when I started teaching on Rikers was that Fresh Start didn't accept inmates who were in KEEP. 'But don't make a general announcement,' my supervisor said. 'Just ask the inmate privately in the interview, and see if he's interested in getting out of the program.' Apparently, various city and state officials supported the program, and we had been warned about discriminating against KEEP participants.

We didn't want them in the program, my supervisor explained, because methadone is a coveted jailhouse item that inmates are known to fight over or barter with. The other reason, she said, is that the men are given such high dosages they're often groggy and high, making working with knives in the cooking class dangerous and learning computers virtually impossible. I thought it sounded reasonable, and when I met Anthony, I was convinced.

ANTHONY

Before Rikers, Anthony had been attending Columbia University, an eye-catching detail he noted on his Fresh Start application. During the interview he explained that his recreational heroin habit had turned into a crippling addiction. The problem, he said, was that every time he came to Rikers he was steered into KEEP, and as a result he never got straight. He was released with a habit that was as bad as the one he came in with.

The good news was that he wanted to join Fresh Start and was willing to stop taking methadone.

'That's great,' I said. Not only was Anthony tremendously likable, but he also wrote like a pro. In fact, the first article he submitted was a trenchant critique of KEEP. We couldn't publish it in the *Rikers Review*, but *Prison Life* magazine was pleased to accept it. Titled 'Rikers Highland,' it reveals the problems with methadone maintenance in jail:

At Rikers Island, at least in the two jails (C95 and C76) where I've spent time, if you've got the commissary or the cigarettes, you can always find some drugs to help pass the time. For me, this was a mixed blessing, because it was my drug addiction that kept catapulting me back to the island.

Heroin was my drug of choice. Before my most recent bout, I had been straight for several years, which had rewarded me with a good job, a long-term relationship and a Manhattan apartment with all the trimmings. My downfall began when I visited a buddy in London. The plan was to indulge for a couple of days and then resume my sober life when I returned to New York.

Problem was, after I got back, I conned myself into thinking I could continue shooting heroin recreationally. To make a long story short, within six months I'd lost my job, my apartment, my girlfriend and most everything I owned. Then I started getting arrested. My habit had me so strung out I couldn't do anything in the morning before feeding the monkey. This included attending community service and making it to court. So one by one my arrests turned into warrants, until eventually jail time was the only alternative the judge could consider. I blew every chance the court gave me; I'd gotten so used to kicking dope on the floor of Manhattan Central Booking that the nurses knew me on a first name basis. I got used to arriving at Rikers like the walking dead with one goal in mind – METHADONE!

Dope fiends like me were always amazed to find that the city's liberal attitudes toward criminology extended to the detoxification of heroin addicts via methadone, a synthetic form of heroin. Most amazing, methadone is offered for *entire* sentences at Rikers. Methadone is so powerful it keeps addicts 'straight' for over 24 hours, whereas heroin lasts only 4 to 6 hours. To describe the program as popular with prisoners would be an understatement at best.

There are, however, some serious problems with methadone maintenance. One is that an addict can leave jail with a worse habit than he came in with. For me, I could have used jail time to kick the habit and get a sober perspective on life, but I never got to the point where I was able to 'say no' to dope. It's far more difficult to make the decision to be drug-free if you haven't had a drug-free day in years. Historically, jail provided that period of sobriety from which countless alcoholics and addicts have been able to see there's another way to live, and then choose that way.

But for new detainees like myself going through withdrawal on the bullpen floor, methadone was the light at the end of the tunnel. I would tell myself that if I could just hold on until I saw the doctor, everything would be all right. And sure enough, my time would come: The doctor would take one look at me and within a few hours, the pain would be gone.

And once you're on the monkey juice, as it's known by the inmates, Rikers isn't such a bad place. You can sleep 16 hours a day; you can eat, or not eat, the prison food. Even if the days drag on a bit, you're half in the bag anyway.

Prisoners, like all of society, cannot afford to be confused about the ultimate effects of methadone. At best, those on methadone settle down to a life of quiet addiction. But many do not. They inject cocaine instead of heroin and continue their criminal activity. While methadone is neither a substitute for sobriety nor true treatment for drug addiction, it may still be preferable to no intervention at all. It is virtually free when compared with the cost of true drug treatment – and this makes it particularly seductive to bureaucrats under pressure to do something about the drug problem. Methadone can be part of a rational response to addiction, but don't kid yourself – it's no panacea.

You don't find many firsthand accounts like Anthony's in the literature because the majority of methadonians live on the fringes of society. Indeed, they are among the most marginalized inmates I've met on the Rock.

In the fall of 1997 I asked my captain friend if he could take me to the 'KEEP line' so I could interview some inmates for a research paper I was writing.

'No problem,' he said, and escorted me to the corridor in C-76, where two hundred inmates lined the wall. The few white guys were horribly skinny and pale, shaky albino scarecrows. Nearly all of the inmates were perspiring despite the early winter draft.

I conducted random interviews with five men, lasting about fifteen minutes apiece. I spoke with the CO who oversees KEEP and the nurse who administers the methadone. Everyone was eager to talk; few had anything good to say about the program.

The first man I speak with is Tomas. 'There's no "h" in that,' he says, pointing to my pad. Tomas is a thin and toothless African American, thirty-one years old. He's been an addict for eight years; in the past eleven months, he's been to Rikers seven times. On each of his bids, he signs up for KEEP. His current dosage is seventy milligrams a day.

I ask about the high dosage. When Magura evaluated the program, inmates were maintained on thirty milligrams a day if they weren't enrolled in a methadone program on the outside and forty milligrams a day if they were. Supporters of KEEP say that heroin today is purer, thus the higher dosages.

'I started on twenty milligrams but the clinic raised me up and now I feel great,' he says, grinning a gummy smile.

I ask if he gets a referral to a clinic in the community before he leaves.

'I don't remember.'

Some medical lollipop, I think. A referral to a clinic was supposed to be the cornerstone of KEEP, and this guy doesn't even remember if he got one.

'Actually,' he adds, 'I think you can get a referral, but I don't bother 'cause the clinic's too far for me to go and I don't have Medicaid [health insurance for the poor, which is required at some clinics to receive methadone]. Then I usually don't have car fare, either, so that's a problem too.'

'Great system, huh?'

'Yeah, well.' He shrugs. 'When I'm here, I get KEEP. When I'm out, I just go back to heroin.'

Because he's released with a seventy-milligram habit, he adds, 'I need seven to eight bags of dope a day just to feel well. I don't even like getting high anymore. I just don't want to feel bad. I don't want to feel the pain.'

Reginald is in his late forties. He's more animated and healthy-looking than Tomas. In fact, he's rather engaging. I start by asking him if he's been to Rikers before.

'When you mean? This year or total?'

'Total,' I say.

'My God, woman! Now that's a hard one.' He squints and looks toward the ceiling. 'I musta been to Rikers *at least fifty times* in the past fifteen years!' The number seems to surprise him as much as it does me.

'Doesn't all this jail time get to you?' I ask. 'Aren't you tired of being bossed around and eating mess-hall food?'

'Well, not really. I mean, it's easier to come here, get high, and get fed than to have to hustle on the streets for a fix.'

'You don't have to tell me, Reginald, but can I ask why you're here?'

'Boosting,' he says, not missing a beat. (Boosting is jailhouse slang for shoplifting.) 'But I used to be a stickup guy – you know, rob people so I could buy dope, but then I realized that stickups mean five years upstate, and there's no methadone up there, so I learned how to boost, and it's actually more fun.'

'Fun?'

'Yeah, 'cause I get to use my brain. Feels *good* to use your brain, know what I'm sayin'?'

'Yes, yes,' I agree, 'it does feel good to use your brain, and it's less dangerous than stickups, I bet.'

'Right! So, as I was sayin', boostin' gets me just as much money and less time in the joint. I get sentenced to jail time 'stead of prison, and once I'm here I get my methadone.'

Since the conversation is going so well, I ask him about 'methadone diversion,' the Department's fear before the program was implemented.

'How do you know 'bout that? You been locked up, too?'

'No, not really. I teach a class here. My students tell me about it.'

Reginald confirms that methadone is 'a hot item for sale.' It wasn't always so popular, he said, but when new inmates started getting surcharges in the mid 1990s, the guys in KEEP had a chit to bargain with.

As part of recent get-tough legislation, inmates now begin their sentence with a $150 surcharge, meaning that their commissary accounts open with a negative balance of $150, leaving them no money to purchase such jailhouse staples as deodorant or cigarettes. I once asked a deputy warden if he didn't think it was rather harsh, not to mention gross, to deprive inmates of deodorant. 'It's in the soap,' he said testily. When I raised my eyebrows, he returned a steely stare. 'Why are you looking at me funny? I *told* you, the soap we give them has deodorant *in* it.' He enunciated every consonant.

Ever since the surcharge was introduced, not an issue of the *Rikers Review* is published without one of the inmates writing a story about the 'infamous surcharge.' The first-timers talk about the shock of arriving on Rikers to discover that they have a surcharge that will take ten weeks of menial labor to pay off. In the meantime, if they don't have someone on the outside to send them money, and many of them don't, they do things like wash another inmate's clothes, write letters for illiterate inmates, or draw cards in exchange for cigarettes or deodorant.

If an inmate fails to pay off his surcharge by the time he's released, a warrant is issued for his arrest. My current group of students say they know several inmates who are serving jail time today because they did not pay their surcharge from a previous incarceration.

'But us guys on KEEP are lucky,' says Reginald. 'We can sell our methadone when times are hard.' He explains how it gets back to the dorms. 'When the guard's not looking, you don't swallow. You go back to the dorm and spit it up in a cup and sell it. It's easier to do this when the regular CO's not here – the guys who fill in never watch and don't make you talk, like he sometimes does.' He points to the CO at the front of the line.

Then he mentions something I've never heard of, and which sounds pretty hard to pull off. Called the 'gypsy switch,' it works like this: The inmate attaches a plastic bag to the front of his shirt, and when he gets his methadone, he throws back his head in a straight-down-the-hatch kind of motion. The methadone, however, goes straight into the bag, which the inmate twists shut and sells quickly back in the dorms. Methadone buyers appreciate the hygienic touch and apparently pay more.

The CO watching over the KEEP line has also been watching me. As I wrap up the interview with Reginald, he taps me on the shoulder. 'Don't forget about me.' He winks. After two years on the post, he has a lot to say.

He begins by saying he's 'seen it all,' and describes the program as 'ridiculous.' 'How can it be doing any good? I'm always seeing the same faces.' He illustrates his point with an example. 'Once an inmate is released, it takes two or three days before his name is deleted from the list.' He holds out a computer printout of inmate names and ID numbers. 'Sometimes a guy is released and back here before his name's even crossed off the list.'

Another problem he sees is the high dosage. 'I have guys here getting a hundred milligrams a pop. The doctor gives 'em a hard time if they want to reduce it.'

I mention that some researchers believe that high dosages block cravings.

'Baloney,' he says. 'What a bunch of garbage. You believe that?'

'Well, I'm not a doctor –'

He cuts me off with a wave of his hand. 'Listen, this is the deal: These guys come here, get high, and then get released with an addiction, usually without a home, with three tokens to their name and no skills, and we wonder why they keep coming back to KEEP. Hey' – he laughs – 'that's a good one!'

My field research is becoming dark comedy.

I speak with the nurse who hands out the methadone in small paper cups from behind a window. She shares the CO's cynicism. 'I don't see the purpose of this,' she says. 'They're not getting off heroin when they get out and they keep [the word is beginning to annoy me] recommitting crime. All they have to do is play a good game and the doctor gets them into KEEP.'

By this time I feel like I need KEEP myself.

My next stop is the administration office on Rikers that coordinates the program. I ask if the director's around and might have a few minutes to speak with me. A counselor, eating a sandwich at her desk, says he's out. I leave a note with my phone number, explaining that I'm doing research for a paper on methadone.

The counselor offers to answer my questions, which helps because the director never does call me back, despite two more messages.

I ask why inmates are given such high dosages and why they're discouraged from getting out of KEEP.

'We encourage people to be on seventy milligrams because that's the blockage dose,' she says as if reading from a script. 'They need that amount so they won't suffer withdrawal symptoms. At that level the urge to get high is completely suppressed. We encourage people to detox on the outside. Whatever changes need to be made can be made on the outside. We don't detox here.'

'Why? Isn't jail as good a place as any?'

'You'll have to ask the director.'

Back then, I was horrified. Nothing about the program made sense. Even Magura's evaluation study showed that '88% of KEEP participants and 85% of controls reported returning to heroin and/or cocaine use after release from Rikers.' With an evaluation like that, you'd think the program would be shut down.

Today, I know there is much about prisons and jails in this country that doesn't make sense, and wise advocates choose their battles carefully. But with regard to KEEP, I am glad we broke the rules and bucked the system. I'm glad we told Anthony and many others that they couldn't join Fresh Start unless they left KEEP. I doubt Anthony would be where he is today if he hadn't.

After leaving Rikers, Anthony entered a residential drug-treatment program where abstinence, not methadone, is the goal. Today he's a computer networker with a six-figure salary. He's going on five years clean.

TYRONE

September 5, 1999: Tonight I had dinner with Tyrone and his grandmother in the Bronx. It was the first time a graduate invited me to his home for dinner, and I was flattered. Tyrone said he wanted to cook. In fact, he said, he loves to cook. 'I used to cook for sixty kids at a time in the group home where I grew up.'

'Grandma,' he tells me later, is not his real grandmother. She's actually the grandmother of his ex-girlfriend, Katrina. The three of them lived together before Katrina got lost in the drug world and Tyrone got sentenced to a year on Rikers for auto theft. Nevertheless, Grandma asked Tyrone to live with her when he got out. Katrina was bouncing between the streets and the psych ward at Bellevue, but Grandma was fond of Tyrone and could use a man around, she said. He was glad to have a home to return to when he left jail.

Tyrone was something of a cook, I recalled, and a fine writer as well. He once wrote a hysterical review of the mess hall for the *Rikers Review* modeled after *The New York Times*' 'Dining In' section, the title of which seemed particularly fitting for diners confined on the Rock. The idea was actually suggested by journalist Michael Massing, author of *The Fix,* whom I brought to Rikers for a special meet-the-author class. He ended up brainstorming with the students – and he told me repeatedly how much they impressed him – about articles for the *Rikers Review*. Mimicking the highbrow tone of a food critic, Tyrone wrote:

Here we are at the famous CIFM mess hall, one of the busiest restaurants in all the five boroughs. Over a thousand diners eat here daily. This restaurant does not discriminate.

CIFM has many hosts, all in matching uniforms. Sometimes they physically escort you to your seat. Because this restaurant is so popular, it is often crowded and noisy. The hosts can be known to rush people out.

Appealing to budget-conscious diners, tips are completely unnecessary. In fact, everything – including both meals and service – is on the house. What a deal!

Allow me to let you in on a little secret: Every Sunday and Thursday the restaurant features 'the catch of the day.' I suggest you try it because it tastes like nothing you've ever had, and I dare say you probably haven't. You might think it's chicken, but it's not – it's seagull.

The one dish I won't recommend is the beef chunk stew. At first glance it looked delicious, but I must say I could hardly chew through all the gristle and fat. When I tried to leave my table to speak with the chef, one of the uniformed hosts stopped me in my tracks and told me to take a seat. I called upon another uniformed host and asked if I could exchange my meal. In the rudest of tones he replied, 'If you don't like it, throw it out.' In all my years of dining out (I mean 'in') I have *never* been spoken to in such a hostile manner.

A final quirk I should also alert you to is that the restaurant closes and opens very early. One night – it was around 8:00 P.M. – I dropped by for a little snack to tide me over 'til morning. To my surprise, the restaurant was closed. At eight o'clock? 'How can this be?' I asked. A uniformed host told me to come back the next morning, when the doors reopen at 5:30.

On the way to the Bronx to meet Tyrone and Grandma, I stop at 149th Street and Grand Concourse to change trains. I notice how grubby and desolate the station appears compared to (some of) the gleaming and busy stations in Manhattan. More than twenty min-utes go by before the Number 4 train finally arrives – another hazard of life on the outskirts. As the train pulls out of the tunnel and ascends the elevated tracks, my stomach tightens with the sick feel-ing that overcame me when I worked in the Bronx two years ago. Outside the window junk-filled lots and graffiti-covered buildings whiz by. Even going fast the decay smacks you in the face. A hulk of a housing project looms across the tracks, looking more like a prison than a residential dwelling. Sheets on a clothesline, drawn between two windows, flap in the wind. 'Why would anyone dry clean sheets in dirty city air?' I once asked Angel Rivera, who lives in the Bronx. 'Because they can't afford dryers,' he said.

Liquor stores and check-cashing centers punctuate the streets, reminding me of a bleak, wintry day when my colleagues and I posted flyers in a check-cashing center announcing our job-training program for welfare recipients. We knew that welfare recipients cashed their checks there, and we were desperate to find clients, as our program was beginning in two weeks. The city's sprawling wel-fare agency, the Office of Human Resources Administration (HRA), was a funder of the program and had promised to send us interested clients, which was appropriate since HRA is the clearinghouse for welfare recipients. The promise didn't pan out. There were morn-ings while jogging in the park when I'd approach workfare people (welfare recipients whom the city pays $68.50 every two weeks in order to receive public assistance) and ask if they'd rather learn to cook instead of pick up trash.

Fresh Start's 'training-first' program, the brainchild of Fred Patrick, a progressive deputy commissioner at the Department of Correction, was a novel idea in the new era of welfare reform. In an unusual collaboration, three city agencies, the Department of Correction, HRA, and the Department of Employment, contracted with Fresh Start to recruit and train 100 welfare recipients for insti-tutional cooking positions in the jails. Unfortunately, by the time the contract was signed there weren't as many cook openings as pre-dicted, so much of the job development for a population known as 'the hard-core unemployable' had to be done in-house. The con-tract stipulated that we find jobs for 65 percent of the trainees.

(Most welfare-to-work programs consider a 40 percent placement rate to be high.)

Oddly, on the first day of training, a third of our carefully screened and seemingly eager participants didn't show up. How could this be? I wondered, thinking that ours was the most popular workfare assignment in town, offering training, counseling, and the promise of a job. Even though the jobs were on Rikers, because they were city jobs they came with a pension and a $30,000-a-year salary. In fact, over 250 welfare recipients had come to the open house we'd held the month before. The line trailed halfway down the block.

The students didn't show up, we learned, because HRA had failed to transfer them from their previous workfare assignment into our program, leaving them in welfare-land limbo and without the transportation money they needed to get to the training site. To be fair, the size of the city's welfare population is massive, and despite drastic reductions over the past five years, keeping track of the caseloads of roughly 725,000 parents and children is no small undertaking. But my colleagues and I soon came to see that training the participants, even finding them jobs, was far easier than battling the bureaucracy of HRA for the simplest things we needed to make the program work. I used to think that people on welfare had it easy, but my attitude changed when I saw how the system worked and how tough new reforms fully discouraged people from accessing public assistance. (These hurdles are documented in detail in a 1999 study by the Association of the Bar of the City of New York.) Many days I wondered how the trainees in our program and my clients from Rikers managed to fill out the endless paperwork and comply with the complicated regulations when their college-educated director couldn't cut through the red tape.

Someone like Stanley comes to mind, a recovering addict who felt he was ready to re-enter the job market and work as a cook. He called one day to say he'd be late because he'd burned himself ironing his shirt. (We had an employer coming that day and he wanted to look professional.) When Stanley arrived – I'll never forget this – half of his face was covered with a burn in the shape of a triangle.

His eyes were tearing from pain, but he didn't want to miss the class. Stanley explained that he was ironing his shirt when the phone rang. He put down the iron, went to pick up the phone, but somehow his signals got crossed and he ended up with the iron to his ear. Two years later I bumped into Stanley on the subway. The burn mark had faded but he was still unemployed. He had TB, he said, which barred him from working in a kitchen. The welfare agency had assigned him a job picking up trash in the park, which he didn't seem to mind. 'It's better than sitting at home,' he said. For 'hard-core unemployable' people like Stanley, a job such as this is probably better than nothing, and at $68.50 every two weeks, the city's got a deal. However, the words of HRA's new commissioner, Jason Turner, seem particularly harsh when it comes to people like Stanley – and the other individuals in our program who were just as disorganized and ill prepared to enter the workforce as he was:

Many individuals we try and help have had an absence of boundaries; they have had excess freedom. . . . What we need to create is something that was not possible in the old entitlement system – an urgency to take action. We need to create, if you will, a personal crisis in individuals' lives which can be [used] constructively as a tool for helping them.

A more hopeful encounter was meeting a former trainee from our program on Queens Plaza. Mira was from Russia and could barely speak English when she came to us. She applied for welfare when an injury left her husband out of a job. They had two young children, whom he looked after while Mira cleaned city office buildings as part of her workfare assignment. We almost didn't accept her into the program because of her limited English, thinking she would be unable to read recipes or understand the instructors. But she turned out to be one of the best students, reading a dictionary during her lunch hour and landing one of the coveted cook jobs on Rikers. When I saw her that night on Queens Plaza, she was still in her uniform, on her way home from work after eight hours in jail. It was a week before Christmas and she burst into tears when we hugged hello. For the first time in three years, she said, she was able to buy

Christmas presents for her children. 'Thank you,' she said, over and over, 'thank you for believing in me.'

We were able to believe in Mira and the other welfare recipients who went through our training program because, back then, city officials emphasized a 'training-first' versus 'work-first' approach to welfare reform. Training-first programs begin with 'tough love' and changing attitudes. They offer life-skills classes – how to manage money, get along with co-workers and resolve conflicts – and then move on to real-life job training in fields where viable employment opportunities exist. After training and job placement, there is follow-up and counseling to help ensure job retention. This approach enabled us to reach our goal of training and finding jobs for sixty-five welfare recipients in less than a year.

When Tyrone asked me to dinner, I told him I'd go if he'd let me buy the groceries because I knew he was broke. He had applied for public assistance after he left Rikers, but it takes forty-five days for checks to be processed. Tyrone, like most of my clients from jail, needs public assistance immediately – and temporarily – to get on his feet. They need money to get transportation to interviews and maybe buy a shirt and tie. He had visited the HRA office, filled out the paperwork, and been to the new 'Job Center' to find work. (Mayor Giuliani and Commissioner Turner began converting HRA's Income Support Centers to Job Centers in 1998.) 'It's getting harder and harder not to go back to the game [selling drugs],' he said. 'I've borrowed what little money I can from Grandma.' Her telephone service was temporarily disconnected. 'And that was the phone number I put down on job applications,' he told me.

After fifty days went by, I called an old contact from HRA, hoping he'd accept my call. (I used to badger Lloyd almost daily when I was directing the welfare-to-work program.) Lloyd was a senior-level manager at HRA who had access to all the files of public-assistance recipients in New York City. With a few taps on his keyboard he could call up a case and make an adjustment. I called him the Wizard of Welfare, envisioning him at a great console, the lives of a million people in his hands, their fates within striking distance of his fingertips.

'Just like old times,' I sighed when he told me that the caseworker assigned to Tyrone had quit and his application got lost in the shuffle. 'Tell him to be patient,' Lloyd said. 'Call me back in a week if he doesn't receive a check.' Well-meaning advice, but it doesn't mean much to a person whose phone has been disconnected.

I arrive at Burnside Avenue and call Tyrone from a pay phone. He's on his way, he says, and I wait outside a bodega, staring at the potholes in the street, the traffic under the elevated subway platform, the train overhead that screeches so loud it's painful; at the obvious dealers on the corner, the shopkeepers pulling heavy metal gates over their doors, just like we used to do at closing time, usually breaking a nail in the process; at the men standing next to me, staring, because I stared briefly at them, thinking I recognized a face from Rikers Island. Even the Indian summer sun and blue sky can't punch a hole in the misery of this place.

Tyrone and I head to the supermarket, which is clean and well stocked. He shows me the cube steak he wants to cook and says it's delicious. He has the menu all planned: pan-fried steak, rice with green peppers, corn bread, a vegetable. We buy an Entenmanns's chocolate cake and Turkey Hill vanilla ice cream. I throw in a basket of strawberries, thinking of Grandma.

We walk with our groceries to Grandma's building, about ten minutes away on a quiet residential street. The grass is lush and mowed, surrounded by a chain-link fence, with a sign saying KEEP OFF THE GRASS! Inside, the apartment is sparsely furnished and devoid of all but essentials. Tyrone explains that's because Katrina, his old girlfriend, destroyed the place one night in the throes of a mental breakdown – her children had been taken away from her and the foster family was planning to adopt them. Given Katrina's history of self-mutilation, crack use, and mental illness, she knew her chances of getting her children back were slim to none.

'She broke all Grandma's china,' Tyrone says, plus the mirrors, pictures, and knickknacks. The only wall adornment I notice is a two-year-old calendar, advertising a local deli, hanging on a nail in the hallway. In the main living area there's a sagging couch, some chairs, a coffee table, and two cots with rumpled blankets. A 'dresser' made of milk crates contains neatly folded clothes and doubles as a nightstand. On the top are toiletries, deodorant, Johnson's baby powder, perfume, and a hairbrush. A TV and stereo are stacked against a wall. There isn't a book in sight.

I go to the bathroom to wash my hands before we start cooking. Despite a few roaches near the faucet, it's as clean as it can get. There aren't any towels so I dry my hands on my pants. I peek in the shower: no bottles of shampoo or even a bar of soap. Nothing except a water bug stuck in the drain. It's alive, I notice, trying to escape.

7

STRAIN OF TWO CITIES

Society itself contains the germs of all the crimes committed. It is the social state, in some measure, which prepares these crimes, and the criminal is merely the instrument which executes them.

— Adolphe Quételet, *On Man,* 1835

Finally, the most certain but most difficult way to prevent crimes is to perfect education.

— Cesare Beccaria, *On Crimes and Punishments,* 1764

ANGEL: PART II

On a snowy evening in 1994, Angel Rivera was released from state prison. He had a bus ticket home and a thin brown trench coat, courtesy of the Correction Department. It was better than nothing, and at least he had a place to go. His sister, who lived in a small, fourth-floor walk-up in the Bronx, had offered him the couch.

Angel stayed with her for a while and went to an employment agency that helps ex-offenders find jobs. I made a call on his behalf to a director I know there and asked him to take care of Mr. Rivera. At an agency deluged with clients, calls like this matter; in Angel's case it did. They found him a job, at eight dollars an hour, as a handyman in a hospice for people with AIDS.

He stayed for a year and did well: arrived early, worked overtime when needed, and did everything from changing lightbulbs to installing electrical wiring. But when the agency lost a contract, his schedule was reduced to part time. I know this because I spoke with his supervisor, just to make sure there wasn't something they could do. He didn't want to reduce Angel's hours either, he said, but the matter was out of his hands.

I was happy to help Angel when I could, not only because he was the first 'criminal' I met and my early penology tutor, but also because he'd always treated me with decency and kindness, and because opening a door for him was what people had done for me.

He showed his appreciation in more ways than I can name, but one incident stands out in particular.

I was moving from Manhattan to Brooklyn, and although I had hired a moving company, Angel insisted on helping. He showed up with two cups of coffee and dressed in his maintenance uniform. Because of the uniform, the movers thought I'd hired a special 'overseer' for the job, and Angel was delighted to take on the role. He coordinated the entire move, made sure they handled my belongings with care, and rode with them in the truck to Brooklyn. 'I'll make sure they don't stop for coffee and doughnuts and blame it on the traffic,' he said, knowing I was paying them by the hour. 'It takes a crook to know one,' he joked.

By this time Angel had his own place: a dark basement apartment in the South Bronx with a bathroom down the hall he shared with three other tenants. He chose it because the rent, at $100 a week, was affordable while he was working full time. When he was reduced from full time to part-time hours, I was amazed he didn't return to crime.

On his days off he filled out job applications and went on interviews. At the time, New York City had a high unemployment rate (approximately 9 percent); the felony conviction on his rap sheet and the gaps in his résumé only made matters worse. 'I feel like I'll never stop paying for the past,' he said. 'I've done my time, but it doesn't seem to matter.'

Luckily, a volunteer at Fresh Start, Shiela Rosenblatt, referred him to a maintenance job in a building owned by her husband. To spare Angel the anxiety, Shiela told the personnel manager in advance that he had a record but that he'd been out and working for the past year. Because the maintenance team was unionized, however, the best she could offer was work on an 'as needed' basis.

Angel was paid ten dollars an hour and, on good weeks, was given four days of work.

Several months later Angel and I met for breakfast, and the minute I saw him I knew he was sick. Even through his coat the weight loss was noticeable. 'I can't hold down any food,' he said. 'I've lost almost twenty pounds.'

I asked if he'd seen a doctor, and he reminded me that he didn't have health insurance. 'I'll just wait 'til it's bad enough and then go to the emergency room,' he said. He'd almost passed out on the subway the night before, but felt better when he got home. 'I fell asleep and hoped it would pass by morning,' he said, as he'd done every night for a month.

Like many of the 'working poor,' Angel wasn't poor enough for Medicaid, which in New York usually requires that a person be on welfare. But now that he was sick, his job was in jeopardy and he could end up on welfare after all.

I called my friend Dr. Peter Meacher, who's a family practitioner at a community clinic in the Bronx. Through a federally funded program, the clinic can treat patients like Angel who have neither Medicaid nor outside health insurance. Angel wasn't a drug user and never had been, but still I feared the worst.

'What's depressing about his ailment,' Peter told me after he saw Angel, 'is how treatable it was. I wish he'd seen me a month ago.' He gave Angel antibiotics, and within a few days he could hold down food. 'Please tell him to come back and see me if he has any more problems,' Peter said. 'He's such a sweet man, and his life is more stable than most of my patients.'

The first thing Peter does with new patients is a 'geneogram,' where he asks them to sketch their family tree. 'Every single person will have lost one, two, or maybe three family members to AIDS, gunfire, or some other violent incident,' he tells me. 'Nearly all have a relative who is incarcerated. It is absolutely striking.'

On any given day, he adds, 'armies of grandmothers' with small children crowd the waiting room. The children's mothers have died of AIDS or are in prison. The grandmothers become their de facto caregivers.

'The level of stress in their lives is huge,' he says. 'Their personal experience with trauma is astounding.' Several months ago, he started a smoking cessation clinic. Every day the sign-up sheet was filled with names. 'At the first session a man got up and thanked us profusely. He said it was the first time the South Bronx offered a group like this.

'For people in Manhattan, where I live,' Peter says, 'it would simply be a matter of choosing which group to go to. Here, a smoking cessation group is a novel concept because people have far more pressing needs.'

Angel continued to work on an 'as-needed' basis for three years, making ends meet as best he could. Then one day he received a call from the woman in Personnel. She felt badly that they hadn't been able to hire him full time, she said; when a colleague at a prestigious Manhattan ad agency asked if she knew any maintenance workers for a soon-to-be-vacant position, she recommended Angel, and he got the job.

He now has medical coverage, three weeks' vacation, and a $23,000 salary. And he recently gave me a gift: a business card with the title 'maintenance specialist' under his name. 'I feel like I'm finally starting my life,' he said on his fiftieth birthday. 'Now all I need is a new place to live, with a bathroom all to myself.'

I was leaving my office for a game of squash one evening when I received a call from a Fresh Start graduate. 'I got the job!' he said, referring to a dishwasher position in a Manhattan restaurant. A volunteer chef in the cooking program had given him the lead, and he'd followed up on it when he was released. 'And it's no minimum-wage job, either,' he said. 'I'm making eight dollars an hour.'

Less than an hour later, my squash partner and I exchange hellos on the court. He's a dealmaker (that is his word) on Wall Street and elsewhere and appears as elated as my client sounded over the phone. 'Great day!' he says between stretches. 'Made half a million dollars. This market's incredible!'

Half a million dollars in one day, I'm thinking when he asks me how my day was. 'Great. One of my clients got a job making eight dollars an hour as a dishwasher.'

Like my father, who also worked on Wall Street, Eric laughs when I refer to my students as 'clients.' In their world, clients wear suits and ties and pay high fees for expert advice. In my world, clients wear jailhouse greens and receive our services for free. And I know from experience that the advice I give is far from expert: It's listening and following my gut, and it's wrong as often as it's right.

After the squash game, I am Eric's lucky dinner guest. We go to a four-star restaurant – for no other reason than the fact that he has a refined palate and the money to pay for it. As always, I'm happy to accompany him.

Tonight we're at Lespinasse, an opulent restaurant in midtown Manhattan. A tower of lilies and roses rises from the floor in the center of the main dining room. I stop briefly to smell a lily and, hours later, the attentive maitre d' surprises me with a bouquet of sprays when we leave. The entire room sparkles from the gold-framed mirrors, the huge chandelier, the diamonds flashing on earlobes and fingers. The menu is equally rich: foie gras, white truffles, quenelles, gianduia mousse. For the price of an appetizer, it occurs to me, my ex-inmate student would have to wash dishes for four hours. (It's true: In some Manhattan restaurants, appetizers cost more than thirty dollars.)

Moments such as these provide a real-life context for understanding a central New York paradox: the pockets of ultrarich and ultrapoor that dot the city's landscape, sometimes co-existing within blocks of each other. I've had the opportunity to visit both worlds, occasionally on the same day, but these days it seems as if the pockets of the rich are growing deeper, while those of the poor are remaining just as shallow. Several new studies confirm this.

'The Wall Street boom is widening the income gap between the poorest and richest U.S. families – and New York has the biggest spread,' says an article in the *New York Post,* citing a joint study by the Center on Budget and Policy Priorities and the Economic Policy Institute published in February 2000. 'The gap between the rich and the poor was widest in New York, with the poorest fifth earning $10,770 in 1998, down $1,970 since 1988, and the wealthiest fifth earning $152,350, up $19,680 during the same period.' The study attributed the widening gap to Wall Street's long-running bull market, which favors wealthy investors; lower-paying service jobs replacing manufacturing jobs; and the largely stagnant minimum wage. 'The benefits of this [economic] growth have not been equally distributed,' said Elizabeth McNichol, one of the study's authors. 'The incomes of the poor and middle class have fallen or stagnated.'

The New York Times also covered the study. 'Despite the strongest economy in years, nearly one out of four New York City residents had incomes below the Federal Government's poverty threshold in 1998,' it said, a rate that has 'barely dropped since the last recession,' and that 'is twice as high as the national average.'

Indeed, Census Bureau data on poverty rates in the largest metropolitan areas in America confirm that New York's economy is 'lagging behind in lifting the incomes of the poor.' A senior economist with the Bureau of Labor Statistics found it 'striking' that the 24 percent poverty rate of the New York–New Jersey metropolitan area in 1998 was higher than that in the greater metropolitan regions of Los Angeles (22.5), Chicago (17.3), Detroit (22.4), Washington (23.8), Philadelphia (8), Boston (22.1), and Dallas (17.1). Only Houston, with a poverty rate of 28.1 percent, was higher.

'The financial pages report daily on a stock market boom, but the median household's wealth is falling, not rising,' writes Lester C. Thurow, a professor of economics and former dean of Massachusetts Institute of Technology's Sloan School of Management, in *USA Today*. 'The bottom 20 percent of the population owes more than it owns. Ninety percent of the economy's capital gains goes to the top 20 percent.' The potential problems of income inequality, he states, are political, not economic. 'Capitalism, it should be remembered, happily co-existed with slavery for much of America's history. . . . Maybe America will just have to live with much higher levels of inequality,' he adds. 'India does – and it is, after all, a democracy.'

How does income inequality affect crime? One need only glance at any criminology text to find countless studies that reveal a correlation. Some of the best commentary on the subject is from criminologist Elliott Currie in *Crime and Punishment in America* (1998). He writes:

While we were busily jamming our prisons to the rafters with young, poor men, we were simultaneously generating the fastest rise in income inequality in recent history. We were tolerating the descent of several million Americans, most of them children, into poverty. . . . At the same time, successive administrations cut many of the public supports – from income benefits to child protective services – that could have cushioned the impact of worsening economic deprivation and community fragmentation. And they also removed some of the rungs on our already wobbly ladders out of poverty.

Indeed, in spite of economic expansion since 1993, the only superpower in the world still has about one out of every four children aged five and under living in poverty, according to the National Center for Children and Poverty at Columbia University. By comparison, the corresponding child poverty rate is about 15 percent in Canada, 12 percent in Japan, 7 percent in France, 4 percent in Belgium, and 2 percent in Finland.

JOHN

John Wareham is an international executive recruiter, an industrial psychologist, author of several bestselling business books, and a prominent business lecturer. I met him on Rikers five years ago, when he came to a Fresh Start graduation. He was the guest of a friend in greens and offered to give us a contribution. 'A contribution of time,' he said, 'if you'll allow me.' At first I hesitated at the proposition, figuring that like other volunteers he'd burn out after a few round trips to the Rock. But he offered to give a few sessions on public speaking, then, if they went well, an adaptation from his leadership-development classes for senior executives. Five years later, he's still with us, every Monday morning, from 9:30 to noon.

With typical insight into what attracts an audience, John calls his Rikers class How to Break Out of Prison. His purpose is not to help the inmates effect a physical escape from Rikers, but, rather, a mental and emotional release from the conditions that put them there, 'namely, lack of information, faulty thinking, and self-doubt,' he says. The class features parliamentary debates; readings from the world's great philosophers from Plato to Jung; and political teachings from Martin Luther King, Jr., to Malcolm X. 'Authorities initially said that this material would be too sophisticated for prison inmates,' he says. 'In fact, with just a little coaching, the men quickly grasp the principles involved, and then go on and apply them to their own lives.' John's goals are threefold: 'to help the men think clearly, express themselves confidently in any situation, and to create and live satisfying and rewarding lives.'

John and his wife, Margaret, recently established a foundation, The Eagles, which invites an elite core of Fresh Start graduates to join upon release. The mission is to develop them into bona fide social leaders. They share in discussions at his country house; he includes them gratis in corporate executive retreats, and he exposes them to relevant Broadway shows. He also makes them 'Eagles' business cards and appoints them counselors for other inmates, meeting them at the prison gates upon release – their most vulnerable moment. The Eagles also become featured guest speakers at colleges and the like, using the public-speaking skills they learned from John on Rikers to bring the message of redemption to a wider audience.

In one of the most unusual 'outside events' held on Rikers Island, John once brought three senior executives to the Rock to discuss the issue of economic opportunity. The event was not a lecture, but a parliamentary debate between the executives and the inmates. Both teams knew about the debate in advance and had the opportunity to prepare. The statement they debated was: That it is better to rob a bank than work at McDonald's.

In a clever role switch, John assigns the three executives to argue the affirmative (it's better to rob a bank) and the inmates to argue the negative (it's better to work at McDonald's). He's typed up programs for the event and lists the participants as follows:

Emile (Tovi) Kratovil, writer and retired New York maritime courtroom and appellate practitioner;
John McClean, courtroom criminal attorney turned international corporate lawyer with twenty-five years in practice between Hong Kong and New York; and

Tom Morgan, senior vice president at Smith Barney, syndicated New York radio-show host, and writer.

Clifton Powell, warehouse manager, eighteen-month incarceration for sale of controlled substance, and prior conviction for same;

Herbert Berry, a sheetrock taper, sixteen-month incarceration for drug sale to undercover police officer, and prior conviction for assault; and

Jonathan Hutchinson, shipping and receiving warehousing, seven-month sentence for domestic violence.

Tovi Kratovil begins by arguing that a job at McDonald's offers little pay, few benefits, and minimal job security. 'If you want some money to run your life and you want independence and you want a hope of getting ahead,' he says, 'I think, like Willie Sutton, that you should rob a bank.'

Clifton Powell counters that 'the old days are over' and makes several points using his best convict knowledge. 'When Bonnie and Clyde and their crew robbed banks,' he says, 'they robbed the whole bank. Nowadays, when you rob a bank, you rob one teller. And when you rob that teller, you usually get only two or three thousand dollars, which goes pretty quick in the fast life. Then what do you do?' he asks. 'You've got to rob another bank. And like I mentioned before, even Willie Sutton got caught.'

John McLean makes a compelling case, beginning with a quote from Karl Marx: '"It is the history of mankind to create systems whereby the rich and powerful can live by the toil of the powerless."' Now, McLean says, 'political powerlessness is one thing. It makes it difficult to breathe. But economic powerlessness is another thing altogether. It makes it difficult to *live*.' He adds that robbing a bank is a victimless crime.

Herbert Berry rises to the challenge. He asks the opponents what they'd do if their son or daughter came to them and asked, 'Dad, I'm thinking about robbing a bank. Should I do that or get a job at McDonald's?' He points out that 'the first black mayor of this city, David Dinkins, once worked at McDonald's. So did another man: Martin Luther King,' he adds. The inmate debater ends by asking the executives to look at themselves in the mirror. 'What do you want to see? A man who's trying to better his life, or a thug?'

Tom Morgan, of Smith Barney, is next. Fittingly, he focuses his premise on the concept of capitalism. 'We live in a capitalist society,' he says, 'which means you've got to have *capital*. Capital ain't six bucks an hour. Capital is a hundred thousand dollars, which you can get from robbing a bank.' He turns to Herbert Berry. 'Mr. Berry raised the question "How am I going to answer my child?" I'll tell you how I'd answer: This is capitalism – you've got to have capital.'

When the formal part of the debate concludes, John Wareham opens it up to speakers from the floor. Two of my students, Reggie Michaels (a.k.a. 'Lord Blacque') and Mark Hollins, rise to the challenge. We had a class the night before but departed from the curriculum so they could practice.

Reggie, who's twenty and doing a year for drug sale, does an about-face and sides with the executives. 'I'm for robbing the bank,' he says unapologetically: 'They talk about Martin Luther King and how he worked at McDonald's. Now here's a man who spent a lot of hard time devoted to our people. And what happened to him? In the end he got killed. By who? Probably the government. We don't know. So my suggestion is: Rob a bank. Get back at them. Do it for Martin Luther King.'

Mark is in his mid-thirties and is troubled by Reggie's remarks. He stands and pauses before he speaks. He puts down the notes he's prepared and decides to speak from the heart:

'There's a serious, serious situation going on in our society right now, and it involves me and most of the African-American and Latino brothers in Rikers and other prisons. We're incarcerated at a rate that's eight times that of our white counterparts. If we decide to rob a bank, we'll be showing a willingness to go into a situation that's already designed against us. The despair that arises from that is not something we can afford or our kids can afford.

'One of the things I've learned on Rikers is that the people we call criminals and inmates are just as intelligent, just as strong, just as talented as anybody who's living a productive life on the outside. We've just been conditioned to think otherwise, and it's time we redirect that negative conditioning into the positive.'

Everyone applauds, even the COs by the door.

'Each week in this class,' John Wareham tells the audience, 'a man gets up and says, "Excuse me, my English is so bad." But then, of course, he wins your heart, and you say to yourself, "This guy is so smart and so switched on that despite the broken English, or even *because* of the broken English, he's going to be a winner in the debate." The men here who spoke for the negative were speaking from their hearts, and their hearts won the day.'

What endears John to the inmates is not just his engaging curriculum or his capacity to empathize, but that he speaks to them straight. 'The cat keeps it real!' as one of the men remarked. Like John, I teach on Mondays, and I'm glad to have the students after his class. Not only are they more upbeat, but they often have funny stories to share from their morning with John.

One day, for example, he gave the men an assignment: 'Prepare a three-minute speech to the parole board arguing for your immediate release. Use everything you've learned. Make it compelling.'

One after another the students went to the front of the room and said things like: 'My wife needs me . . . I need to be home for my kids. . . . I miss my girl. . . . Jail time's hard on a man.'

John stops the exercise midstream and tells the men a joke. 'Now listen carefully,' he said: 'There's a point to this.

'A man goes to the doctor for a checkup, and after the exam the doctor tells him, "I have both bad news and good news. Which do you want to hear first?"

'"The bad news," the patient says.

'"Okay, the bad news is that you have cancer and will die in six months."

'"Oh, my God!" the patient says. "How can you possibly have any good news? I'm going to die."

'"See that lovely nurse over there?" replies the doctor. "The one with the pert lips, the fabulous figure, and lithe, long legs?"

'"Yes, yes I do," says the patient.

'"Well, the good news" – the doctor smiles happily – "is I'm screwing her."'

Some of the inmates chuckled; others were confused. 'Get it?'

John said. 'See – you guys are just like the doctor. You're talking about your *sexual* needs but you're missing the point! Society couldn't care less about that, and, frankly, I couldn't either. What the parole board needs to hear is that you've addressed the cancer that's brought you to this place – that you've looked at yourselves, treated the offending infection, and that you're now a different person, someone who knows the meaning of the word *remorse,* someone truly ready to go out into the world and support yourself.' And next week, he tells them, they're going to talk precisely about how to achieve that 'happy goal.'

KENNETH

In *The Rich Get Richer and the Poor Get Prison,* author Jeffrey Reiman, a professor of philosophy at American University, makes an interesting comment about crime and punishment in America. 'The criminal justice system is sometimes thought of as a sieve in which the innocent are progressively sifted out from the guilty, who end up behind bars,' he writes, 'but the sieve works another way as well. Its sifts the affluent out from the poor, so it is not merely the guilty who end up behind bars, but the *guilty poor.*'

Not surprisingly, there is evidence that a high proportion of people from all walks of life have at some time or another committed serious crimes. Sociologist Jessica Mitford, in her book *Kind and Usual Punishment,* gives us a striking example, straight from New York: A study of 1,700 New Yorkers weighted toward the upper-income brackets who had never been arrested for anything and who were guaranteed anonymity revealed that fully 91 percent had committed either a felony or a serious misdemeanor. Sixty-four percent of the men and 27 percent of the women had committed at least one felony, for which they would have been sent to state prison had they been caught.

My former student, Kenneth Johnson, didn't think he'd get caught the night he stole, and he was relieved that he didn't end up back on the Rock. 'That woulda broke John's heart,' he tells me, referring to John Wareham, who's stuck by Kenneth since the day he left Rikers in 1996.

At the time of the incident, Kenneth had been at Project Renewal for six months and had made it to the second phase of the program. If he stayed out of trouble for another few weeks, he'd be rewarded with a room at the YMCA. Most people would consider a room at the Y punishment, but for Kenneth it was an improvement over the chaos at the treatment facility. Kenneth writes poetry, and he needs peace and quiet.

'Things was going great,' he says one evening over coffee. Kenneth is a big man – legs the size of tree trunks, the chest of a linebacker – but declines the offer of pastries. A gunshot in the stomach sometimes gives him indigestion.

'I'd been drug-free nearly a year and was makin' good progress in the program,' he says. 'I hadn't stolen anything in months.' But when he saw that book in Barnes & Noble . . .

'Takin' a little thing like a book wouldn't hurt nobody,' he recalls. 'I mean, what the hell? I done a lot worse. I've stabbed people. I've shot people. What's stealin' a stupid book got to do with anything?'

Kenneth wanted to teach himself Spanish, and there in front of him was a book with a learning tape attached to the cover. 'So I took the tape off and put it into my Walkman,' he says. A security guard saw him do it.

'As I was walkin' out, the toy-cop told me to turn around. I didn't give him a fight 'cause I really didn't think anything was gonna come of it. But when he said they were gonna arrest me, my heart sank. I saw everything I'd worked so hard for fly out the window. They took me to the manager's office, said they was calling the police.

'Luckily for me,' he says, 'two lady cops showed up. I was also lucky 'cause I'd just gotten paid.' In fact, he had over $250 in his pocket.

When the police officers asked Kenneth to empty his pockets to make sure he wasn't carrying a weapon, they saw the money. 'Why didn't you just pay for it?' the lady cop asked. 'This doesn't make any sense.'

The funny thing, Kenneth adds, was that 'these white lady cops said they didn't think they should arrest me – maybe they didn't wanna go through all the paperwork, I dunno. Anyway, they tried to convince the manager to let me go. Now the manager, a *black* man, is hell bent on having me arrested! He's tellin' *them* to arrest me and I'm like, C'mon, man, cut me a break. I'll pay for the damn book.'

But the manager thought that was too easy. Meanwhile, the cops still didn't want to arrest him. So in a version of 'community justice' the police and the manager put their heads together and made Kenneth a deal: He'd pay full price for the book, but he couldn't keep it.

'Can I have the tape?' he asked.

The incident was a turning point for Kenneth, and I include it here because it represents a post-incarceration experience that defines the journey of many of our graduates as they try to 'go legit.' Like most people who attempt to change a behavior or break a habit, the process isn't always linear and uninterrupted. Three months in Fresh Start and abstinence from drugs doesn't suddenly 'cure' them of years of criminal thinking and behavior – in Kenneth's case seventeen years.

'When I left that bookstore,' he says, 'It hit me – I knew then and there that my time was up, that it would never work the same for me again. I promised myself I'd never go back to jail, and that night I realized how close I came.'

Kenneth says that Fresh Start gave him exactly what he needed – 'It opened me up to people I never would have interacted with in the past' – but it took a close call like the one he experienced to convince him that his criminal days were over. He was also now a stakeholder in society with something to lose. 'Every time I left jail in the past,' he says, 'I never had nobody like John in my corner. The only people I knew helped me to be self-destructive, how to be a better criminal.'

Besides the Barnes & Noble incident, Kenneth decided to 'just do everything different' when he graduated from Fresh Start and left Rikers. 'In the past, I'd get out and not even think about joinin' a drug treatment program, so this time I did. I signed up the week I got out. In the past I'd never get in touch with my family, but this time I called my mom from jail and told her she'd see me real soon.'

Then he looks at me and laughs. 'And I stayed in touch with white folks. . . . You know I didn't like white folks much, but with people like John and you, how could I hold on to that racial stuff?'

There was something else, he says. 'All the time I was out there in the street gettin' high, I still had a feeling inside of me, an image of what I wanted to become. Everyone has that feeling. I'd look at people in restaurants and wish I could do that – eat and pay without runnin' out. . . .

I thought of how peaceful it would be to sit on a bench in the park without canvassing the place, wonderin' who I could rob to get my next fix. If I could just stop getting high for one day, I'd tell myself, maybe I'd be all right.'

Now, he says, 'I can go to a restaurant and pay. I can sit in a park and relax. I can see someone drop something and give it back to them.'

Today he's back on Rikers as a counselor for Fresh Start inmates, and when I see him at the front of the room, holding forth in a dress shirt and tie, it's hard to believe that four years ago he was in my class wearing inmate greens. I'd actually turned him down when he interviewed to be in the program. 'I thought you were crazy,' I tell him.

'I thought *you* all was crazy,' he says, 'runnin' around Rikers tryin' to help a bunch of criminals.'

'Yeah, all of us white folks,' I tease.

We can talk about racial issues now, conversations neither of us could have had before Rikers, before Fresh Start. I grew up not knowing many black people, really, and admit that 'criminal' was the image that came to mind when I thought of blacks. Kenny saw most white people as 'racists,' he says, and there's still a grain of ambivalence. The problem he describes is understandable.

'Sometimes it seems like every black man like me who's gotten ahead has had a white man in the background,' he says. 'I look at my job now – and sometimes I feel like the only reason I got that job is because John recommended me. It's not what you know, it's who you know, but the problem is that most black folks don't know any-body in a position to help them. So we always have to go to white folks to get the jobs, the training, the things we need.'

He tells me about a recent conversation he had with the inmates in the program. 'I told the couple of white guys, "I don't mean nothin' against you, but society accepts you for who you are because of your race. You'll leave this jail and you'll be all right because society expects you *not* to be in jail. Let's face it – for a white man to go to jail he gotta be a real fuckin' idiot."

'But for us black men,' he says, 'society *expects* us to be in jail, and that's what we've come to believe – like jail doesn't mean nothin' to us 'cause we're black men, like we rob and we steal because that's what black men do. We've come to believe that's what we do. Self-destruction is so deeply rooted in us.'

When Sergeant Hall speaks to minority youths in the inner city, he offers a type of 'suck-it-up' advice, which, he admits, 'isn't necessarily the right way to look at things, but it's reality.'

'As a black male,' he tells them, 'you should know that the odds are stacked against you. You knew that day one. You knew that before you were eleven, twelve, thirteen years old, so by the time you're nineteen, you shouldn't be bitchin' about it. If you didn't do what you needed to do to prepare yourself to compete, then shame on you.'

Kenneth's and Sergeant Hall's comments remind me of something Jesse Jackson said that I've never forgotten: 'There is nothing more painful for me at this stage of my life than to walk down the street and hear footsteps and start to think about robbery and then look around and see it's somebody white and feel relieved. How humiliating.'

Richard Simpson is the director of education at the renowned Peter Kump Cooking School in Manhattan. He has volunteered with Fresh Start since its inception, and has hired some of our graduates. Besides noticing that the inmates he met in the jail kitchen 'were some of the biggest guys I've ever seen; there wasn't anybody whose upper arm wasn't bigger than my thigh,' he says, 'it wasn't until I got with my students in the classroom that I realized that they were just like any other students I've taught. They wanted to learn and it worked. It was great,' he says.

'On the other hand,' he adds, 'it gave me a lot of sympathy for them, because I realized what they couldn't do. They couldn't read well. They couldn't comprehend well. They couldn't do math, and it made me very aware of a fundamental difference between people like us and people like them. It made me aware that it's probably not an accident they're on Rikers. Their basic cognitive skills are so lacking. I remember I took to rewriting recipes in monosyllabic words and printing them in large type. I didn't know if it would be a good thing to do, but I asked if anyone wanted to read aloud. And they all wanted to. So we'd read the recipes as many times as it took so that everyone got a chance at reading. It was a big deal to them. You and I take it for granted that we can read. They can't. They were so excited it was almost like working with kids – except that most of them were the size of ice cream trucks.'

Because of the higher literacy requirement for the men who work on the *Rikers Review*, the students in my class usually have better reading skills than the inmates Richard describes in the cooking program. But in each class there are always several men whom I look at and wonder how they'll ever make it in the world. Joe Carter for example, wrote the following bio on himself for the magazine. Joe was nineteen at the time I knew him. He had a sweet, loopy smile and rarely said a word. He wanted to go to college when he left Rikers, he told me. On the piece of paper he tore from his notebook, he wrote:

Am 19 old and want to go back to school to get my ged and get my live together so don't have to come back to this place and show my brother good way to go but people put down think guest I use to put myself down but thank god for gives me seound changes.

Even if Joe could get into college, funding would present another barrier. The dollars New York has spent on corrections has resulted in less money for other public services, the most vital of which is education. Today, New York spends almost twice what it did to run its prisons a decade ago. Since 1998, 'New York's public universities have seen state support for their operating budgets plummet by 29 percent – while funding for prisons has increased by 76 percent,' according to a 1999 study by the Justice Policy Institute. 'In actual dollars, there has nearly been an equal trade-off, with the Department of Correctional Services receiving a $761 million increase during that time while state funding for New York's city and state university systems has declined by $615 million.'

Another significant effect of expanding the prison system is the shift of economic resources from urban communities to other locations. Not only does incarceration remove 'social capital' (men, parents, and guardians) from the communities that are least prepared to handle the loss, but it transfers critical economic capital as well.

Few people know that prisoners are counted as residents of the *place where they are imprisoned,* not where they come from and where their families live. 'Until recently, this qualified as an interesting but not especially important factoid,' writes *The New York Times* about the study issued by the City Project in March 2000 that highlighted this census quirk. 'But the explosion of the prison population during the last couple of decades has changed all that. It is creating a noticeable shift in government dollars and political influence, generally to the advantage of rural areas at the expense of big cities.'

New York's prisons house approximately 71,000 inmates. The vast majority of these prisons, 90 percent, are located in upstate communities. However, seven out of ten state inmates come from New York City. 'As a result,' writes the *Times,* 'a felon from the South Bronx doing time at Clinton Correctional Facility is recorded as belonging to Dannemora, near the Canadian border, and not his home city. . . . It does not require great imagination to see how there would be a transfer of poverty funds and other census-based federal payments from the five boroughs to upstate towns.'

To complete the grim picture of disenfranchisement, consider the fact that more than 6 percent of black men in New York cannot vote because they are in prison or on parole. Nationwide, fully 13 percent of the black adult male population (1.4 million African American men) have currently or permanently lost the ability to vote because of a felony conviction, according to a 1999 report by Human Rights Watch and the Sentencing Project. 'Given current rates of incarceration, three in ten of the next generation of black men will be disenfranchised [unable to vote] at some point in their lifetime,' write the authors. 'In states with the most restrictive voting laws, 40 percent of African American men are likely to be permanently disenfranchised.'

One of New York's early prison reformers, a prominent businessman by the name of Thomas Mott Osborne, founder of the Osborne Association, spent a week as a voluntary convict in Auburn prison to get a sense of what happened to men within prison walls. Before he left, the story goes, he threw himself on his knees and prayed for the strength to spend the rest of his life trying to reform the prison system. Until his death in 1926, he spoke out against the senseless brutality of prisons and sought to turn what he referred to as the 'scrap heap of the prison system' into a 'human repair shop.' Almost a hundred years later, many criminal justice advocates are still having the same discussion.

My work in the prison system began with a similar desire, and I believe that prison conditions, generally, still need improvement. Nonetheless, progress has been made: The reduction of violence and expansion of services in jails on Rikers are perfect examples. I can count a good number of state prisons in New York as places where 'human repair' is taking place.

It is easy for outsiders and prison reformers to blame the problems of prisoners on the facilities in which they're housed. This is a natural reaction: When you see a person in pain, you look to his immediate surroundings. My journey in writing this book took me outside the prisons and into the communities where my students live and were raised. They do not look like the communities of the 'average American' by any standards or means. They suffer from dysfunctional schools, woefully insufficient medical care, substandard housing, and high rates of violence and substance abuse, all of which result when despair sets in and there's little left to lose. In the vacuum that's created, prisons have stepped in, becoming our anti-poverty policy, our drug-treatment policy, our mental-health policy, and our education policy.

My early description of Rikers as 'the dirty secret' of New York refers not to the jails themselves but to the shameful social problems they hide. The marginalized people I see on Rikers and in many state prisons were not created on the inside, but in communities forgotten by elected officials.

In the eighteenth century, English philosopher Edmund Burke said: 'Evil happens when good men do nothing.'

ACKNOWLEDGMENTS

One of the many challenges new authors face is finding an agent to sell their work. I was lucky: Noah Lukeman, agent nonpareil, found me. Noah even came to Rikers Island to meet my inmate-students and speak to them about the world of publishing.

I thank my editor at St. Martin's Press, Michael Denneny, for his steadfast encouragement and excellent judgment, and my previous editor, Dana Albarella, for her belief in this book. Special thanks as well to assistant editor Christina Prestia, a consummate professional who kept me focused and the project on track.

I acknowledge the many individuals at the New York City Department of Correction who have supported Fresh Start since its inception. The inmate-graduates and I wouldn't be where we are today without the benevolence of former commissioners Michael Jacobson and Bernard Kerik; Deputy Commissioner of Strategic Planning and Programs Roger Jefferies and his predecessor, Fred Patrick, all long-standing friends of Fresh Start. Correction Officers Dwight Gray and Rachel Sellers oversee Fresh Start on Rikers; their warmth and professionalism are the glue of the program. Special thanks, too, to Correction Officers Delbert Beasley, Jerome Garlick, Glenn Miller, and Henry Rohr for always treating our students with fairness and compassion.

At the Austin H. MacCormick high school on Rikers Island, I thank Deputy Superintendent Timothy Lisante for being the best role model a 'correctional educator'-in-training could have, and Frank Dody, principal, for continuing the tradition. And I speak for hundreds of students in thanking instructors Helen Clerici and Martine Scannavino for their vast contributions over the years.

ACKNOWLEDGMENTS

I owe a debt of gratitude to author Jonathan Kozol, who inspired and helped me from the start. I thank authors Steven Donziger and Ted Conover for their encouragement and expert advice. I am grateful to Alessandra Alecci, Janine de Vogelare Baron, Carol Ferry, David Hammer, Kenneth Johnson, and Peter Schmidt for their insightful and speedy review of the manuscript.

Several professors at John Jay College of Criminal Justice have enriched my thinking through their bold ethnographic work and the generous time they extended to me. In particular, I thank Barry Spunt, an early catalyst in my academic career, as well as Charles Bahn, David Brotherton, Todd Clear, Rick Curtis, Steve Sifaneck, and Richard Wolf.

There are many individuals, too many to list, whom I thank for the opportunities they have given me and their friendship over the years: Rachel Amols, Carlos Batista, Ralph and Peggy Brown, Mickeni Caldwell, John Chiarkas, Don Colbert, Hilton Cooper, Chris Cozzone, Laura Davidson, Nancy Duggan, Eddie Ellis, Malik Folsom, Gennifer Furst, Jason Gerald, Frank Guzman, Clay Hiles, Leonard Hughes, James Jiler, Kenneth Johnson, Lynwood Jones, Alice Layton, Donald Matusik, Peter Meacher, Joseph Messineo, Anthony Papa, Fred Patrick, Elizabeth Payamps, Juan Pietri, Patricia Ritchings, Eric Rosenfeld, Marianna Shturman, Adolf Smith, Dwayne Speight, Richard Stratton, Herbert Sturz, Earl Swindel, John and Margaret Wareham, and Ilene Wittner.

My highest appreciation goes to my mentors, Robert Gangi, executive director of the Correctional Association of New York, and Elizabeth Gaynes, executive director of the Osborne Association, who have influenced my life profoundly.

Finally, I want to thank my family: my grandmother, Collette Ramsey-Baker, for lighting the spark of public service in me through her work as founder of the Deafness Research Foundation; my sister, Carin Wynn-Dupuis, for her special friendship and insightful advice, whether book- or life-related; my brother, Brooks Wynn, for keeping me laughing and showing me that change is possible; my brother-in-law, Richard Dupuis, for his generosity to me and my students; and, most of all, my parents, Charles and Collette Wynn, for 'giving me roots and giving me wings,' and for teaching me the value of an open heart and mind.

RESOURCES

One of the most sobering and insightful updates on criminal justice in America can be found in a 1999 report by the National Commission on the Causes and Prevention of Violence. The report offers a retrospective analysis thirty years after President Lyndon B. Johnson impaneled the commission in the wake of the assassinations of Senator Robert F. Kennedy and Martin Luther King, Jr. Since the late 1960s, the report reveals, violent crime is up 40 percent in big cities, the number of people possessing firearms is up 120 percent, and prison construction has increased sevenfold.

'How do we stand on justice today?' ask the authors. 'Almost a quarter of all children five and under live in poverty. America is the most unequal country in the industrialized world in terms of income and wealth. The "digital divide" is accelerating the gulf between our haves and have nots. The average CEO makes 419 times as much as the average worker, and this ratio has greatly increased over the last three decades. The states spend more on prison building than on higher education, whereas the opposite was true at the time of the Commission.'

The good news, the authors note, is that America today has both the knowledge and the resources to launch an 'effective attack on the violent crime that still afflicts us.' The report cites a number of programs as good public-policy approaches to crime prevention. Equally important, the authors provide a blueprint for financing a national urban and criminal justice policy and the ways in which concerned citizens and organizations can work to create the political will necessary to effect meaningful and lasting reform. The study was conducted by the Milton S. Eisenhower Foundation, a nonprofit research group located in Washington, D.C.

Another excellent primer for laypeople and professionals alike is Elliott Currie's *Crime and Punishment in America*. 'A society that incarcerates such a vast and rapidly growing part of its population, but still suffers the worst violent crime in the industrial world, is a society in trouble,' the author writes. Currie's lucid and readable book cuts through reams of statistics and studies to show why current approaches to America's most stubborn social crisis have not worked and, more important, what will.

The Real War on Crime, a report by the National Criminal Justice Commission, is a far-sighted account of the forces behind current criminal-justice policy. Published in 1996 and written in the same jargon-free style as Currie's *Crime and Punishment in America, The Real War on Crime* covers the gamut of contemporary criminal justice issues, from the prison industrial complex to the myths and realities of crime and violence in the United States.

Specific to Rikers Island, the New York City Department of Correction offers a detail-rich Web site covering Rikers' history, inmate characteristics, charts, statistics, organizational briefs, and program highlights (*http://www.ci.nyc.ny.us*).

For general criminal-justice information, an excellent place to begin is the home page of the Justice Information Center, a service of the National Criminal Justice Reference Service (*http://www.ncjrs.org*). NCJRS is one of the most extensive sources of information on crime statistics, crime prevention, and research and evaluation in the area of crime control.

SELECTED BIBLIOGRAPHY

Akers, Ronald. *Criminological Theories*. 2nd ed. Los Angeles: Roxbury Publishing, 1997.

Amnesty International. *Rights for All*. London: Amnesty International Publications, 1998.

Anderson, Elijah. *Code of the Street*. New York: W.W. Norton, 1999.

Association of the Bar of the City of New York. 'The Wages of Welfare Reform: A Report on New York City's Job Center.' *The Record* 54, 4 (1999): 472–492.

Beccaria, Cesare. *On Crimes and Punishments*. Translated by David Young. Indianapolis, Ind.: Hackett, 1986. (Original work published 1764.)

Beirne, Piers. *Inventing Criminology: Essays on the Rise of 'Homo Criminalis.'* Albany: State University of New York Press, 1993.

Bourgois, Philippe. *In Search of Respect: Selling Crack in El Barrio*. Cambridge: Cambridge University Press, 1996.

Braithwaite, John. *Crime, Shame, and Reintegration*. Cambridge: Cambridge University Press, 1989.

City Project. *Following the Dollars: Where New York State Spends Its Prison Moneys*. New York: City Project, 2000.

Clear, Todd. 'Backfire: When Incarceration Increases Crime.' *Journal of the Oklahoma Criminal Justice Research Corporation* 3 (1996): 7–17.

——. *Harm in American Penology: Offenders, Victims, and Their Communities*. Albany: State University of New York Press, 1994.

Cole, David. *No Equal Justice*. New York: New Press, 1999.

Conover, Ted. *Newjack: Guarding Sing Sing*. New York: Random House, 2000.

Correctional Association of New York. *The Troubles They Cause: Double-Celling and Program Cuts in New York State Prisons.* New York: CANY, 1998.

Currie, Elliott. *Crime and Punishment in America.* New York: Henry Holt, 1998.

Donziger, Steven R., ed. *The Real War on Crime: The Report of the National Criminal Justice Commission.* New York: Harper/Perennial, 1996.

Felson, Marcus. *Crime and Everyday Life.* 2nd ed. Thousand Oaks, Calif.: Pine Forge, 1998.

Flateau, John. *The Prison Industrial Complex: Race, Crime, and Justice in New York.* New York: Medgar Evers College Press, 1996.

Foucault, Michel. *Discipline and Punish: The Birth of the Prison.* Translated by Alan Sheridan. New York: Pantheon, 1978; reprint ed., New York: Vintage, 1995.

Haas, Kenneth C., and Geoffrey P. Alpert, eds. *The Dilemmas of Corrections.* 3rd ed. Prospect Heights, Ill.: Waveland Press, 1995.

Jacobson, Michael. 'Trends in Criminal Justice Spending, Employment, and Workloads in New York City Since the Late 1970's.' *Crime and Justice in New York City.* Andrew Karmen, ed. New York: McGraw Hill, 1998–1999 edition.

Justice Policy Institute and the Correctional Association of New York. *New York State of Mind?: Higher Education vs. Prison Funding in the Empire State, 1988–1998.* New York: CANY, 1998.

Kauffman, Kelsey. *Prison Officers and Their World.* Cambridge, Mass.: Harvard University Press, 1988.

Kozol, Jonathan. *Amazing Grace.* New York: Harper, 1995.

———. *Savage Inequalities: Children in America's Schools.* New York: Harper, 1991.

Mauer, Marc, and the Sentencing Project. *Race to Incarcerate.* New York: New Press, 1999.

May, John, P., ed. *Building Violence: How America's Rush to Incarcerate Creates More Violence.* Thousand Oaks, Calif.: Sage, 2000.

Menninger, Karl. *The Crime of Punishment.* New York: Viking Press, 1966.

Milton S. Eisenhower Foundation. *To Establish Justice, To Insure Domestic Tranquility: A Thirty Year Update of the National Commission on the Causes and Prevention of Violence.* Washington, D.C.: Milton S. Eisenhower Foundation, 1999.

Mitford, Jessica. *Kind and Usual Punishment: The Prison Business.* New York: Alfred A. Knopf, 1973.

Osborne, Thomas Mott. *Within Prison Walls: Being a Narrative of Personal Experience During a Week of Voluntary Confinement in the State Prison at Auburn, New York.* New York: D. Appleton, 1914.

SELECTED BIBLIOGRAPHY

Parenti, Christian. *Lockdown America: Police and Prisons in the Age of Crisis*. New York: Verso, 1999.

Reiman, Jeffrey. *The Rich Get Richer and the Poor Get Prison*. 5th ed. Boston: Allyn and Bacon, 1998.

Robert, Albert, ed. *Critical Issues in Crime and Justice*. Thousand Oaks, Calif.: Sage, 1994.

Robinson, Randall. *The Debt: What America Owes to Blacks*. New York: Dutton, 2000.

Walker, Samuel. *Sense and Nonsense About Crime and Drugs*. 3rd ed. Belmont, Calif.: Wadsworth, 1994.

Welch, Michael. *Punishment in America: Social Control and the Ironies of Imprisonment*. Thousand Oaks, Calif.: Sage, 1999.

INDEX

INDEX

INDEX